Crawl-Space Computing

Crawl-Space Computing

Lawrence J. Dickson

Cooperating programs
that don't hide your data
while they are working on it

(including a guide to the Connel toolset)

This book was published with the crucial aid of several people.

Thomas L. Dickson	Production and Typesetting
Alice K. Dickson	Art and Illustrations
Elizabeth M. Dickson	Cover Art

My thanks go also to my wife Jeanne C. Dickson, without whose encouragement I would have bogged down, and to the Kickstarter organization, which provided me a path out of the post-2008 funding desert.

This book was typset using pdfLATEX on 7″ × 10″ paper using LATEX and the `memoir` package (among others) on May 6, 2014. This is revision 253.

Printed in the USA and other locations

Fierce Press
National City, CA
United States

   ISBN-13:   978-0-9666440-1-2
   ISBN-10:   0966644018

Dedication

This book is dedicated to my father and mother:

LAWRENCE EDWARD DICKSON
September 17, 1913–January 9, 1981

ELIZABETH MARY HELINA DICKSON
November 14, 1920–August 8, 1976

They brought me and my sisters up, without deference to prevailing trends, on an acre in north Seattle. Everything that is pithy and countercultural in my book and life arises from their original inspiration.

Major Contributors

Partner
Adrianus Warmenhoven

Angels
Alexandru Nedel
Kyle Cassidy

Patrons
Roger Wagner
Dennis Roos
Richard Miller
Rob Fryer
Elizabeth Dickson

This book is part of a Kickstarter project. Without the support, and the guidance on priorities, of the above major backers, it could never have happened. For whatever enduring value you find in these pages, please thank the people above.

Preface

The growth of scientific knowledge has obviously spurred a massive explosion of technology. But, the driving spirit of science is not to change the world but to understand it.
    —Kwame Appiah, quoted by Bill Cowan, University of Waterloo, Canada

The purpose of this book is to leave a legacy.

This purpose connects to a situation in which we, the world of creative programming, now find ourselves. Together, the purpose and the situation are going to determine the shape of this book. I'm saying this right here, early on, because it is rather an unusual shape, more tilted (at first) toward "creative" than toward "programming." So bear with me while I explain.

Recovery from monoculture

For the last two decades, I have been like a guide keeping open the trail to Nova Scotia while the covered wagons all go thundering off to California. Nothing about the science of computing has changed, but the way people talk has gradually altered, year by year. Computer programs and even computing languages are a subset of "the way people talk." And many years of slow change can sum up to quite a shift.

My roots go back to the seventies and earlier, to an "age of science." People were discovering the Van Allen Belts and bringing back rocks from the Moon. Computing was in its infancy, although the *science* of numerical algorithms, as represented by Donald Knuth, was well underway. By contrast, in 2014 we have been for many years in an "age of technology," and computing is a trillion-dollar industry. But positive feedback, typical of commercial success, has led to a narrowing of technique.

Computers obey both command and nature, but command has been the focus of development since the early 1990s. Physical nature has a wide, accessible, village-like structure of territorial entities communicating across boundaries over time. This is deliberately hidden in the deep, centralized, legalistic command structure called "abstraction," which thus easily appears to produce instant, universal results at will.

The results are easy to see. Things like multiple choice, picking from a list, filling in the blanks, doing what the user interface wants—these all go fast and easy. But what if the task is different? What if the data does not fit, or you need an ellipse instead of a rectangle, or the mouse can't do a fine enough job? Then although it is clear that all the necessary data and capabilities are there, ease of use becomes extreme lack of flexibility. All of a sudden, THE PROGRAM STANDS BETWEEN YOU AND YOUR DATA.

It's important here not to be deceived by appearances. A massive increase in quantity (not to mention flashiness) can leave the impression that "things are busting out all over" when in fact nearly the opposite is true. It's like the huge increase in supply of potatoes in pre-1847 Ireland, but they were all one kind of potato, susceptible to one rot. And since the coding problem is all one kind of thinking—a monoculture of the mind—I needed to step back and take thought myself about how to leave a legacy that fights it.

First, it's clear I have to use tools that date from before the convergence. Practically speaking, that means C, a 1970s-era language that still is supported almost everywhere, thanks to its low-level flexibility. In addition, there are operating system usages, like `bash` (in Linux/Unix/BSD) and `BATCH` (the old name for scripting in DOS and Windows), that have proved remarkably persistent. The reason is mainly that the programming of servers demands them.

In addition, I have to use an approach that can ease the modern programmer out of the monocultural mindset. This means going behind programming to things and what they actually do. That is why the first few chapters of this book will have an almost artistic feel. Only after assembling these kindergarten blocks can I re-enter the world of programming, this time with specific instructions on how to make it do what Wide Computing wants.

Luckily, it turns out that is a pretty good description of what my legacy teaching is trying to save: things, and what they actually do.

What do you need to know?

Because of my artistic lead chapters, the answer to this question is: *not much*. In fact, all I really ask is a scientific bent of mind. Things have consequences! Also needed is your willingness to have patience while you work out these consequences.

An experienced programmer or computer science student may actually need to *unlearn* some things. Almost always, when a word has a modern computing meaning and a more general naive meaning, I mean the latter. I do my best to avoid these. For instance, I use "piece" where the more natural term would be "component," which unfortunately has an object-oriented meaning quite different from what I want to say. Still, some will sneak through.

If I succeed at my task, the complete newbie will find himself or herself able to program more and more as the chapters advance. This is because the thing, and what it needs to do, cause questions to arise. These, in turn, require research and design, before a word of code is written. The program will break into more than one piece, and data will flow between them, with data rate requirements. Each piece is simple (even if its algorithms are not), and the data passing between pieces is also simple. Each piece can be tested *by itself,* and when all are put together, you will suddenly find you have a working device.

After all, I'm not really a programmer. I'm a mathematician, and I like to know why things work. Since I'm a lazy mathematician, I like it to be *obvious* why things work. It's amazing how easy programming becomes when you break it down into little things that obviously work. That includes fast, powerful, rocket-science programs, because power and mystery are not the same thing!

Connel

The C toolset Connel goes with this book. Although Connel is not necessary to apply this book's techniques, it makes things easier, especially when a modern, UI-centered operating system has to talk to hardware and embedded code or code on other machines. Connel, which is named after "connector link," compiles and runs *without change* both on Linux and Windows, and the resulting programs can communicate (Windows to Windows, Linux to Linux, or Windows to Linux). Connel is also designed to communicate with "alien" code and hardware, whether it's a UI-based program in any language, or embedded code running on hardware that may not have an operating system or even a standard compiler. Connel also cooperates with virtualizers like VMWare to allow programs on different virtual machines to talk to each other.

The beauty of Connel is that you don't have to learn a new protocol for each communicating application. Often, you don't even have to recompile the code. This is because the talking machinery of Crawl-Space Computing behaves the same (in the state machine sense) between any communicating pair, whether software or hardware. In fact, you don't even need both sides of the communicating pair: you can substitute a *dummy* on one side, and the other side will run at full speed and not even know the difference. In addition, you can "mix and match" real working modules at will, and all your data is always completely under your control as it passes from one module to another.

Acknowledgements

The amazing success of my Kickstarter is what makes it possible for me to try to hand over this legacy. Credit goes to a lot of people. I've listed some tersely in the preceding pages, but it does not do them justice.

This project would not be where it is without the work of many others. I wish to thank my daughters Elizabeth and Alice and my wife Jeanne for all their help with the video. It could not have happened without them. Also, I thank my son Tom and my colleagues William and Dave Swanson, Rob Fryer and Trey Hunner for advice in development, and especially for the chance to do real robotics and satellite science. I am more of a theoretician, but with these other creative people pitching in, some real and impressive things are getting done.

I wish to recognize the contribution of the scientists, mostly from England and Europe, of the occam-com list. For decades, since before the eclipse of the Transputer, they have carried the torch for Communicating Sequential Processes (CSP) and related Wide Computing projects, while to be sure allowing a little abstraction to creep in. Discussions with them have stimulated me, both in my work leading to this book (including errata found by Anne Van Rossum), and in my ITOCA patent work. In particular I wish to remember my colleague Michael Poole, author of the Transputer Development System (TDS), who passed away recently.

Several major contributors, of technology and exposure as well as finances, are already carrying this beyond anything I could have anticipated. I've asked around among them about setting up a Wide Computing community to accomplish more than I can alone. Of these, four wish their work to be publicly mentioned, while others prefer to remain behind the scenes.

Adrianus Warmenhoven is the leader who, among other things, came up with the Raspberry Pi stretch goal. Contacting him thousands of miles away shows what a brilliant thing Kickstarter is. He already has a group of people who, in many cases, state what I am after better than I can myself.

William Swanson is my longstanding colleague at MeasureBot3D LLC, the robotics invention startup whose computing side he has been leading and I have been aiding. As a brilliant young embedded programmer, hardware designer, and language creator, he has made frequent contributions to my design thoughts. The latest was an introduction to XCB and to Windows graphics, which helped get the Graphics Slave off to a good start.

Trey Hunner is the San Diego organizer who has put me in touch with so many key people, including Roger Wagner and Tero Kukola, not to mention a local business incubator that may be in a future bigger than one desk at home.

Without Trey, I would never have set about Kickstarter.

Rob Fryer is an eager inventor and engineering pioneer whom I've known for years. He widens my horizons to things like the Kicksat project which will include a satellite by Rob's team. This challenge has been a fertile source of Wide Computing ideas - as my WORLDCOMP 2013 presentation showed.

There are others, whom I can't mention here, but you know who you are, and please be assured of my gratitude! They have provided even more directions, like OSC. I must focus on the promised rewards, so the more initiative you all take, the happier I am.

We made it - and I must say that the response was far better than I ever really expected! I look forward to working with you all, and going beyond the mere posting of the rewards. I think I will be able to declare some "skosh room" and do the Raspberry Pi port anyway. One generous backer has already provided hardware, and others have expressed great interest. I may have to call for help or stretch the time a bit.

Finally, I'd like to thank the Kickstarter organization itself. Reaching all around the world to a group of people who don't know each other but are trying to save the same thing is an amazing accomplishment, and it is the Kickstarter design that made it possible. Funding anything countercultural in the post-2008 desert is also an amazing accomplishment, and the Kickstarter design made that possible too. Every call for help to Kickstarter personnel got a prompt and effective response, and their advice, in FAQ and elsewhere, was unfailingly wise, as unfolding events proved to this business newbie.

Contents

Introduction to Wide Computing   1

Abstract

The purpose of this chapter is to introduce a 2014-era computing enthusiast to Wide Computing—the why, the how, and the theory. I will follow an elementary, even naive, approach for two reasons. First, I want to reach as wide an audience as possible. And second, a key feature of Wide Computing is that it reduces abstraction to a minimum. You get your hands on serious data and do useful projects without mastering a six-volume API.

α—time, space, and parallel from hobbies to space science

β—get rid of hiccups

γ—hardware/software equivalence

δ—natural data and timing gatekeepers set you free

ϵ—flatten out the difficulty curve for complex projects

ζ—the duality of Wide versus Deep

η—tools that open doors

θ—terms that everyone can understand

1.1 Approach

The practical approach taken in this book, and in this introduction, is "advancing waves." Each wave reaches a certain level of utility, with a number of forward references and partially worked-out concepts. These raise a number of questions, which lead to a discussion of theory and specifics that illuminate the foundations of the next wave.

The usual Deep introductory approach is to offer hands-on coding (or at least filling in the blanks) of a tiny, restricted "Hello World" program, and then to proceed through targeted features. (Compare [9].) The Wide approach embraces the entire world of computing from the very beginning, and focuses in by stages on details that will allow actual programming of the project. This will support *any* project, and gain control of *all* the data, not just what the author or language designer discloses.

Each task under this approach therefore starts with a design stage (like essay-writing instead of filling in the blanks), and the design is based on theory. So my first job will be to introduce you to the theory. The beauty of this theory is that it is simple, naive, and short—the opposite of what people now expect of a computing paradigm! And it is capable of doing every computing task.

ITEM	DEEP EMPHASIS	WIDE EMPHASIS
Resource allocation	Shared Dynamic System-controlled Infinite pool	Distributed Static Explicitly programmed Explicitly limited
Configuration decisions	Run time	Load time
Initial state	State of all enclosing callers	Explicit load-time setup parameters
Component life	During call only	Eternal
Typical task ordering	Stack	FIFO
Normal stack state	Deep	Empty
Information passing	Calling sequence, global variables	Process-to-process (channel) transmission
Program control	Serial	Parallel
Model	Compiler parse	Connected hardware

Table 1.1: Contrast between paradigms

1.2 What is Wide Computing?

Wide (Crawl-Space) Computing is the technique of programming independent pieces, and exposing, at the top level, the communication and timing connections carrying all their shared data. It contrasts with Deep (Concrete-Slab) Computing, which exposes a single face of control and underlays this with many hidden layers of callable program components able to perform parts of the tasks desired. Wide is naturalistic, while Deep is legalistic.

To drill down into the implications of this, see Table 1.1. This is, except for the column headers, identical to a table I published in a 1996 paper [3]. The Deep trend established then has (except for a few outliers like map-reduce, GPGPU and Go) only continued, adding one or two layers in many computing languages, as in [9].

Every one of the rows in Table 1.1 is related to independence of the pieces and/or exposure of the communications. For instance, deeply nested calls (which correspond to multiple inheritances in object-oriented languages) are easily done deep in a stack, but those deep stacks are not friendly to context switches that support independent program pieces (multitasking).

To take another example, the independent pieces of Wide Computing clearly require parallel program control. By contrast, the single face of control (typically a graphical user interface) preferred by the Deep model imposes a single timeline and is therefore locked into the methodology of serial programming. This is the source of the common opinion that massively parallel programming is a task of fantastic difficulty. That's only true if you insist on the Deep model. Non-programmers (like shoppers in a store) do massively parallel tasks all the time without thinking.

The rest of Table 1.1 will become clear as we progress. Right now, there are already questions that need to be answered.

1.3 Why?

To get started on the **why** of Wide Computing, I'd suggest you glance at two references. First, look at the 2014 cutting edge of Deep in [1] (thank you, Roger Wagner), and then look at Wide as done in 1993—[10] Figures 13 and 17. On the one hand you have extreme obscurity based on convoluted design (callbacks), while on the other you have a design picture that anybody can understand, with arrows meaning real data flow between real entities. Think of them as villages with roads carrying traffic.

You can do any computing task with the Wide approach, as is rather obvious, since both microprocessors and human society are built that way. But after twenty years of monoculture, the computing world "speaks Deep," leaving the problem of getting from here to there. This book, and Connel, offer shortcuts to make this happen. This section will introduce you to the reasons why it's worth the effort.

1.3.1 α—Time, space, and parallel: from hobbies to space science

Wide computing works within time, while Deep computing is designed as if everything were instantaneous. Because delays do exist, and are significant, Deep computing requires *callbacks*. The low-level, "reused" system driver code that hides timing and data input/output must call high-level user functions to deal with the specifics of the program, as in Figure 1.1.

Notice that this requires passing a function as an argument to a driver (so-called "first-class functions"), which has bad implications for security and

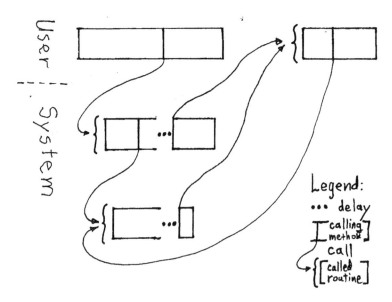

Figure 1.1: Deep calling structure with callback

predictable behavior. This introduces variability in the hidden drivers, which in Object Oriented programming is called "inheritance" and "polymorphism," thus making a namespace-centric feature out of a design flaw. Notice also the existence of circular paths, which can lead to resource trouble, especially since the deeper behavior of driver code is usually obscure.

Wide computing handles the same problem in Figure 1.2. Here the context-dependent method calls are eliminated, and replaced with independent programs ruling distinct resources ("pieces"). Notice that the top piece subsumes *both the user method and the callback*. In place of call arrows we get data-flow arrows, allowing natural control of all the state complexity that gets scattered among the Deep methods and drivers. Each piece can be tested separately, and all the data flow through the arrows is accessible.

Because **time** is OK in Wide programming, the pieces of Figure 1.2 are relaxed about blocking. In fact, they deliberately exploit it for control purposes, which can easily be programmed in. And **space** (in the territorial sense of ownership, rather than sharing, of resources) comes natural to independent "workers" tasked with parts of a project. Finally, the entire structure of Figure 1.2 is obviously **parallel**, in contrast to the Deep structure, which is straining to preserve the metaphor of nested calls on a single CPU.

There it is, in a nutshell. **From hobbies to space science** should be obvious now. Think of any project of that sort, and it breaks down, *and breaks*

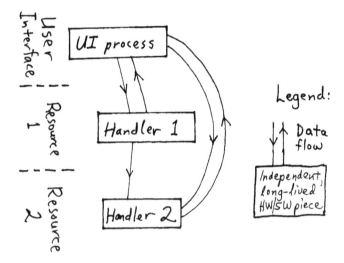

Figure 1.2: Wide structure of independent pieces

down naturally, into a more extensive version of Figure 1.2. In fact, Wide pieces improve on code reuse. They allow whole device reuse, independent of version and operating system, and complete control of data flowing between program parts.

The only question remaining is: can you do this kind of stuff—with modern tools? And the answer is: you are forced to do it, because time and resource-space dominate every project. You can follow the dictates of "advanced" tools and agonize through every step, struggling upstream against the tools' Deep bias. Or you can deliberately impose Wide structure *from the beginning of the project,* selecting tools that fit the design. Making this possible is the purpose of Connel, and of this book.

1.3.2 β— Get rid of hiccups

Building software to race as fast as possible through a problem leads to hiccups, or glitches in the flow, because irregular input and natural variation cause batches to come ready all at once, with time gaps in between. The Deep paradigm refuses to deal realistically with time, and therefore it keeps falling into this trap. It's built into Deep DNA, so to speak. Remember the early computer games that were ruined when X86 CPUs *increased* their clock speed?

Only Crawl-Space Computing can assure no hiccups, because only Crawl-Space Computing puts the data flow plumbing on the outside. Once all the data flow (video, music, robot actuator feedback) is there where you can pass

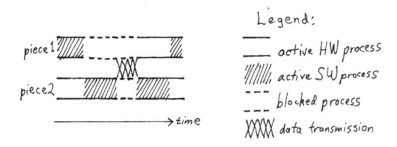

Figure 1.3: Hardware/software equivalent communication

it through your traffic meter, you can design exquisitely smooth production. I'll detail the solution later in the book.

One point needs to be made. Some people complain that the data passing overhead of the Wide model kills the efficiency of the program, causing Figure 1.2 to limp along behind Figure 1.1 forever. This is rarely so, and any random-intensive database case that suffers from such a Deep requirement can be enclosed in one box in Figure 1.2 (a so-called *harness*) and the rest of the world can treat it as a source. For everything else, communication overhead can be made minor, because immense hardware and protocol effort has gone into making that so.

The best is the enemy of the good. If you insist on the highest altitude, you have one possible point and no room for maneuver. My rule of thumb is that one to five percent can be yielded to Wide overhead, as this is vanishingly small compared to Moore's Law variations.

1.3.3 γ—Hardware/software equivalence

The mighty Communicating Sequential Processes (CSP) model (see [8]), as expressed in occam ([6]) and the Transputer, leads to hardware/software equivalence. This means equivalence of multitasking (lots of programs running under the OS) and multiprocessing (lots of embedded thingies helping you out), and interchangeability within these classes. In the book, I develop this even further with "move"-type operations such as the swap caddy, the flip driver, and the slider slot, described in the Second Wave chapter.

Figure 1.3 shows a simple case of hardware/software equivalence, an unconditional point-to-point communication. The direction is unimportant; what matters is that `piece1` came ready before `piece2`. The hardware version could be on two separate processors connected by wires; the software version could

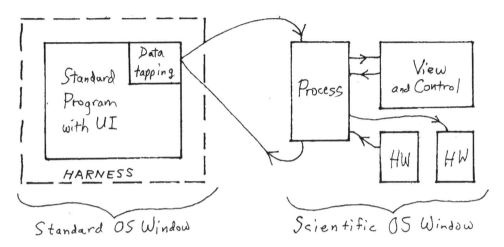

Figure 1.4: Harness with data rerouting

be multitasked on a uniprocessor. The machinery of data transmission could tie up both, one, or even neither (DMA) of the processes' CPU cycles. The state-machine behavior is not implementation-dependent, though speed is.

All the other occam-like constructs used in Wide programming, such as parallels and alternations (`select()`), show similar hardware/software equivalence. Connel is also designed this way. The power of this is immense, as it yields also hardware/hardware equivalence and software/software equivalence, allowing easy mix and match operations with Wide pieces, often without even a recompile.

1.3.4 δ—Natural data and timing gatekeepers set you free

Modern apps and mystery programs (the kind found on the "cloud") cause discouragement, because the programmer or artist feels trapped in the labyrinth hiding his data. But every program has to output at some point. This is where Wide designs can gain control. You draw a line around the big, tangled thing, and start to extract what you need.

What I call *gatekeepers* are the focus of Connel. They live in very general programming spaces (Linux and Windows) and are meant to operate in tandem with undigested hunks like UIs and UI-based programs. Each program has a way of packaging and outputting data, whether a "save" or an export, and each OS has ways of transmitting this from program to program, even if scripts and canned UI sequences have to be used. GUIs even offer ways, like Automator in the Mac, to script their UI sequences, though this capability is little known

7

(thank you, Tom Dickson).

Drawing a line around the standard "app" in this way, and causing controlled data flow in both directions across this line, is called a HARNESS. Once the data has passed coherently under control of your Wide pieces, which live outside the harness on the right-hand side of Figure 1.4, and are connected with connector links (connels), you can shout out **"FREE AT LAST!"** and begin to really create.

Here I define a (lowercase) *connel* to be a practical, explicitly named or addressed device for carrying data in blocking FIFO fashion from one piece to another. It can be either hardware or software.

The two OS Windows of Figure 1.4 can be windows in one OS, or whole virtual machines, or connected physical machines. Because the gatekeepers (like `select()` among sockets or serial channels) are responsive, you do not have to restrict yourself to batch runs. You can display it, you can watch it flow, you can do science on it, you can do subtle modifications and then pass it back to the app.

The image of *villages connected by roads* is the complete picture of your project. The reason I created Connel, and the way it works best, is to make the app or UI be just one village and give freedom to make several other villages, all totally according to your specs, and responsive to whatever kind of independent software or embedded hardware you want to connect up. It turns out that the important data can always be reduced to a simple form, it flows fast down the "roads," and you can watch all of this flow and time it precisely.

1.3.5 ϵ—Flatten out the difficulty curve for complex projects

Everyone has heard of major disasters in software projects, the latest at this writing being the $500,000,000 "Obamacare rollout" in 2013. Less well known is the relative fruitfulness of computing development in the Space Age of the 1960s and early 1970s, with fewer engineers and far poorer equipment. Figure 1.5 is the result of some research I did for DARPA in 2007, showing that *development viscosity,* defined as amount of effort per unit of improvement, has conservatively increased 60 times (not 60%) since 1966.

The reason is the factorial (worse than exponential) difficulty of Deep development, where everything has to relate to all of past history, taken in any order. Typically, user-level developers throw up their hands at understanding the consequences of all the hidden code invoked by their modules. If the target project is anything but incremental, this leads to "Obamacare disasters." You will notice this almost always, when an important customer utility installs major new software.

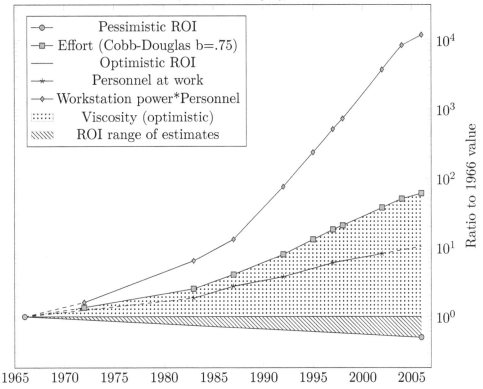

Viscosity Index Graph
(Sources: see [11])

Figure 1.5: Massive increase in development viscosity

The Wide, communicating village model flattens this difficulty curve to linear. To convince yourself of this, use Obamacare as an example. Just devise a data flow description of the health care signup, analogous to Figure 1.2. From subscribers to insurance companies, it's not much more complex than Figure 1.2, and its physical bigness is soluble by repetitive construction methods.

With harnesses and completely described data flow, many developers (past and present) can work together and not bog down in each other's complexity. Every piece can continually be tested independently of all others, creating a comfort level that extends across every nested depth of the design. Standardize/send/particularize is a trivial overhead compared to this boon.

As unplanned new requirements pour in, the project adjusts without a complexity explosion. (An analogy that shows this is the expansion of pioneering settlement networks in the 1800s.) All particularizations, such as changing

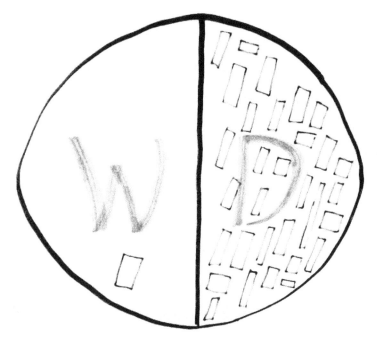

Figure 1.6: Duality

apps, OS versions, and data formats, are quarantined within their harnesses, at worst resulting in packet protocol additions, easily coordinated between two sides of a harness edge. So the easy development leads to trivial maintenance (my DBA name is "Lost Art of Zero Maintenance").

1.3.6 ζ—The duality of Wide versus Deep

My claim of a *duality* is a huge claim, because it implies that the Deep monoculture has neglected half the "development territory." Figure 1.6 is **realistic!**

Close examination of Table 1.1 gives details of the duality. Both in nesting development and spreading applications, each Deep approach has a dual Wide approach. See [7], in which the original Object-Oriented terminology, which is nowadays fully Deep and namespace-centric in its applications, refers in 1993 to the Wide entities implied naively by its nomenclature. (Minor namespace changes in established Deep languages, hiding tools like C `malloc`, hijacked the Object-Oriented approach in the early 1990s.)

Perhaps the most unintuitive example of this duality is call/return, typically a Deep action involving pushing and popping a stack. It's a surprise to most people that there is a Wide dual, fully implemented in Transputer occam, which uses no stack but places the call information in a process workspace, and does a jump/jump-back. (A Transputer has a three-word stack used only for interrupts.) This allows calls to work well in parallel constructs, and can be set up on any processor with a workspace pointer, like the X86 register DS.

Graphical user interfaces display the duality very strongly. The *user experience* of a GUI is completely Wide: the mouse pointer is moved to a **territory** to grant focus or make a selection or an input. The territorialism is 3D, with windows lying under other windows. However, standard GUI *programming* "maps" this Wide experience onto a unified Deep block of code, in which the visible territories do not have an independent existence but are implemented by an event-based Deep call and callback structure.

This Deep abstraction of the GUI can have highly anti-intuitive results if not programmed very carefully (where "very carefully" means "in a way that fits the territorial intuition"). Thus, GUIs are one case where moving to the Wide side of the duality could create a great simplification and increase of robustness at a stroke. Because it's human speed, the overhead caused by extra communications would be insignificant.

1.3.7 η—Tools that open doors

An infuriating experience that is growing ever more common (thank you, Tero Kukola, for making me aware of this) is the tool that acts as a gated community, where you do not control the gate. You have "access" (or refusal of access) taking the place of ownership. You find yourself being moved to the "cloud" where your work is stored mysteriously and dished up only by a program to which you must pay subscription fees. Instead of being located clearly in a file system under your control, it is accessible vaguely by a search.

This is an extension of the click-on-file system, developed much earlier, where a *file* (your created object) is associated one-to-one with a *program* that, by implication, is always used on that file. From a scientific point of view, that is absurd. Your data should lie open to you to use in ways limited only by your imagination. It should be so clear that you can organize work on it by hand.

The Crawl-Space or connected village model of Wide computing is clearly sympathetic with this ideal, while the convoluted Deep model, with its important hidden details, is prone to access limitations. Two "orthogonal" features supported here encourage massively accessible data. One is *pseudocoding,* in which an occam-like dialect is used to define precisely the state machine behavior of the program. I use occam because, line for line, it is much richer than C in state machine capability, being designed to support Communicating

Sequential Process (CSP) program structure. The other is *packet protocols*, which actually define the data as it is passed, allowing complete assurance that the information suffices for the project requirements.

In the book, I go into detail about pseudocoding, but leave the packet protocols (which are well known in standard computing) up to you. In addition, I offer some detail about standard tools, such as the `make` process of compiling, and the text files behind an Integrated Development Environment. By proceeding in this direction, you, the developer, can be freed from dependency on any specific tool.

1.3.8 θ—Terms that everyone can understand

Wide Computing is friendly to a naive approach because its behavior displays a strong analogy to connected *physical* devices. The book bolsters this by insisting on the hardware/software equivalence in its extensions of occam, even if the hardware analogy is rather impractical. The reason for this is that the hardware analogy forms an anchor, imposing behavior limitations that prevent many forms of "going nuts" that are typical of Deep (legalistic) computing algorithms. It also prevents invalid metaphor, a source of deep-seated bugs that is in the DNA of most standard computing. For a detailed discussion of this, see my white paper [4].

Being a mathematician, I have a personal preference for the terminology of mathematics and physical science. I also have a hard time following abstract Computer Science of the sort found in [1]. The entire book is designed for a non-Computer Science major. Anyone who can hack code to do a science project ought to be able to follow my presentation.

I admit that there are places in the book where the mathematics and physics get pretty detailed. These are illustrations of the *applications* of Wide Computing, not essential to the understanding of Wide Computing itself. Similarly, there are lots of code snippets in the book (and a few complete breakdowns) but these are for reference. You can blow past them in a first reading, and go back when you are actually building code.

1.4   Drill down

1.4.1   Wide Computing is general and practical

The ability to do any computing task with Wide techniques follows from an even stronger claim: "You can do anything with Transputers in occam." The Transputer was a 1980s-era embedded chip designed to be programmed in

Wide fashion by its native computing language, occam. On the scale of Wide to Deep, occam is more extremely Wide than Connel or the techniques I will be teaching here. Nonetheless, correcting for the hardware capabilities of its era, Transputer-based solutions showed themselves capable of doing everything. Perhaps the most extreme example is in [5]: an autonomous vehicle travelling the German autobahn in 1993, guided by Transputers programmed in occam.

Though the Transputer is gone, occam still exists. It will be the foundation of the pseudocoding technique taught later in this book.

Some questions now arise.

If modern languages are too Deeply layered, and occam is only to be used for pseudocode, how are we to code our Wide programs?

This is a difficulty I have dealt with for years, and the solution, though not entirely satisfactory, is to use the least abstract language univerally available: C. Consulting Table 1.1 shows that C is already Deep (for instance in its use of a stack), but it is minimal and close to the bare metal. Communication using C libraries is completely general, not restricted to designed-in features as in many more recent languages. Hiddenness can be avoided, as discussed later, by not using `malloc` or C++ constructs.

Having settled on C, it turns out that the standard operating systems Linux and Windows can be adapted to Wide programming. This is because they have been forced to be server-friendly (even Windows had to restore its command-line BATCH-like capabilities because of this). Embedded programming is naturally Wide and, even if the tools available are more rudimentary, can be made to join the model, as long as they are programmed in C so that their communication features can be placed outermost.

What I avoid, or at least must work around, are object-oriented languages and their enforced hiding, as in this code snippet on page 4 of [9]:

```
void draw() {
  w.step();
  w.display();
}
```

This is in Processing, a language developed from Java. I asked William Swanson what he thought `w.display()` does, and he replied, "Magic."

What about code reuse, and economizing programmers' time?

To train C and these operating systems to do Wide Computing, I developed Connel. Used in a strict pattern, clearly modelled on occam, Connel forces the C program to behave in a reliable and understandable Wide fashion. Not only is this code highly reusable, but it relates to a clear data flow model. Knowledge of difficult C and OS-based communication behaviors is encoded in the Connel routines and does not have to be rehashed each time the programmer needs it.

The C code generated by Connel and other Wide Programming techniques is verbose. I do not have the resources to develop a scripting language, though C macros could be used to vastly reduce the number of lines of code. The resulting code blocks, which are completely standard C (not C++) and do not use `malloc`, must force the programming to do Wide tasks which are "stepchildren" of the stacky design of C.

The programmer's time spent on this, however, is minimal. This is because big blocks of code can be lifted from older programs, starting with the sample programs in the Connel distribution. For those who do not have a fold editor, cut and paste works fine. The upshot is a template program in which all the communication "pudding" is already working at full speed and can be tested, even before the algorithmic "plums" are inserted.

Why spend time on communication links when we could be writing real performing code?

There are three answers, and they get to the heart of the technique.

First, in any project, it's a good idea to do the hard part first. Communications are tricky, with complex state machines full of exceptions. A "path through the minefield" should be found. Doing "plum" code first, making assumptions about the comms, and later finding them wrong, can create a real tangle.

Second, the outer connector links can be accessed later without rewriting the program. This is useful for testing, for spying data flows, and for adding new features.

Third, the timing and dependencies of the algorithmic code are usually known before it is written. This means that a template "pudding-only" program can be made quite realistic (using timers and busy loops) and be available to help with construction of other pieces, at the same time as the algorithmic code is being written.

1.4.2 Theory and Critiques

The contrast between Wide and Deep models of computing is the contrast between naturalism and legalism. This makes it clear that both models are universally valid for all programs. Legalism proposes that every action of the machine should be exactly in accord with its programming, and this (short of physical disasters) is always true. Naturalism proposes that every piece of the machine behaves according to the physical laws of its construction, and this also is always true. It is therefore always a matter of emphasis.

The legalistic, Deep model says that the state of the program (data and code) carries within it, as a logical consequence, the output of the program. Thus, if `Sum` produces the sum of two positive integers, and `LargestPrime` produces the biggest prime number less than or equal to a positive integer, then

`result1 = Sum(384290, 1289721)`

and

`result2 = LargestPrime(43982576)`

each fit this model. Creating the computational machinery to find the answer may not be so trivial (especially in the second case), but it is in principle doable. This is the viewpoint of functional programming.

Two problems arise.

(D1) First, what about computing time? The functional programming model ignores it, but it matters in the real world.

(D2) Second, what if not all the state is present at the time the task is triggered? Then delays and communication calls (like "read(x, y)") will have to be sneaked in to achieve success.

The naturalistic, Wide model says that any machine consists of pieces, each of which is itself a machine, which has an initial state, a final state, and ways of affecting the machines or results around it. This is the viewpoint of occam, of hardware design, and of engineering outside the computing world (as of bridges and classic cars).

From the standard software designer's point of view, a choice of two difficulties arises.

(W1) If the machine is programmed in a standard algorithmic fashion, especially with dynamic resources, it is hard or impossible to disentangle the smaller machines and their effects on each other.

(W2) On the other hand, if Wide techniques are used to isolate the smaller machines except for specific, known communications and timing effects, it seems that a crippling restriction is imposed on the options available to the programmer.

There is one weak point in each criticism—one path through which the model's advocates can break through.

(D1) is weak under conditions of Moore's Law, with rapidly increasing raw computing speed. Succeeding advances in chip speed have permitted Deep Computing to sweep all before it until very recently. Lately, the complexity explosion implied by (D2) has begun to take its toll.

(W2) is weak under conditions of cheap computing resources. GPGPU and map-reduce are already demonstrating this on the fringes, and non-uniform memory access (NUMA) is pressing it into center stage, but it is still viewed more as a problem than an opportunity. In fact, it is very much an opportunity, because of a second-order effect I have not discussed yet.

In Deep computing, by the very fact that all programming options of the major machine are left open, any part of the program can affect any part of the machine, no matter how distant its functionality. (This is a trait of legalism: some weird codicil can make the Alternative Minimum Tax apply to a low-wage worker, so everyone needs to check everything all the time.) This means that programming effort and complexity increase as a function of what every other programmer has done everywhere else through all of history. Also, internally, as a program's size increases, its difficulty increases nonlinearly because of the entanglements.

In Wide computing, on the other hand, every piece is self-contained and unaffected by history. The difficulty of expanding a program is linear. *This is an effect that shows itself very early, even in programs maintained by only one person.* All that is needed is to figure out how to apportion the work among the independent pieces, using planned communication paths, without significantly affecting total efficiency. And great leeway is offered by modern hardware, which now cheaply offers more and more cores that can work side by side, instead of attempting to increase clock speed.

1.4.3 Knowledge, hiding, and predictability

Before going on, I must issue a warning to readers who are not quite so naive in the terminology of Computer Science (CS). Many common terms are in use in CS, especially in object-oriented programming (OOP), in a way that means almost the opposite of their naive meaning. Understanding this is critical to critiquing and understanding Wide Programming.

I use the word "piece" because both "object" and "component", which seem that they should mean the same, have become tainted in this way. They refer more to namespace entities than to physical things or analogues thereof. In particular, their "methods" are designed to *hide* the "plumbing" through which data and timing are transmitted. Consider the line

```
w.display();
```

in the Processing example I quoted from [9].

Inheritance and polymorphism increase this hiding effect. The result is ease of programming, but only up to a point. This point is reached when lack of knowledge takes its toll. Code workarounds and branches are then necessary, but increase the problem for later rounds of coding.

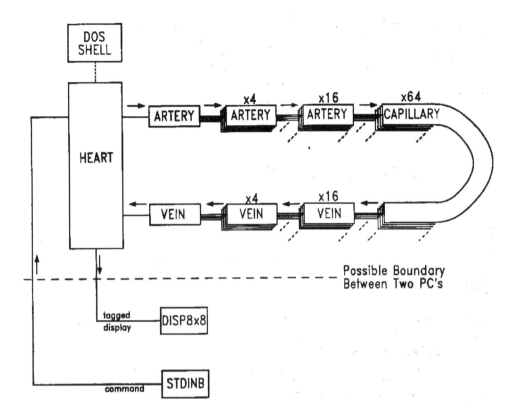

Figure 1.7: HEART3 1MB Palmtop DOS demo

The design in Wide Computing is done the opposite way. Stuff happens within a piece, but it is deliberately set up so that all significant effects that cross the boundary of the piece, both in time and "space," are known and explicitly enumerated. (Notice that this is how all engineering is done outside the computing world.)

An important consequence of this is *hardware/software equivalence*: It does not matter whether a piece is implemented as a separate piece of hardware (multiprocessing), or as a Wide-designed program or process sharing code and timing within a single piece of hardware (multitasking), as long as the resources are sufficient. The significant effects are the same. Therefore these options are interchangeable. As [6] says (page 71): "Configuration [meaning how the processes are mapped onto hardware] does not affect the logical behavior of a program."

This huge claim—whose consequences you can well imagine in the world of massive multicore, GPGPU, and Google-scaled map-reduce—was illustrated by my 1993–1996 work of [3], in which DOS, which is a single-tasking OS with only one megabyte of memory, was tricked into multitasking on the HP Palmtop. Figure 1.7 shows a tiny example (it was extended to up to 128 simultaneous "screens", either multitasked or multiprocessed). The switch between multitasking and multiprocessing is achieved *without recompiling.*

Because all the significant effects going into or out of a piece are programmed on the outside, each piece can be tested separately, and connected pieces can be spied upon as they interact. More important, knowledge about what the piece does is always preserved, no matter how many generations of software development follow. And a piece's behavior is not silently altered by some internal call whose definition is changed by a later version of library or OS. Wide Computing restricts itself to stable, low-level tools.

It remains, then, to answer objection (W2) in more detail. First I will sketch some basics.

1.4.4   Data flow basics

The consequence of dealing with objection (D2) is the concept of *data flow.* This obviously points to an analogy with fluid flow, but we need to justify this.

A resource, such as memory, may have a necessary role in causing a computing machine to put out the correct result. Here we are concerned with a resource that is *writable* in the context of the program. This implies that at one time (before being written to) it may have a different state from later (after being written to).

If this change of state involves progress in setting up for a correct program output or behavior, then clearly in some sense the "after" state must be better than that "before." Data flow happens when the resource changes from an indifferent state (either undefined or useless) before to a specific and useful state after. If it's a byte of eight bits, then any of them can be either 0 or 1 before, and we don't care. A full-byte write puts each of them into a specific state (either 0 or 1, but decided correctly).

Typically (but not always) this state is a copy of the state of a similar byte somewhere else. Then it is said that *data has flowed* from the *source* byte to the *destination* byte. Notice that in the case of a "copy," the analogy with a flow is not exact, because afterward the data still exists in the source byte.

It is possible to have a "move," in which the source byte degenerates to an undefined or useless state. This could be modeled as a turntable with a byte on each side turning 180 degrees. More commonly, it may happen that the source memory is not used further with that value after its data has moved on, and waits to receive more data from yet another source before being useful again.

This would then be part of a "pipeline." But in general we cannot necessarily assume this, and the term "data flow" permits one-to-many copies and refers specifically to the advancing state of the receiver.

A critical part of data flow is its *timing*. Use of the data may not start until after it has flowed in. (Failure to assure this is a common source of program bugs.) In fact, transmission of a timing event alone is a form of data flow. It changes one bit of information, causing "After event?" to change from FALSE to TRUE. Even though no bit of memory may contain "After event?", this change is capable of affecting program flow, as by an interrupt. Therefore the term "data flow" is synonymous with "timing and data flow."

A final point is the pipeline model of data flow. In fact, in all the ordinary output/input combinations (voltage on a wire or wires, transmission through wave action, writes to memory) the datum input rubber-stamps the datum output, and the time received is substantially the same or at least in time order of sending. This substantiates the usual model of ordered pipeline flow.

The modelling of programs as collections of single sequences of actions which can emit or receive data or timing signals to or from other such sequences was pioneered by C.A.R. Hoare in Communicating Sequential Processes, or CSP. The computing language occam was modeled on CSP, and the Transputer embedded processor was built to run occam.

However, occam IO is synchronized and unbuffered (with one exception: the first byte sent through a wire link). Due to the difficulties of coding explicit FIFOs everywhere, most standard data channels are ordered and buffered. A number of outputs may be standing in a queue, not yet input by the receiver. Because Connel is designed for practical use, we go with "ordered and buffered" even in our "almost-occam" pseudocode. It is always possible to create the synchronized and unbuffered design if necessary by using an explicit acknowledge (ACK) message going in the opposite direction to the main one.

1.4.5 Algorithmic basics

The great challenge to the Wide Computing model in (W2) is algorithmic efficiency. By deliberately limiting the ability to influence other pieces of the general program, the Wide programmer has reduced his options in performing the task. This includes not only branches and writes to the alien pieces, but even reading information from an alien piece, if that information is either subject to change (race condition), or is too far away (NUMA). Therefore special program or hardware elements called *communication channels* come to the fore, and are used to move data from one piece to another.

Thus the two main efficiency challenges to Wide Computing are:

(C1) Is the burden of data transmissions (called "communications over-head") required by the Wide algorithm so great that the system is bogged down by it?

(C2) Even apart from communications overhead, is the restriction enforced on the design of the algorithm itself so that its work can be done in several independent processes (called "cost of parallelization") so great that it ruins performance?

The answer, of course, is, "It depends." The goal of the Wide Programmer is to find as many tasks as possible for which these challenges can be met. And the surprising thing is how many of them there are. The fact is that raw size makes problems more parallelizable, *often by the crudest methods,* even when by nature they are very entangled (like a compiler parse).

I will explore three dualities in the world of algorithms. They are related but not identical. Then I will give a simple example, that shows how parallelizability can creep in where not expected.

First duality: top-down versus bottom-up. This is usually a duality of design. In top-down design, the large-scale problem pre-exists the small-scale components used to solve it, and usually determines their character. In bottom-up design, the small-scale components are a "given" and by connecting them (or a subset of them), the large-scale solution is found.

Second duality: intensive versus extensive. This actually refers to physical units, but I'm using the terms more naively to refer to those problems where the interconnections are relatively very numerous compared to the amount of data (intensive), as opposed to those with few or no non-local interconnections between massive data (extensive). An example of the first might be a deep expression evaluation:

```
x = (((x1+x2)*(x3+x4))+((x5+x6)*(x7+x8)))/((x9-x10)*(x11-x12))
```

An example of the second might be a multiply-accumulate:

```
w = (y1*z1)+(y2*z2)+(y3*z3)+(y4*z4)+(y5*z5)+(y6*z6)
```

Frequently, intensive expressions hide what must be an extensive implementation. An example is the recursive definition of factorial:

```
unsigned integer fac(unsigned integer n) {
  return (n > 0) ? n*fac(n-1) : 1;
}
```

Unwinding the evaluation of this formula reveals that an array or stack of n "black boxes" is needed. A bottom-up approach is more economical:

```
unsigned integer fac(unsigned integer n) {
  unsigned integer k = 1;
  unsigned integer i;
  for (i=1; i<=n; i++) k *= i;
  return k;
}
```

The third duality is deep versus wide, as defined above. An intensive problem could be analyzed by top-down methods and performed by deep techniques, with a single "outer face" and "black boxes" which, each in their turn, are resolved into deeper problems with black boxes until finally they have real data that can be evaluated. (This is how compilation is typically done.) An extensive problem with a repeating bottom structure can do those evaluations first and then combine them. (This will work for the multiply-accumulate or dot product.) Thus intensive problems tend to be recursive, stacky and deep, and extensive problems array-oriented and wide.

However, an array-oriented extensive problem may have an order imposed on its resolution, in which case a wide approach may be harder to find. An example of this is standard long division. Even in these cases, when a large number of similar calculations are required, vector (pipeline) programming makes Wide computing usable.

1.4.6 Algorithm example

I will now fully analyze one apparently simple problem, showing how subtle these issues can be. It is addition of two unsigned binary integers.

cin	0	0	0	0	1	1	1	1
a	0	0	1	1	0	0	1	1
b	0	1	0	1	0	1	0	1
	--	--	--	--	--	--	--	--
sum	00	01	01	10	01	10	10	11

The above table shows the complete single-bit results, including a carry-in. The left bit of the sum is a carry out, the right bit the modulo sum. Two N-bit numbers can be added, giving an N-bit modulo sum and one carry out bit, by feeding the carry out of sum K into the carry-in of sum $K + 1$. This is an extensive algorithm, the "ripple carry," but due to the order of dependency it takes time N.

Now we carry out a top-down analysis. If a and b are N-bit integers, and c is 0 or 1, then we define

```
s(a,b,c) = a+b+c = c(s(a,b,c))|m(s(a,b,c))
```

where c is 1 bit and m is N bits. Here | does not refer to "or" but is a join between left bits and right bits in a binary number, so that

```
1b|0100b|1001b = 101001001b
```

for example.

If $N = 2M$, a = aL|aR, and b = bL|bR, then the carry out of the aR+bR sum is the carry-in of the aL+bL sum. Hence we get

```
s(a,b,c) = s(aL,bL,c(s(aR,bR,c)))|m(s(aR,bR,c))
```

Hence if we have the four incoming values (with their carries out) of s(aL,bL,0), s(aL,bL,1), s(aR,bR,0), and s(aR,bR,1), we can construct s(a,b,0) and s(a,b,1) by selecting one of the left sums based on the right carry, and then throwing away the right carry.

In fact, since c(s(aR,bR,0)) $\leq$ c(s(aR,bR,1)), we can copy s(aL,bL,0) over s(aL,bL,1) if c(s(aR,bR,1)) == 0, and we can copy s(aL,bL,1) over s(aL,bL,0) if c(s(aR,bR,0)) == 1. In the rare case where the two right carries disagree (which only happens if aR and bR are bitwise complements), we need do nothing.

Carrying this logic all the way down to the single bit adds, we discover that with enough parallel adders, we can finish our addition in $\log(N) + 1$ steps instead of N steps. Here $\log(N)$ is, as usual in CS, the log base 2 rounded up to an integer. This "conditional sum adder" is as good as the best adders in use in actual hardware, such as the Kogge-Stone adder.

For those who are conversant with the problems of transistor-level chip design, I may add that with one extra step, every carry bit can be made to agree with the carry out of s(a,b,c) for the two maintained sums. This eliminates fan-out problems and breaks the data at each reduce step into independent sets of eight bits, two of which are neither read nor written.

This adder is a trivial example of the "map-reduce" approach to parallelizing problems. This, where applicable, reduces a problem of size and time N to a problem of parallel size N and time $\log(N) + 1$. The "map" part is the bunch of parallel operations (time 1) and the "reduce" part is the joining of the results (time $\log(N)$). For example, a problem of size 256 is done in time 9. Most really large problems are either outright local and hence completely parallelizable, or susceptible to map-reduce, which by being a little wasteful in transistors (cheap) is able to save immense amounts of time (very valuable).

1.4.7 The Connel crawl-space strategy

I will conclude this chapter by returning to questions of practicality.

The purpose of this exercise in Wide Computing is to put scientific computing power, equivalent to the actual ability of the hardware that is so cheap nowadays, into the hands of ordinary "hackers." In particular, it should be possible to open the gates to a yard as big as you want—working from the problem that you want to solve, and not from the capabilities of available UIs, "apps" or languages.

So I don't care if I waste a few cycles, or generate a few extra lines of code (though I do not want to waste the programmer's time). And I am not anxious to keep everything up to the purest occam-level CSP standard. All I want is that it should work, and it should be obvious why and how it works, and all the working bits and pieces should be easily and clearly accessible.

Connel doesn't do threads, but it does `select()`. Connel stays coarse-grained, adapted to C machines and operating systems, and remains in the realm of full processes. If shared memory is needed, it's kept under control of terse negotiating commands sent over the standard, explicit communication channels. You don't get responsiveness by using fine-grained threads, you get it by using `select()`—a fact that seems to be forgotten even by hardware designers these days (e.g. Arduino).

The CSP people discovered decades ago that there is no substitute for `select()` (called ALT in occam) when you have a single process that needs to respond to several asynchronous communicating partners. Without it, you can spawn fine-grained threads until the cows come home, and you will still get hesitation. The coarse processes spend a moment starting, but then respond just as fast. They are understandable, and there are not many of them. And all the OS tools help you keep track of them, and Connel spies can watch the data.

Connel select also supports timer expiration. The newest development of it is capable of supporting graphics events, either in Windows or in Linux (XCB).

Connel deals with OS-accessible, named data channels. We have keyboard and screen, serial ports (including virtual ones via Bluetooth, USB and VMWare), Windows named pipes, and Linux sockets. We could do more, but that seems to be enough to get universal connectivity, both within an OS and between systems, including embedded.

Reconfiguration involving data channels of the same type does not require recompilation. Reconfiguration that changes the type of channel (say from socket to serial) usually requires only minor, methodical changes on the outside of the code, in the "pudding." This is all that is needed for changes from multitasking to separate hardware assist, or from OS-based components to embedded ones—a prime use of Connel in a successful commercial software project.

This strategy puts all the difficulty of communication hookups firmly on the outside and at the start of development. Take lots and lots of detailed notes! Make HOWTO files, and keep adding to them! Then you will come back months later and boot up all the pieces of your complex system in proper order, and it will work, and you will know why.

Multiple terminals and scripts are your friends. This is the easiest way to develop code either in Windows or Linux. Again, take lots of notes, and avoid the trap I have fallen into—which is to rely too much on history files. This is especially seductive in VMWare virtual machines, which suspend and therefore never shut down.

Using redirected spies and dummies permits you to send and receive data at full speed. Accurate timing reads—which can be arranged at microsecond accuracy using RDTSC—can be used to detect even the smallest hesitations. Simple command-line programs can do fast post-mortem analysis of the redirected output and spy data.

Design sketches (First Wave) and pseudocoding (Second Wave) are critical to any project. The Wide Computing approach is front-loaded with enough design to make sure of the power to finish the job. Each piece gets its sketch, and is a live thing that pulls in input and pumps out output with a certain rhythm during its lifetime. You are never caught short because you add enough CPU and communication to make sure of staying ahead of the demands of the task.

Wide Computing offers a number of rather obvious top-down techniques for project design. There is simple worker parallelization for completely distributed tasks, like CDMA channels or the well-known prime searches. There are partly distributed map-reduce calculations, as in the above example, and pipeline calculations. In the latter case the workload may break down into large chunks, with an alternating communication and computation "breathing" structure that produces batches of output at a varying delay. See [10] and related references. Finally, and most obviously of all, there is the breakdown of a project into parts of different kinds, which are then handled by different pieces with needed data passing between them, as in Figure 1.2.

All of the above are used as needed until each piece is clear enough so that a bottom-up analysis of the piece estimates its computational needs, communication bandwidth, and delays. Then it's all combined and a total estimate made. This works over the whole lifetime of a project.

Long-lived projects find themselves using the last technique (parts of different kinds passing or shunting data flows) more and more as features are added. An example would be a movie editor with inventive feature addition. Dummies (that pass data and do nothing) are your friend during such add-on developments. These include insertion of new hardware that passes data much faster than needed without changing program behavior until their added capacity is used.

The key thing about Wide Computing is that there is no point at which increasing complexity locks up the project. Each updated replacement piece, even if of completely different design and date, is slipped in to perform according to the same specifications as the old, like a new alternator replacing an old alternator in a classic car. Then a new capability can be spliced in without disturbing the old. It's like a village expanding into a city, and yet "Chicken Street" remains.

1.5 References

[1] Alboaie, Sinica: "Harvests: From now is possible to call asynchronous functions in a declarative way and to get almost the same experience as with synchronous code," GitHub, circa January, 2014.
`https://github.com/salboaie/harvests`
README.markdown

. . .

`Harvests` library is an experiment to sort out the ugliness of the asynchronous `callbacks` without `promises` or `control flow libraries`.

. . .

```
//on success harvest.myFileContent will contain the content
//you can start as many calls and they will be executed when
their dependencies are fulfilled
```

[2] Choisser, John P., and John O. Foster: *The XT-AT Handbook.* Annabooks, San Diego, 1989–1992. Booklet (3.5" by 6"), 94 pgs.

[3] Dickson, Lawrence J: "occam (TM) Road Map for the DOS PC." *Proceedings of the 1996 International Conference on Parallel and Distributed Processing Techniques and Applications* (PDPTA'96), Hamid R. Arabnia, editor. CSREA, Sunnyvale CA, 1996.

[4] Dickson, Lawrence J.: "Transparent Analogy as a Foundation for Language," September 12, 2007. `http://www.tjoccam.com/tacliwhp.pdf`

[5] Franke, U., and H. Fritz, A. Kuehnle, and J. Schick: "Transputers on the Road," Transputer Applications and Systems, Proc World Transputer Congress 1993, Vol 1, IOS Press 1993, p 1–17.

[6] INMOS Ltd: *occam 2 Reference Manual.* Prentice Hall International Series in Computer Science, C.A.R. Hoare, editor, Prentice Hall, 1988.
http://www.transputer.net/obooks/obooks.asp

[7] Justo, George R. R., and P. R. F. Cunha: "Deadlock-Free Configuration Programming," 2nd Int. Workshop on Configurable Distributed Systems, March 21–23, The IEEE Computer Press, pages 147–158, 1993.
http://www.cpc.wmin.ac.uk/~justog/GeorgeJusto-Publications.html

[8] Roscoe, A. W.: *Understanding Concurrent Systems,* Texts in Computer Science, Sprinter, 2010.

[9] Shiffman, Daniel: *The Nature of Code.* http://thenatureofcode.com, 2012.

[10] Welch, Peter, and George Justo and Colin Willcock: "High-Level Paradigms for Deadlock-Free High-Performance Systems," *Transputer Applications and Systems '93,* Volume 2, IOS Press, 1993, p 981-1004.
http://www.cs.kent.ac.uk/projects/ofa/kroc/high-level-paradigms-1993.pdf
This is a beautiful and intuitive solution for any number of problems, deadlock-free. Vertically there is a client-server cascade, and horizontally a massively parallel "heartbeat" system, with hybridization, therefore control and status, possible. All results are proven, though the CSP terminology may require some study. See [8].

[11] Standish, Stacey: Mathematics and Computer Science employment statistics (communication). Bureau of Labor Statistics, 2006.
Lamoreaux, Naomi R, and Kenneth L. Sokoloff: "The Decline of the Independent Inventor: A Schumpeterian Story?" 2005.
Odlyzko, Andrew: "The Decline of Unfettered Research." AT&T Bell Laboratories, October 4, 1995.
Wikipedia: "List of Intel Microprocessors," 2006.
http://www.sparcproductdirectory.com/history.html ca 2006.
Viscosity = Effort/ROI indexed from 1966, Cobb-Douglas Production Function (geometric mean) with labor weighted 75%, total workstation computational power 25%.

First Wave: Design The Major Pieces   **2**

Abstract

The purpose of this chapter is to describe the First Wave of Wide design, which consists of wrestling with the problem from a Data Flow point of view until it is clear that we have a path leading to a successful solution. I will illustrate with two real-life examples: the timed display of an array of temperature and humidity sensors in an orchard (thank you, Roger Wagner), and the CDMA decoding of signals from 120 weakly transmitting satellites (thank you, Rob Fryer). Each of these will suggest further needs which will be worked on in later Waves.

2.1   First Wave technique

The First Wave does not yet involve coding or even pseudocoding, though it may involve the study of existing code and pseudocode. It is focused instead on issues of intense practicality. You do not exit the First Wave until you are confident that the tools you have settled on are sufficient to solve the problems presented by the project.

This requires primitivism: data flows, timing, and cycle counting. But it also involves drawing pictures and diagrams that help make clear what the demands of the problem are. The standard technique of counting up the time required by the central calculation and multiplying it by the data rate is, as experienced programmers know, not good enough. Issues such as delays, data rate irregularity, and dependencies have to be faced clearly.

In a problem of any complexity, you will not escape without dealing with priorities. Calculation has to take place, but data needs to get in to be calculated upon, and the results have to get out. These operations create resource contention, and the tools and chips to be used have to be measured up against their needs. Otherwise as simple an operation as serial input could trip you up, especially in embedded work. As a rule, the first step in prioritizing is to place essential communication at a high priority, calculation at a lower.

The key to success is breaking up the problem into simpler parts. These are Wide Computing pieces, not dependent calls or methods. A piece stands alone and is equivalent to a piece of hardware. It starts, inputs data and timing according to a certain rhythm, outputs data and stimuli with a certain rhythm, and ends. The methodology of getting from input data to output data can be left vague, as long as the dependencies and effort required can be conservatively estimated.

This means that First Wave work involves doing a lot of searching of existing technology, whether hardware or software. It is the only way that "dependencies and effort required can be conservatively estimated." Sometimes the search reveals bad news, and pushes you "back to the drawing board" to find another path to goal. All of this is happening before you type a single line of code or even pseudocode.

The breakdown into parts is not restricted to big, app-level pieces. Small, humble things like FIFOs and communicators get First Wave attention too. It's a temptation to cry out, "Well of course I will get the data in there somehow! The bandwidth is not that great!" When tempted to think this way, recall how you feel when one of these "trivial" communicators refuses to work in software that you have to use.

Because of this, the First Wave returns to that most characteristic of Wide Computing features: the communication channel on the outside. So before we plunge in, I am going through a few details about the behavior of this communication in the real world dealt with by Connel, and by embedded programming.

2.2 Basic communication

As mentioned in the Introduction, the best model of communication to start with is ordered pipeline flow. This is a sequence in time of output/input data-copying events, from one piece (program or hardware) to one other. All the data goes in one direction and arrives in the same order as it left. In the case where there is a First-In First-Out (FIFO) buffer, it may arrive later than it left, perhaps much later. Typically data arrives in characters (8-bit bytes). Object-Oriented languages reach for this by "serializing" data, but in Wide Computing it is natural.

For bidirectional communication, one simply postulates two of these pipelines flowing in opposite directions. They may or may not be related, as message and ACK, for instance. Questions of ordering and synchrony dominate. One pipeline may have extra characters left over to input; then the ACK will not work properly. And of course communication parameters must match (baud rate in real serial transmissions, for example).

The surprising thing is that this obvious list summarizes the main difficulties with point-to-point communication: (a) the existence of the pipeline at all; (b) communication parameters; and (c) pipeline contents, which usually means emptiness as an initial state. These difficulties tend to cluster at the beginning, when connection is being established. Once past them, properly programmed communication goes smoothly, unless the channel itself is unreliable. Many hardware-based protocols, such as TCP/IP and Bluetooth, fight such unreliability with hidden retries, trying to abide by the model of a buffered pipeline of ordered characters.

The foundational model of a unidirectional pipeline—an occam "channel" if we ignore the buffering—is very strong for most purposes. It does not directly cover the need to broadcast data (one to many) or to merge data streams (many to one) though these can be done, perhaps inefficiently, using helper programs. It also does not deal with shared memory, but that is not a big problem. Using the liberal extension of occam in Wide pseudocode, two programs sharing memory can negotiate its use with short messages sent in the standard pipeline fashion.

Outputting to, and inputting from, a pipeline can be modeled on the "write()" and "read()" calls found in most standard languages, including C. One pushes into a pipeline, the other pulls out. A loop can easily be imagined that does a broadcast, or a one-to-many:

```
int fdin, fdout[4];
unsigned char b;
int i;
/* setup code here, such as file descriptor opens */
while (read(fdin, &b, 1)) {
  for (i=0; i<4; i++) {
    write(fdout[i], &b, 1);
  }
}
```

This is extremely inefficient one byte at a time, but analogous more efficient broadcasts can be devised, especially if there is parallelism (such as multithreading). A better expression will be given when we do pseudocode, but meantime drawings like Figure 2.1 can make the data spread clear.

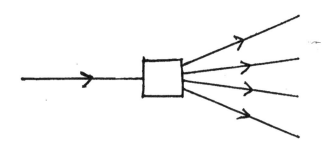

Figure 2.1: Broadcast spreader

2.3 The alternation, also known as select() or WaitForMultipleObjects()

The many-to-one is more difficult. *It requires a basic capability that cannot be composed out of the standard read() and write() even if there are many threads: the alternation or ALT construct, which is implemented by select() in Unix-related systems and by WaitForMultipleObjects() in Windows.* This *irreducible* construct allows the sequential program to respond immediately to the first of two or more unpredictable asynchronous stimuli.

At this point it is best to anticipate pseudocode, which handles it more clearly than select() or WaitForMultipleObjects() loops. The general purport (using Python-like indentation) should be clear.

```
WHILE notdone
  ALT
    a ? adata
      -- perform action involving adata
    b ? bdata
      -- perform action involving bdata
```

Here x ? xdata refers to a read of xdata on channel x. The way this will actually be executed is something like this:

```
WAIT
a ? adata
-- perform action involving adata
b ? bdata
-- perform action involving bdata
b ? bdata
-- perform action involving bdata
WAIT
b ? bdata
-- perform action involving bdata
a ? adata
-- perform action involving adata
b ? bdata
-- perform action involving bdata
WAIT
b ? bdata
-- perform action involving bdata
WAIT
a ? adata
-- perform action involving adata
...
```

The two independent channel inputs are racing, and can come in in any order, with or without waits. If new input data comes ready while "perform action" is still running, the following ALT immediately chooses an input, while if not, a wait takes place at that ALT.

The inputs may be a timer expiration or an event, as well as data. The program responding to the stimuli is purely sequential. No polling is used, but the response is as timely as possible. This is the right way to program processes that have multiple asynchronous inputs or stimuli, and eliminates much uncomfortable multithreaded code, leaving the design far simpler.

First Wave design can simply have multiple data arrows coming in, and a single action block dealing properly with whatever data has come in, in whatever order. Frequently, very little code is included in the "perform action" blocks inside the ALT, perhaps only a few state settings, and most of the action is done afterwards, as in the following pseudocode:

```
WHILE notdone
  SEQ
    ALT
      a ? adata
        -- perform action involving adata
      b ? bdata
        -- perform action involving bdata
    -- perform action involving either adata or bdata or both
```

In occam, code sequences are represented by a special symbol SEQ, because an equally valid way of composing code—in parallel or PAR,—is also possible. Please also note that the channels (a and b) always have to pre-exist their use, and unlike adata and bdata have to be declared outside the WHILE loop, because they are shared with a parallel program, not shown. This is why occam totally fits the model of Wide Computing.

This ALT-based code is the heart of Connel and of Wide Computing. It makes code extremely responsive to multiple stimuli, eliminates most of the need for low-level multithreading and shared variables, and leaves the core of most projects in a set of simply structured pieces, often purely sequential.

2.4 Some kinds of communication channels and events

Connel has implemented a set of communication channels in Linux and Windows that, by experience, are enough to accomplish most purposes. It can be expanded at need, or Wide Computing programmers can write their own native code, guided by Connel source.

2.4.1 The keyboard and the text console screen

This simplest of all IO for text-based programs is carefully implemented in Connel. For maximum responsiveness, Connel offers character IO rather than line IO.

The true tty consoles, rather than the redirected sort, are used in both Windows and Linux. This is because redirection is a blunt, incomplete tool, incapable of important needs like multiple inputs. Also redirection hides the communicating channel, which according to Wide Computing theory should be explicitly defined. For both these reasons, Connel usage prefers OS-internal program connections to use SOCKLOCAL declarations, which are named pipes in Windows and sockets in Linux.

2.4.2 The serial connection

Connel offers buffered serial connections, leaving it to the operating system to implement these. Therefore, they are in fact implemented not only by serial cables, but also by Bluetooth, by USB, and by VM-to-VM serial connections in VMWare. They are always expected to pre-exist the program on both sides of the communication. Serial connections are bidirectional (have two pipelines, one moving in each direction) whether or not their implementation is full-duplex or half-duplex.

Once the serial connection exists and the communication parameters like baud rate are agreed upon, buffering is expected, so programs may need to be able to drain leftovers from the channel. Following that, the channel operates in character mode, though buffering means that actual tranmissions are usually much more efficient than that. Serial IO is most useful between different machines, including embedded boards, which are typically programmed "by hand" to be able to handle buffered serial IO.

2.4.3 The SOCKLOCAL connection

The current version of Connel does communication internal to an OS on a machine via SOCKLOCAL, which means named pipes in Windows and sockets in Linux. Each is restricted to bidirectional communication between a server and a client, one client at a time. Activity is started by the server, which may open or create a SOCKLOCAL entity in the file system. From time to time a client connects, communicates, and disconnects. This operation is also called "connect" from the server's side, though traditionally "accept" is the term used.

Connel has thus far avoided the server's spawning multiple client connections, because it violates the static (outer) nature of the Wide connector links. A SOCKLOCAL has one name and can be picked up and relinquished by various communicating partners in sequence. This is versatile enough for operations that are not excessively dynamic, including most scientific and robotics applications. The reason is that multiple serving channels can be created, each handling one client at need.

A server that creates a SOCKLOCAL is a slight violation of the Wide design, permitted because of convenience. The server runs first, and its initialization, when it is creating the SOCKLOCALs, is treated as "outside" the effective program run, as in this pseudocode:

```
SEQ
  --initiate server              --  \
  CHAN SOCKLOCAL thesock :       --   \    This is server code
  PAR                            --      > that creates a
    WHILE serving                --     /   SOCKLOCAL then uses it
      -- do server IO with thesock  -- /
  SEQ
    client1(thesock)             --  \    These are sequentially
    client2(thesock)             --    > connecting and
    . . .                        --  /    disconnecting clients
```

2.4.4 Timer

The timer is not a communication channel but an event. It is extremely useful, especially in select() loops, where it provides a timeout branch when needed. It must be programmed with great care, because its misuse can cause near-misses and other hard-to-reproduce bugs.

Connel timers always use microseconds. The real-time clocks of most non-embedded systems are much coarser than this, so a timeout happens after, not at, the specified time.

2.4.5 Graphics

Graphics primitives are treated as communication events. In Windows we have the standard Msg events (detected by MsgWaitForMultipleObjects, counted and all peeked), while in Linux XCB is placed over X, and an XCB file descriptor triggers select() responses which are then read.

It is expected that most Connel programs will not include graphics, but will when necessary communicate with a special graphics handler that will be explicitly and separately programmed. This prevents the code tangle that results from centralizing all control in a Graphical User Interface (GUI).

2.4.6 Interrupts

Interrupts are events, and the collection of all active Interrupt Service Routines (ISRs) can be understood as a big ALT loop running at highest priority. Wide Computing principle applied to these can be used in the construction of embedded code, but Connel does not as yet implement interrupt responses, except for those that are available to the select() loop.

The pseudocoding techniques are extremely useful, even as is, for the design of completely reliable embedded code.

2.5 Example: orchard sensors (thank you, Roger Wagner)

This is the first of my examples, which are presented with a bias toward simplicity, and use existing capabilities. For instance, I am unmoved by the possibility that Bluetooth 4 may someday support mesh topologies. This is hidden, and the Wide approach prefers existing and understandable (and therefore design-robust) parts.

A small orchard lies just outside of view of the homestead, on hilly terrain. There is a water system, but it gets plugged now and again, and the temperatures need watching on colder days. On hills and vales, sensors poke six inches into the ground to keep track of dampness near the fine root system, and shaded thermometers watch for extremes. Twenty sensors may be enough, and data once an hour is more than sufficient.

The mission control station will be like a combined display of security monitors, not action-packed, but we need data for at least 24 hours. A glance will then show trouble spots before the trees can be damaged. We certainly have no wish to string long wires, and Bluetooth in some variations has enough range.

2.5.1 (A) Sketch the basic design

One graphics slave program plots the slowly moving data, as fed to it by a master data capturer running on the main computer. This is also capable of minor calculations and can detect and send some alerts. The data from all 20 sensors is sent hourly via Bluetooth to the data capturer.

In each sensor system, an embedded chip reads temperature and dampness (and possibly other variables such as battery charge) and transmits them hourly via Bluetooth to the master at mission control. This is a battery-powered low-power system, with the battery either replaced periodically or recharged by a solar panel. It therefore is as crude a chip as possible, and spends much time in sleep mode.

2.5.2 (B) Critique the basic design

A good start is to focus on Bluetooth, since it's the critical connection between a reasonably-priced main system with a good screen, which is standard equipment these days, and a reasonably priced embedded design using a low-power CPU and a standard development tool like Arduino or Energia.

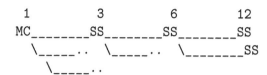

```
   1           3           6           12
  MC_____SS_____SS_____SS
    \_____..    \_____..    _____SS
        \_____..
```

Table 2.1: Fan-out of depth 3 sensor system with connectivity 3

This embedded design, with Bluetooth included, can already be found in existing products like the Kickstarter sensor Flutter (see [1]). But Flutter appears designed for single sensor use, and is veering toward complexity and high power usage, so it will probably only serve as a guide. We need to do some basic Bluetooth design.

There is no problem with the data throughput, but we are assuming a connectivity of 20 will be available to the master at mission control. This is rather demanding and must be checked. References [2] through [6] are obtained from the search "bluetooth serial maximum number of connections" and quickly supply the bad news: The number of connections may vary from 1 to 7 according to the spec, and for low-energy Bluetooth, the maximum is just 3. It's hardware, so multitasking in the control center will not help. Thus, it is back to the drawing board.

2.5.3   (C) Redo the design, correcting the communication

The thing favoring us here is the extremely low bandwidth: twenty bytes per sensor per hour, maybe. So there is no trouble with placing the sensors in sequence around the hour. Perhaps one could close and reopen a Bluetooth connection to each sensor in turn. That's not very robust (if one hangs, it could stall the whole system, like a string of Christmas lights). For the purpose of this exercise, I'll demonstrate a solution that generalizes from a Wide point of view and uses fixed links. Even a connectivity of 3 is good enough for a fan.

As shown in Table 2.1, even with connectivity only three a depth of three is good enough to connect 21 sensor stations to mission control. How this might work for actual placement in an orchard is shown by Figure 2.2.

Since each Bluetooth device has a worldwide unique identifier, it is possible with this setup to preprogram each device (MC and every SS) with the identifiers of its three (or fewer) communication partners. MC has three slaves; each of the 12 depth-3 SSs in Table 2.1 has one master; all the others (3 depth-1 and 6 depth-2) have one master and two slaves. This design is clearly extensible to further depths for bigger orchards.

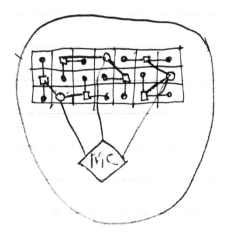

Figure 2.2: Orchard sensor connectivity

For First Wave purposes, we will assume that the problem of programming these connections and triggering their startup has been solved. (Bluetooth notes exist in the Connel package distribution.) An even more interesting programming problem, which will be put off until further Waves, is how to install a replacement part at any depth, and get communication partners to work with it. This is obviously doable. The key to usefulness will be to devise a way to do it easily.

The design in Table 2.1 clearly implies that each Bluetooth transmission will move only one depth level. Commands move to a greater depth, and data moves to a lesser depth. Thus, a communication between master control and a depth-n sensor station requires n Bluetooth transmissions.

The question arises how many of these will be happening at the same time. In many fanout applications we would try to get this kind of parallel use as high as possible, using point-to-point hardware. In this case, it will be a good idea to force them into being sequential or nearly so, for two reasons: (1) The point-to-point design conceals a major shared resource, the local broadcast transmission area, which Bluetooth deals with in a hidden fashion using message filtering. So as not to overburden this capability with potential interference, we want to keep the simultaneous transmissions as few as possible. (2) The problem has an undemanding data rate, so spacing out the transmissions has little cost. We just have to design a way to synchronize the timings.

Figure 2.3 shows the result of these considerations. If a depth n sensor receives data from K sensors of depth $n + 1$, it must pass on all the data it receives, plus one block of data from its own sensors. If $n_{\max}$ = the maximum

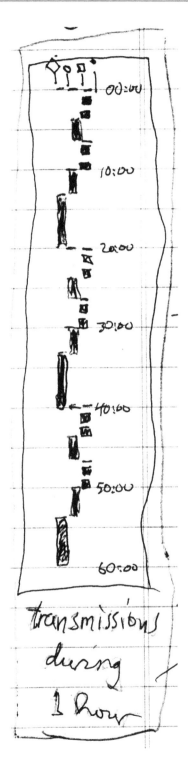

Figure 2.3: Orchard transmission timing

depth (here 3), and $m = n_{\max} - n$, then

$$\text{datasent}(0) = \text{datasize}$$
$$\text{datasent}(m) = K * \text{datasent}(m - 1) + \text{datasize} \quad \text{if} \quad m > 0 \qquad (2.1)$$

It is easily confirmed that this is equivalent to

$$\text{datasent}(m) = \text{datasize} * (K^{m+1} - 1)/(K - 1) \qquad (2.2)$$

In our case $K = 2$, so we get

$$\text{datasent}(m) = \text{datasize} * (2^{m+1} - 1). \qquad (2.3)$$

If we ignore the time required to send commands as small compared with returning data, then we need only add a setup time (meaning everything except data transmission: wakeup, command, data uptake, calculation). This needs to be added only to the maximum-depth sensor times, since other sensors will have even more time before they have to return data, and therefore should have plenty of time for setup. If $t_d = t_d(0) = $ the data transmission time allocated to a maximum-depth sensor, and $t_s = $ the setup time for such a sensor, then for constant data rate datasize/t_d we get

$$\text{time}(0) = t_s + t_d$$
$$t_d(m) = t_d * (2^{m+1} - 1) \qquad (2.4)$$
$$\text{time}(m) = 2 * \text{time}(m - 1) + t_d(m) \quad \text{if} \quad m > 0.$$

This forces the data returns not to overlap. An analysis similar to the above gives

$$\text{time}(m) = t_s * 2^m + t_d * (m * 2^{m+1} + 1) \qquad (2.5)$$

It follows that for the case of Figure 2.3,

$$\text{timeCycle} = 3 * \text{time}(2) = 12 * t_s + 51 * t_d \qquad (2.6)$$

If we arbitrarily assign 45 seconds to t_s and 1 minute to t_d, which should be more than enough, we get the timing arrangement of Figure 2.3.

By assigning an in-time wakeup for each SS based on this cycle, leaving a little leeway for timer drift that may happen over one hour, we can assure that each SS is awake to hear its command, and yet allow it to sleep most of the time.

2.5.4 (D) Protocol, display and output

Before leaving the topic, it is a good idea to begin sketching the data protocols. This is not as urgent a task as the communications and the hardware, because protocols can be expanded at will without disturbing the ones that are already functioning.

Central, of course, are the "in operation" protocols:

(D1) Command to take data

This one fans out as it moves deeper, so that one command to a Depth 1 node spreads out into $1 + 2 + 4 = 7$ actual data uptakes before it is done.

(D2) Data return

This one includes a note as to its source along with the values. In the case described in Figure 2.3, of course, time order would identify source, but this will not always be true, and explicit identification usually takes relatively little space and forms a cross-check. Timing order will also lead to problems if one of the sensors cuts out.

Also basic, but less frequently used, are setup and error messages:

(D3) Revise address

A replaced sensor station will have a new Bluetooth address, and its master needs to be notified of this. Also, if not at maximum depth, it needs to be told of its slaves' addresses. An active slave will advertise and be contacted by its master.

(D4) Error

Any sensor station misbehavior ought to be reported if possible, and not just because its data is missing from its master's transmission.

Once mission control has anyone's data it needs to display it:

(D5) Update

This is passed from mission control to graphics slave and causes a change in the display.

(D6) Alert

This is passed out into the external world, if desired, and may be in the form of an alert email or activate other alarm systems.

2.6 Example: satellite CDMA receiver (thank you, Rob Fryer)

Though supercomputers stand ready to analyze the output of Zac Manchester's Kicksats, several backers would like to have the capability of doing this on their own, with hardware that a HAM radio operator can put together. As with the orchard example, Wide techniques allow such a system to be designed with complete understanding of each step and open, top-level access to the data flow between them.

The Kicksat satellite project will probably launch around the time this book comes out. It will release a CubeSat from the International Space Station, and this CubeSat (about 1 foot cubed in size) will adjust its orbit and then eject a number (about 120) of tiny Kicksats which are capable of doing simple measurements and radio communication with Earth. Each Kicksat is about the size of a soda cracker, with two five-inch ears of thin wire.

Every Kicksat will transmit in the same 437.24 MHz band, and they will at least initially be in a cloud near each other, so that raises the question how the signals of individual Kicksats will be distinguished. The answer is CDMA, in particular a 640-bit version of the Sidelnikov, Lempel, Cohn, Eastman (SLCE) variant on the Gold-codes scheme. See [7] and [8]. Since it allows 320 distinguishable channels, and each satellite will use only two (for a zero bit and for a one bit), this is good enough.

It is decreed on the revised Link Budget and other public documentation of the Kicksat that the data will be encoded in MSK at 64 kbit/second (64kb/s) which implies the effective message rate will be a maximum of 100 bits/second. This leaves the problem of reception and demodulation, especially the timing of the message bits (each 640 symbol bits).

2.6.1 Basic design need

John Armstrong found some block diagrams of the ICs in the Nooelec DVB Dongle, which feeds via USB into a Linux system running GNURadio. The R820T does analog conversion of the radio input to get Intermediate Frequency (IF) In-phase and Quadrature (I and Q) data sampled at 28.8 MHz. The IF is between 1 MHz and 4 MHz. This is passed to the RTL2832U, and A to D converted at the inadequate resolution of 8 bits to give I and Q baseband, which must then be demodulated and CDMA filtered. A good-quality receiver, which is the target of this First Wave design, will pick up 16 bits at the 28.8 MHz A to D point, and continue at high quality from there.

The point of this design is to qualify (or not qualify) certain CPUs and data channels for a real-time demod device that picks up the radio transmissions and outputs the data being sent by a particular Kicksat, or by more than one Kicksat. This is a downward-streaming cascade, with data rates getting smaller the farther from the raw signal, but there is a lot of calculation going on to challenge the CPUs. Massive multiprocessing, as by the Parallella board, will prove to be quite useful even for one satellite, as we will discover.

A high frequency signal of the kind coming from the satellites is usually demodulated to baseband by a two-step process involving an intermediate frequency F_I. Suppose $C(t)$ is the carrier frequency plus data signal and $C_0(t)$ is the pure (cosine) carrier frequency, $C_0(t) = \cos(F_C * t)$. Then the IF signal $(I_I(t), Q_I(t))$ is the low pass filtered part of $C(t) * (\cos((F_C - F_I) * t), \sin((F_C - F_I) * t))$. If this is applied to $C_0(t)$ we get $(I_{I0}(t), Q_{I0}(t)) = 0.5 * (\cos(F_I * t), -\sin(F_I * t))$. To get a baseband signal we define $(I_B(t), Q_B(t))$ as the low pass filtered part of $(I_I(t) * I_{I0}(t) + Q_I(t) * Q_{I0}(t), -I_I(t) * Q_{I0}(t) + Q_I(t) * I_{I0}(t))$. In the special case $C(t) = \cos((F_C + dF) * t)$, we get $(I_I(t), Q_I(t)) = 0.5 * (\cos((F_I + dF) * t), -\sin((F_I + dF) * t))$ and $(I_B(t), Q_B(t)) = 0.25 * (\cos(dF * t), -\sin(dF * t))$. Thus a delta frequency in the carrier+data signal corresponds to a (negative) rotational frequency in the baseband (I,Q) vector.

The challenge starts by presuming the IF data is digitized to 16 bits by the receiver board, and then passed to our device to get baseband data at 192 kHz. (This is well over Nyquist for the goal of 64 kHz symbol bits.) The first piece of our device has to be capable of doing this reduction to baseband, and handle the input and output data.

The target frequency F_I of the intermediate frequency signal is typically between 1MHz and 4MHz, according to John Armstrong. Demodulation as far as IF is done by analog hardware, outputting the (I_I, Q_I) analog signal vector which is rotating at a frequency around F_I. This is called *heterodyning* and uses a *local oscillator* of frequency $F_C - F_I$ and its quadrature (90 degrees off phase). Usually, as in the RTL2832U, digital computing begins at this point, with I_I and Q_I samples at a much higher rate than F_I. In the case of the RTL2832U, as noted above, it is a 28.8MHz sampling rate. In the case of the 2-channel AD9650 (see [9]), some hardware work will give us 16 bits at 25MHz.

2.6.2   First problem

We want input at 28.8 × 4 megabytes per second, or 115.2MB/s. This is a problem. Gigabit Ethernet is available on the Parallella board, but this is right at the edge of its capability, and way beyond the rated capability (60 MB/s) of USB 2.0, of which Parallella has two ports, only one for peripherals, and Raspberry Pi (RPi) has only one.

This leaves us with two possibilities: accept analog IF input and do our own high-speed ADC (see [9]), or accept 8-bit output from the RTL2832U. According to the original discoverers of the RTL2832U software radio capability (see [10]), 8 bits gives surprisingly good quality. Unfortunately, the RTL2832U appears to depend on frequency feedback to "lock on", which is problematic

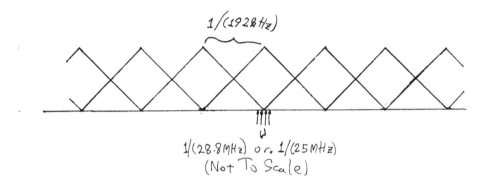

Figure 2.4: Hat function low-pass filter

with multiple summed signals. For the sake of this exercise, we will imagine the AD9650 onboard and dumping 16-bit streams of I and Q into circular buffers.

Figure 2.4 shows a hat-function for averaging the outputs

$$I_{Braw} = I_I * I_{I0} + Q_I * Q_{I0}$$
$$Q_{Braw} = Q_I * I_{I0} - I_I * Q_{I0} \tag{2.7}$$

from the sampled values to 192kHz values. In the case of 28.8MHz, the hat step is exactly 150 sampling steps, while in the case of 25MHz, the hat step is $3125/24 = 130.20833\ldots$ sampling steps. However, even the latter case is tractable if a discretization is used that assigns weight to a sample equal to the area of the hat that lies over the interval that is within half a sampling step of the sample, as shown in Figure 2.5.

The high-frequency component of (I_{Braw}, Q_{Braw}) is between 2MHz and 8MHz, and less than 1% of it is left after filtering by this hat procedure, according to a Fourier analysis which I will not detail here. If storage is tight, even the 25MHz case can be programmed using 24 values of each of the following: end multiplier, center multiplier, and ramp start multiplier. This presumes one allows the multiplier to be incremented by $(24/3125)$ between steps. Then for most samples (in the 25MHz case)

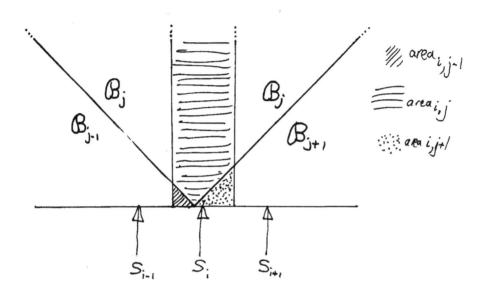

Figure 2.5: Center and end multipliers

```
Mi += (24.0/3125.0);
temp = Mi*IBraw[i];
IB[j+1] += temp;
IB[j] += (IBraw[i] - temp);
temp = Mi*QBraw[i];
QB[j+1] += temp;
QB[j] += (QBraw[i] - temp);
```

The 28.8 case is simpler. Therefore, incrementing the accumulators for I_B and Q_B requires (including Equations (2.7)) 6 multiplies, 6 adds, and 3 subtracts, or 15 floating point operations, for most samples. Also I_I and Q_I must be transformed from integer to 32-bit float.

Worst case is therefore 17*28.8MFLOPS = 490MFLOPS for the high-frequency loop. Some more calculation (such as a scaling multiply, transformation from float to int, and indexing calculations) must happen at the low frequency, 192kHz. So we are talking about 500MFLOPS to support the transformation of I and Q to baseband.

The incoming I_I and Q_I data from the ADC will arrive at most at 2 x 2 x 28.8MB/s or about 120MB/s. Getting the baseband data off the board will take 16 bits x 192kHz for each of I_B and Q_B, or about 800 kilobytes per second total.

If we ignore the lack of an AD9650 on a Raspberry Pi, we can see whether it could keep up. Its processor is the ARM1176JZF-S. Each floating point operation counts as one cycle except for a multiply that is not part of a multiply-accumulate (MAC). Such a multiply is two cycles on the ARM1176JZF-S, according to [11]. That works out to four extra cycles, or about 620 MHz total (actually 535 MHz if you take account that it samples at only 25MHz), and the ARM1176JZF-S is rated at 700 MHz. The 800kB/s data transmission easily fits within the 480 Mbits/s or 60 MB/s capabilities of USB 2.

So the Raspberry Pi is a good board for this A-to-D IF-to-baseband IQ radio data demodulator, except for its lack of a fast dual-channel ADC and fast analog input ports. According to [12], a TCM arrangement with DMA to a circular buffer fed by an AD9650 should cost 1 cycle per 16-bit datum, or 60MHz to keep up with 120MB/s digitized data. That still leaves us under 700MHz.

2.6.3   Second problem

Leaving aside for the moment the problem of soldering these in, we proceed to the 192kHz part of the design. Figure 2.6 shows the appearance of pure MSK data from one satellite after demodulation to baseband. It corresponds to adding or subtracting 16kHz (one-fourth the symbol frequency) from the carrier frequency of 437.24MHz. This speeds it up or slows it down by a quarter-wave over the time of a symbol bit. The waveforms stay continuous, and so do I_B and Q_B in Figure 2.6.

A major problem presents itself at this point. Even after a move to a more accurate crystal [13], the temperature-dependent frequency error is still +-2ppm. After generating the 437.24 MHz frequency, that is about +-900Hz. Because many satellites are transmitting, probably with different errors, it is not possible to "lock on" via feedback as in the RTL2832U. The error is in Hz and its ratio to the frequency goes up as demodulation decreases the frequency. The drift is small over a single symbol bit at 64kHz, but can amount to thousands of degrees of phase error over a message bit that is composed of 640 symbol bits.

The CDMA technique depends on a lock on frequency, integrating the product of the (I,Q) of a template wave, PRN0 for the zero message bit and PRN1 for the one, with the (I_B, Q_B) pair. This should give a sharp peak when it matches (see [7]), but it won't work if the received (I_B, Q_B) pair twists through several full circles due to error over the duration of the message bit. If we can assume the error stays steady over time of the order of a second, a

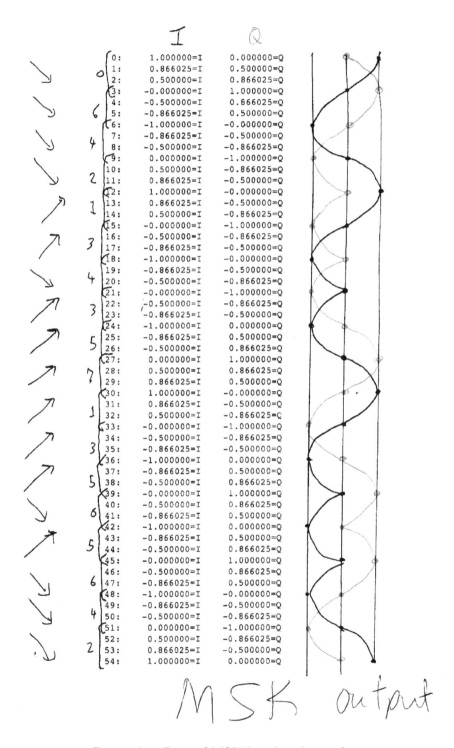

<table>
<thead>
<tr><th></th><th>I</th><th>Q</th></tr>
</thead>
<tbody>
<tr><td>0:</td><td>1.000000=I</td><td>0.000000=Q</td></tr>
<tr><td>1:</td><td>0.866025=I</td><td>0.500000=Q</td></tr>
<tr><td>2:</td><td>0.500000=I</td><td>0.866025=Q</td></tr>
<tr><td>3:</td><td>-0.000000=I</td><td>1.000000=Q</td></tr>
<tr><td>4:</td><td>-0.500000=I</td><td>0.866025=Q</td></tr>
<tr><td>5:</td><td>-0.866025=I</td><td>0.500000=Q</td></tr>
<tr><td>6:</td><td>-1.000000=I</td><td>-0.000000=Q</td></tr>
<tr><td>7:</td><td>-0.866025=I</td><td>-0.500000=Q</td></tr>
<tr><td>8:</td><td>-0.500000=I</td><td>-0.866025=Q</td></tr>
<tr><td>9:</td><td>0.000000=I</td><td>-1.000000=Q</td></tr>
<tr><td>10:</td><td>0.500000=I</td><td>-0.866025=Q</td></tr>
<tr><td>11:</td><td>0.866025=I</td><td>-0.500000=Q</td></tr>
<tr><td>12:</td><td>1.000000=I</td><td>-0.000000=Q</td></tr>
<tr><td>13:</td><td>0.866025=I</td><td>-0.500000=Q</td></tr>
<tr><td>14:</td><td>0.500000=I</td><td>-0.866025=Q</td></tr>
<tr><td>15:</td><td>-0.000000=I</td><td>-1.000000=Q</td></tr>
<tr><td>16:</td><td>-0.500000=I</td><td>-0.866025=Q</td></tr>
<tr><td>17:</td><td>-0.866025=I</td><td>-0.500000=Q</td></tr>
<tr><td>18:</td><td>-1.000000=I</td><td>-0.000000=Q</td></tr>
<tr><td>19:</td><td>-0.866025=I</td><td>-0.500000=Q</td></tr>
<tr><td>20:</td><td>-0.500000=I</td><td>-0.866025=Q</td></tr>
<tr><td>21:</td><td>-0.000000=I</td><td>-1.000000=Q</td></tr>
<tr><td>22:</td><td>-0.500000=I</td><td>-0.866025=Q</td></tr>
<tr><td>23:</td><td>-0.866025=I</td><td>-0.500000=Q</td></tr>
<tr><td>24:</td><td>-1.000000=I</td><td>0.000000=Q</td></tr>
<tr><td>25:</td><td>-0.866025=I</td><td>0.500000=Q</td></tr>
<tr><td>26:</td><td>-0.500000=I</td><td>0.866025=Q</td></tr>
<tr><td>27:</td><td>0.000000=I</td><td>1.000000=Q</td></tr>
<tr><td>28:</td><td>0.500000=I</td><td>0.866025=Q</td></tr>
<tr><td>29:</td><td>0.866025=I</td><td>0.500000=Q</td></tr>
<tr><td>30:</td><td>1.000000=I</td><td>-0.000000=Q</td></tr>
<tr><td>31:</td><td>0.866025=I</td><td>-0.500000=Q</td></tr>
<tr><td>32:</td><td>0.500000=I</td><td>-0.866025=Q</td></tr>
<tr><td>33:</td><td>-0.000000=I</td><td>-1.000000=Q</td></tr>
<tr><td>34:</td><td>-0.500000=I</td><td>-0.866025=Q</td></tr>
<tr><td>35:</td><td>-0.866025=I</td><td>-0.500000=Q</td></tr>
<tr><td>36:</td><td>-1.000000=I</td><td>0.000000=Q</td></tr>
<tr><td>37:</td><td>-0.866025=I</td><td>0.500000=Q</td></tr>
<tr><td>38:</td><td>-0.500000=I</td><td>0.866025=Q</td></tr>
<tr><td>39:</td><td>-0.000000=I</td><td>1.000000=Q</td></tr>
<tr><td>40:</td><td>-0.500000=I</td><td>0.866025=Q</td></tr>
<tr><td>41:</td><td>-0.866025=I</td><td>0.500000=Q</td></tr>
<tr><td>42:</td><td>-1.000000=I</td><td>0.000000=Q</td></tr>
<tr><td>43:</td><td>-0.866025=I</td><td>0.500000=Q</td></tr>
<tr><td>44:</td><td>-0.500000=I</td><td>0.866025=Q</td></tr>
<tr><td>45:</td><td>-0.000000=I</td><td>1.000000=Q</td></tr>
<tr><td>46:</td><td>-0.500000=I</td><td>0.866025=Q</td></tr>
<tr><td>47:</td><td>-0.866025=I</td><td>0.500000=Q</td></tr>
<tr><td>48:</td><td>-1.000000=I</td><td>-0.000000=Q</td></tr>
<tr><td>49:</td><td>-0.866025=I</td><td>-0.500000=Q</td></tr>
<tr><td>50:</td><td>-0.500000=I</td><td>-0.866025=Q</td></tr>
<tr><td>51:</td><td>0.000000=I</td><td>-1.000000=Q</td></tr>
<tr><td>52:</td><td>0.500000=I</td><td>-0.866025=Q</td></tr>
<tr><td>53:</td><td>0.866025=I</td><td>-0.500000=Q</td></tr>
<tr><td>54:</td><td>1.000000=I</td><td>0.000000=Q</td></tr>
</tbody>
</table>

Figure 2.6: Part of MSK baseband waveform

solution presents itself: Try pre-twisting the template bit over all the possible error values, and testing every one of these.

To keep the net absolute phase error under 36 degrees over the lifetime of the message bit, it is necessary to space the template twists by 20Hz over +-900Hz. This means 91 twist variations of each of PRN0 and PRN1 are needed, or 182 tests total. Each test consists of two integrations, one in phase and one in quadrature, resembling Equations (2.7), since the original MSK wave in carrier frequency may have started at any time relative to phase. So there are 364 integrations to be done.

We start an integration at every step at 192kHz. This gives three integration starts over a symbol bit, better than Nyquist, which should give a good peak for a match between them. Each integration step is 2 multiply-accumulates, and $(192kHz)/(100Hz) = 1920$ accumulations are underway at any time. Thus 364*2*1920 MACs happen at each step, with 192000 steps per second. Put another way, there are 91 twist variations, each resulting in 4*2*1920 MACs at each step.

This works out to 91 twist variations, each requiring 2.5 billion MACs per second, or 182 tests, each requiring 1.25 billion MACs per second. This requires some serious computing power. But there is a great deal of repetitiveness, so a highly parallel design is possible. That recommends one of the massively parallel boards now available, such as the Parallella 64.

2.6.4 Massively parallel solution

Conveniently, a test can be split into two integrations, each integration being 1.25 billion floating point operations per second, or 1.25 GFLOPS. Here a MAC counts as two floating point operations. That fits within the 1.5 GFLOPS capabilities of one of the 64 coprocessors in an Epiphany 64 chip, on a Parallella 64 (see [14, 15]). Six Parallellas (or one board with six Epiphany processors) can keep up with this much, assigning 30 or 31 tests to each Epiphany, one test to two cores. This in fact allows PRN0 and PRN1 to get three dedicated Epiphanys each.

Each Epiphany has at least two cores left over, which if the data flow works out can be used to scatter and gather the 30 or 31 tests. Each test detects the quality of the match of one twist of either PRN0 or PRN1 with the data, checking all carrier start phases at once. The scatter core is capable, if necessary, of distributing a copy of the newly arrived I_B, Q_B datum to the accumulators. The gather core must receive the final result of one accumulation from each accumulator and compare them, emitting the strongest. Each one has over

4000 cycles to perform its job, for each "tick" of the 192kHz "data clock", or over 67 cycles per accumulator core, which should be adequate.

Each Parallella is receiving 32-bit floating point I_B and Q_B each data clock, or 1.6MB/s, for a total of under 10MB/s. If each one emits its three best results, at 6 bytes per result, that gives a total of 22MB/s. A USB 2 should be able to handle both at once, though a cleaner design would be to have one USB receiving from the RPi-like demod board, and another USB sending to a further RPi that handles final output.

The duty of that final RPi will be to receive and interpret all the quality data, 18 "winners" for each data clock, and await a real hit, a very pronounced peak. This determines a rotation (which phase was detected by the test quadrature), an error twist (how much phase error accumulated over the course of the message bit), a start time (up to ticks of the data clock), and a message bit (PRN0 or PRN1). Since the RPi at 700MHz has 202 cycles per "winner", and an entire message bit will involve fewer than 40000 "winners", this discrimination task should not be too demanding.

To do 120 satellites at once we merely have to repeat the baseband design 120 times, using 720 Epiphany chips. There will have to be repeaters on the input, since I_B and Q_B cannot otherwise be broadcast, but output is independent for each of the 120 satellites.

A sketch of the design for a single satellite is shown in Figure 2.7.

2.7 Summary

With a basic understanding of communication, and simple cycle-counting of algorithms, it becomes possible to plan very complex projects. No matter how demanding the whole task is, the First Wave approach breaks the job up until each piece is simple from a data flow and timing point of view. This does not imply that the actual programming will be simple, only that its outcome is predictable.

Communication includes one-to-one, one-to-many, and many-to-one, where the last is the trickiest one, its true solution the little-known alternation, or select(), primitive. Connel offers several types of standard links, explicitly defined in Windows or Linux. These allow OS-internal and OS-external data flows, and are also capable of graphics. Related embedded programming techniques embrace even interrupts.

The first example, orchard sensors, uses a layered (fan) approach which has fixed, exposed connector links and can be expanded to any size project. There are many ways in which this example can be refined: redundancy, self-

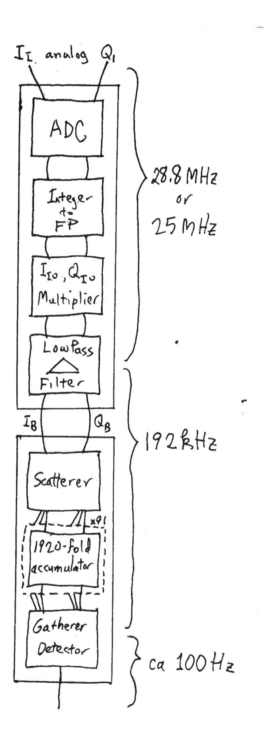

Figure 2.7: Single satellite receiver pieces

organization and self-repair, overlapping timing, and so forth. Having access at the top level to the connectivity is key to dealing with all of these possibilities.

The second example, satellite CDMA, shows how Wide techniques respond to big needs, including a surprise ninety-fold increase in the amount of calculation to be done. Massive multicore systems suddenly become your friend! Wide Computing is not afraid to program these and to use *all their power*. And this example copes, in the First Wave, with the little gotchas that are so often left till last, like scattering, gathering, and total IO needs.

2.8 References

[1] Flutter Wireless:
http://www.kickstarter.com/projects/2021474419/flutter-20-wireless-arduino-with-half-mile-1km-ran

[2] BlueRadios Inc.:
https://www.sparkfun.com/datasheets/RF/BlueRadios_ATMP_Commands_Rev_3.5.2.1.4.0.pdf
2 Multi-Point (MP) Architecture 2.1 Using Multi-Point Mode The ATMP supports any combination of Client/Server connections up to a maximum of 4. The modules are shipped and factory defaulted as Slaves supporting point-to-point connections.

[3] BlackBerry Support Community Forum:
http://supportforums.blackberry.com/t5/BlackBerry-Storm/Concurrent-Bluetooth-serial-port-profile-connections/td-p/176466
Concurrent Bluetooth serial port profile connections Options 03-02-2009 01:38 PM
I would like to know if it is possible to connect to with multiple Bluetooth Serial Port Profile devices at the same time. For example, could the Storm be connected to a bar code reader at the same time as it is connected to a printer? What is the maximum number of simultaneous serial port connections that can be established?
Re: Concurrent Bluetooth serial port profile connections [Edited] Options 06-18-2009 04:51 PM - edited 06-19-2009 11:06 AM
Since noone appears to know what the answer to the above issue is, could someone who actually owns a BB device try getting the following property which returns "The maximum number of connected devices supported":
LocalDevice.getProperty("bluetooth.connected.devices.max");

you would just need to: import javax.bluetooth.LocalDevice;

Concurrent Bluetooth serial port profile connections Options 07-06-2009 03:25 PM

Did this and I got result as "5" on my BB Curve 8310

[4] wirelesslechulla.blogspot.com: "Bluetooth Communication Via PIV16F877A."

`http://wirelesslechulla.blogspot.com/2013/09/bluetooth-communication-via-pic16f877a.html`

`http://elecfreaks.com/store/download/datasheet/Bluetooth/HC-0305%20serail%20module%20AT%20commamd%20set%20201104%20revised.pdf`

M1: The ability to have more than one RFCOMM session operational concur- rently is optional in the RFCOMM protocol. Although support of concurrence is encouraged where it makes sense, this profile does not mandate support of concurrent RFCOMM sessions in either DevA or DevB.

[5] Score Electronics:

`http://www.score-electronics.com/products/connectblue/bluetooth_le/obs421.html`

Features Throughput: 1.3 Mbps (Classic Bluetooth) All software embedded in the module (Bluetooth stack and application) Configurable via AT commands (via Bluetooth or serial port) Maximum number of simultaneous slaves: 7 using Classic Bluetooth only, 3 using Classic Bluetooth and Bluetooth low energy

[6] support.connectblue.com:

`http://support.connectblue.com/display/PRODBTSPA/Bluetooth+Low+Energy+Serial+Port+Adapter+-+Getting+Started`

By default, Bluetooth low energy is disabled for the OBS421 module and it then supports up to 7 parallel Classic Bluetooth links. To enable Bluetooth low energy, the AT*AGLE command is used. If Bluetooth low energy is enabled, the following link configurations are possible.

3 Classic Bluetooth links and 0 Bluetooth low energy links
2 Classic Bluetooth links in parallel with 1 Bluetooth low energy link
1 Classic Bluetooth link in parallel with 2 Bluetooth low energy links
0 Classic Bluetooth links and 3 Bluetooth low energy links

Hence, it is possible, for the OBS421, to have Classic Bluetooth links and Bluetooth low energy links active in parallel. The host transmits data without caring what kind of link it is (except that the throughput is normally much lower for the low energy link). Also note that for the OBS421 module, the Extended Data Mode works both for Classic Bluetooth and for Bluetooth low energy.

MY COMMENT ON THIS DOCUMENT: It has a lot of information relating to multiple sensors. The low energy one uses coin batteries, and has a quicker route to connection. The OLS426 can be subjected to periodic wakeup and then starts advertising.

[7] Wallner, Stefan, and Jose-Angel Avila-Rodriguez: "Codes: The PRN Family Grows Again", Inside GNSS, September/October 2011, European Space Agency. www.insidegnss.com From
     http://www.google.com/patents/WO2013023669A1?cl=en

[8] Manchester, Zac:
     https://github.com/zacinaction/kicksat/blob/master/
     GroundStation/GNURadio/gr-sprite/lib/sprite_correlator_cf.cc

[9] Analog Devices:
     http://www.analog.com/en/analog-to-digital-converters/ad-
     converters/ad9650/products/product.html
     AD9650 25 MS/S 16 bit dual ADC

[10] Palosaari, Antti: "SDR FM demodulation," GMANE, 2012-02-09.
     http://thread.gmane.org/gmane.linux.drivers.video-input-
     infrastructure/44461/focus=44461

[11] ARM: "1.5.9 Vector Floating Point (VFP)," *ARM1176JZF-S Technical Reference Manual.*
     http://infocenter.arm.com/help/index.jsp?topic=/com.arm.
     doc.ddi0301h/Cegdejjh.html

[12] Forums.arm.com:
     http://forums.arm.com/index.php?/topic/13147-what-is-the-
     differences-between-tightly-coupled-memory-and-ordinary-on-
     chip-ram
     What is the differences between Tightly-coupled memory and ordinary on-chip RAM? Rate Topic: #1 0254081
     Member
     Group:Members Posts:34 Joined:23-February 09 Posted 10 March 2009 - 07:36 AM Hi All, I am reading the specification of ARM1176JZ-S and it mentions the concept of Tightly-coupled memory and I have some questions about it. What is the differences between TCM and ordinary on-chip RAM? Can data in TCM be loaded into cache? I notice that each TCM has a base address register. Can TCM be mapped to any aligned main memory address? How should software manage TCM? For example,

where should software map TCM to? When should software replace data with the main memory? Can anybody give me an example? Thank you very much. Dong 0 #2 isogen74

Super Contributor

Group:Members Posts:1157 Joined:20-March 07 Posted 10 March 2009 - 10:00 AM TCM exists in parallel to the L1 caches, so is much faster than on-chip RAM. Typically 1 cycle access, although data accesses to the instruction TCM typically require 2 cycles.

The TCM data is consequently not cachable (which is one of its main benefits - it leaves the cache free for other code / data).

It can be placed anywhere in the address map, with suitable alignment. The TCM base address register is a physical address, not a virtual address, and so can be remapped per-process using the MMU.

> How should software manage TCM? For example, where should software map TCM to? When should software replace data with the main memory?

All very good questions - it really depends on what your software is trying to do. TCM is useful for (1) things that need to run very fast, (2) things that need to run with low interrupt latency, (3) things which are sensitive to timing issues in the main caches (cryptography for example).

Common uses of TCM include CODEC works for audio and video - the built-in TCM DMA transfer engine means that data can be loaded and stored while the processor is off doing other useful things. This post has been edited by isogen74: 10 March 2009 - 10:00 AM

[13] TXC: "SMD TCXO 2.0 × 1.6 × 0.75 mm 7Z Series."
http://www.txccrystal.com/images/pdf/7z.pdf

[14] Adapteva: "Epiphany-IV 64-core 28nm Microprocessor (E64G401)."
http://www.adapteva.com/products/silicon-devices/e64g401/

[15] Parallella Community: "A question of the processor."
http://forums.parallella.org/viewtopic.php?f=10&t=506
Two floating point ops per cycle (800 MHz). FMADD (MAC) counts as two operations.

Tools: Standard Products, Wide Pseudocode, and Connel

3

Abstract

The purpose of this chapter is to give a practical introduction to the tools needed for Wide Computing projects. Most of the tools are standard hardware and software, because Wide design is flexible enough for all kinds of uses. Some of these standard tools are used in surprising ways. Two new tools are detailed here: Wide pseudocode, a variant of the occam language that precisely defines data flow and parallelism, and Connel, a function library that eases Wide construction using the C language.

3.1 Principles behind the tools

In Wide programming there are many centers. This means many independent or nearly independent devices, each of which operates in its own way. That is tremendously liberating, and lets you go straight from each part of a First Wave design to the best device to do that part. But it means that you have to have a firm grasp on how each device is driven, and how they affect each other.

"How each device is driven" operates on two or three levels. When the piece is fully programmed and in use, it is driven by the data and timing. But it is also driven by its programming and even by its wiring, tasks undertaken by you before any input happens. A third level applies to devices with variable programming: the loading of the program is a special form of initial data. There are standard tools adapted to each of these states (compiling, loading, and running).

"How they affect each other" is in place at run time, though it can be altered at load time (which may be something else's run time). Putting all of this together sounds intimidating, but in real projects it is not too bad. It's just one more front-loaded task (like setting up communications), which we have just outlined in its entirety.

The key image is that of pieces that share things. What is the difference between a "piece" and a "thing that is shared"? A piece—like a computer, a sensor, an actuator, or a multitasked program running within one of these—is

```
SEQ
  --initiate server                   -- \
  CHAN SOCKLOCAL thesock :            --  \   This is server code
  PAR                                 --   > that creates a
    WHILE serving                     --  /   SOCKLOCAL then uses it
      -- do server IO with thesock    -- /
    SEQ
      client1(thesock)                -- \   These are sequentially
      client2(thesock)                --  > connecting and
      ...                             -- /   disconnecting clients
```

Table 3.1: Sample of occam-like pseudocode

active and "ticks over" on its own. A shared thing—serial cable, shared memory buffer, virtual connection between virtual machines, socket, pipe, or even a band in the electromagnetic spectrum—is passive and driven by pieces to affect other pieces. Of course this is not a hard and fast distinction. From a higher-level point of view, a FIFO is a shared communication pipe, but from a lower-level point of view, it is a piece with specific programming, which we will discuss in Chapter 4.

Having settled on this key image, which works out differently for each project, we approach it with two sets of tools. The first set is general—compiler/linker, loader (or burner), various testers and debuggers, and programs and design tools that ease the work, avoiding "reinventing the wheel." The second set is specific to Wide Computing: pseudocoding and Connel. We will start with the new and specific set.

3.2 Wide pseudocoding and the structure of occam

To start the description of occam-like pseudocode, it is worth studying Table 3.1, an example already seen in Chapter 2.

Note that occam is a real computer language, which is still supported by several language projects, and can be compiled and used. This sample would fail to compile at several points, as is typical with pseudocode, but it has the correct structure. For more about the real occam language, read [2] (I'm serious; it's only 133 pages long, and can be downloaded as a PDF).

I'll run down a few key points. The use of indentation to denote block structure is very common, found in Python and in well-written C, but in occam it is mandatory. The double dash (--) is the comment symbol, like the C++

double slash (//). SEQ denotes code blocks that happen one after the other in the order given, like curly brackets in C. One difference: local variables that are in scope for the entire SEQ must be declared ABOVE the SEQ and followed by a colon (:). In C, such variables would be declared just inside the curly brackets, before any executable code.

3.2.1 How PAR blocks work

PAR is rather more interesting. It denotes code blocks that run in parallel. This is actually permissive: it really means "run in any order", including overlapped, interleaved, or even sequentially in any sequence.

However, *this is not the same as spawning* in the usual OS sense. Spawning utilizes hidden capabilities of the OS to create child processes which then have an existence independent of the parent. *This is contrary to the design of Wide Computing* or, indeed, of any form of block-structured computing, because the multiple subsidiary (spawned) blocks have no real master, or outer, block. They are uncontrolled once spawned, unless special care is taken to control them.

In occam, on the other hand, the PAR construct denotes subdivision of finite resources. The number of members of a PAR is always finite and known. The master block (the PAR itself) concludes only when every member has concluded. This means that in all implementations of occam, an actual variable must keep track of the number of extant PAR members, and the master PAR block continues until that number drops to zero.

3.2.2 Channel declaration over PAR

CHAN refers to a point-to-point communicator. In occam, it is a *unidirectional* communicator, and its data transmission is (almost) *unbuffered*, but in pseudocode we may be more vague about that. Table 3.1 is non-standard in several ways, but its channel is correctly placed: above the PAR whose members it serves, and therefore *outdented* at least one step before any member that uses it.

This means two things. The channel must pre-exist the running piece that talks through it. And at least two such pieces must exist, two at any time, one on each end of the communication. This means a PAR is an absolute requirement, because occam is not allowed to store a message in a channel and come around later to pick it up.

We will adopt this as a requirement for pseudocode. Since we are allowing buffered channels, it would in theory be possible to transmit, followed by a receive in sequence. This, however, is pointless; why not just declare the message variable as a shared (i.e. handed-down) variable over the SEQ? Wide pseudocode channels exist for the purpose of passing data between pieces that exist side by side, and buffering, if used, is only a convenience or a property of the real communicators.

3.2.3 The use of analogy in pseudocode

It is very easy to understand what an implementation of pure occam does in the case of a PAR. When in doubt, read [1], another short book (161 pages). What the instructions do is very simple, and a small combination of them takes care of each occam primitive.

In the case of a non-prioritized PAR, Transputer occam starts the first member and runs until it deschedules (is forced to wait on event or communication, or is timesliced out, or terminates). Then it starts the second member, and so forth. A running count of number of members running is kept. (A member counts as running, even if in a wait state, until it has terminated.) All members must be started, but the first time the number of running members reaches zero after the last member has started is the end of the PAR block execution.

There is nothing to require they interleave with each other. In fact, the first member may terminate before the second starts, and so forth, leading to the PAR acting as a SEQ! But each time a member deschedules, the PAR is required **promptly** to set another member in motion. This leads to efficiency in use of computing resources.

The usefulness of this in pseudocode is by the principle of analogy: *the real entities referred to by the pseudocode behave substantially the same as would their pure occam counterparts.* Here "substantially" means "in every way that matters." Table 3.1 gives an example of this.

The PAR has two members, as the indentation shows. The first member of the PAR is the WHILE loop, whose contents are omitted, only alluded to by a comment. The second member of the PAR is the SEQ, and client1, client2, and the ellipsis "..." are members of the SEQ. This is seen because the ellipsis is indented the same as client1 and client2.

The first rack of comments (notice that comments are an essential part of pseudocode) tells that the server consists both of the outer code leading to the PAR, including the CHAN declaration, and the server part of the PAR. If we consider "the server" to be its run plus the part of the OS used by its run, we see this is true. It prepares and creates the SOCKLOCAL (causing it to come into existence in the file system, analogous to declaring the channel) and then it uses the channel by connecting with (traditionally called "accepting") communication partners in sequence.

The inner SEQ consists of clients, together with that part of the OS that is needed to run the clients. Clients require the channel to run, which is analogous to "thesock" appearing as a parameter in the client calls. The clients do not begin to operate until after the channel is declared, which corresponds to the location of the SEQ inside the PAR. The resources of the SEQ are "all the rest of the system" including the operator, who may be typing in commands one by one. It does not matter if he goes out to lunch after client1 terminates, and types in client2 afterwards. The SEQ is running in a wait state while he is at lunch.

The counter of currently running members of the PAR is the operator, who does not kill the server until the last client is done—otherwise it will crash. (He should delete the channel from the file system at this point.) So this use of SOCKLOCAL completes a clean analogy with the occam. This would not be true if we used the Linux socket capability of spawning multiple connections and forking copies of the program. That would be somewhat like an ellipsis among members of the PAR, except that there is no control over the closing of the forked copies, and the entire structure is dynamically uncontrolled. Staying with the occam means the real programs will behave in the occam fashion—very robustly, with no leaks or resource overflows.

The sharing of variables among members of a PAR is permitted only when there is no possibility of races. A shared value (VAL) which is read-only can be shared among several members. A variable which is writable may be accessed only by one member; the others may not even read it. Wide pseudocode extends this by requiring that *at any given time* any memory must be either read-only or accessible only to one member. This permits, for example, zero-copy rotating buffers.

3.2.4   More occam/pseudocode primitives

Several more primitives are shown in Table 3.2, an elaboration of an example in Chapter 2.

Much of this is obvious. The code and extra ALT branch involving `clock` are to make sure that at least one input is made every 50000 (time units unspecified). If this fails to happen, the loop shuts down and the code block ends. PLUS and AFTER (and MINUS) are rotating, modulo-2^N operations appropriate to timer outputs. The TRUE/SKIP at the end of the IF block is due to the fact that an occam IF requires a successful test to exit (SKIP is like C "continue"). DATA is a type undefined in occam, presumably understood in pseudocode context.

```
CHAN OF DATA a, b :
[10]DATA adata :
[10]DATA bdata :
TIMER clock :
INT aind, bind, lastime :
BOOL notdone :
SEQ
  aind := 0
  bind := 0
  notdone := TRUE
  clock ? lastime
  WHILE notdone
    SEQ
      ALT
        a ? adata[aind]
          aind := aind + 1
        b ? bdata[bind]
          bind := bind + 1
        clock ? AFTER (lastime PLUS 50000)
          notdone := FALSE
      clock ? lastime
      IF
        (aind > 9) OR (bind > 9)
          SEQ
            batch(adata, aind, bdata, bind)
            aind := 0
            bind := 0
        TRUE
          SKIP
```

Table 3.2: Sample of batching loop

There are no definitions of variables, only of constants, in occam, and pseudocode follows this, because it corresponds most closely to the way embedded code needs to behave, when the code is not reloaded every run.

Of the above, the only primitive that needs to cause you to consult [1] is ALT. This takes place in three stages. First comes "enabling" which checks each of the branches to see if any is ready. Each branch causes an appropriate mark to be made in the branch's local memory. If none is ready, "waiting" happens and that only ends when a branch comes ready. (It is quite possible for it never to end, although the timer branch in Table 3.2 assures an end.) After waiting ends (or, if no waiting was needed, after enabling ends) "disabling" happens. Each branch is checked and the first one found ready is selected. Notice that disabling determines an order of priority.

This approach, in some variation, has to be used by all alternation capabilities, like select() or WaitForMultipleObjects(). It requires more state than a standard blocking read() or write(). It is an irreducible primitive for responsive code.

3.2.5 A few other notes on occam notation

"`flag &`" placed before an ALT branch requires the Boolean "`flag`" to be true before that branch can be selected. This is frequently needed in practical code to prevent overflow or underflow.

"i FROM j FOR k" placed after SEQ, PAR, IF, or ALT defines an INT variable i and replicates it from j through j+k-1. Unlike C, i is not declared above the loop, nor can it be modified within the loop, nor is there any possibility of an early exit. Use WHILE if an early exit is desired. It's best to follow these rules, as they prevent the knowledge about loop behavior from being scattered around the loop.

Sub-arrays, called "abbreviations," also use "FROM j FOR k" (without the i), referring to the index of the array. This is extremely important for the provable correctness of parallel operations. *All arrays in occam have a defined length.* For instance,

`[]INT myset IS [wholeset FROM 20 FOR 10] :`

defines `myset` to be a 10-long subset of `wholeset` starting at `wholeset[20]`.

The CASE in occam is like a C "switch" with slightly different syntax (see [2] for details) and ELSE taking the place of "default". The occam CASE is a true block branch unlike the primitive computed GOTO nature of the C switch.

```
INT, INT, BOOL FUNCTION divides(INT a, INT b)
  INT quot, rem :
  BOOL success :
  VALOF
    IF
      (b = 0) OR ((a = MOSTNEG) AND (b = -1))
        SEQ
          quot := 0
          rem := 0
          success := FALSE
      TRUE
        SEQ
          quot := a/b
          rem := a REM b
          success := TRUE
    RESULT quot, rem, success
:
```

Table 3.3: Essential twos-complement divide

The PROC in occam is like a void-valued function in C, but allows channels as formal parameters and can code an entire piece of hardware. The FUNC-TION in occam is side-effect-free and can allow multiple outputs, a convenient improvement on C. An example is Table 3.3.

Notice that "=" in occam replaces "==" in C, and ":=" in occam replaces "=" in C. There are other subtle differences. Mostly, occam breaks apart multiple-result C operations like "++" and assignments which also have a value. This makes painstaking pseudocode more prolix, but its results are more obvious, and *the real implementation of the pseudocode design may use any equivalent construction in C or in assembly language.* Thus, Table 3.3 can probably be implemented by a single assembly divide (which also yields a remainder).

Finally, occam 2 does not have the analogue of a C struct, but we will allow such an analogue in Wide pseudocode. In its place occam has what is called a "variant PROTOCOL" for communications. This seems to fall between two stools: not quite a struct (it's for communication only), and incomplete from the point of view of a more general protocol (it decides on content based on one tag byte, but does not allow more complex or bidirectional state machine definitions). Wide channel notation allows these more general options, usually via documentation, depending on the wish of the designer. Later versions of occam allow structs under the name of RECORDs, and denote a member as if it were an array subscript (the period "." cannot be used because it is allowed internally to an occam name, just as underscore "_" is in C).

3.3 Folding editor

A folding editor is an extremely useful tool in any form of structured programming, or other organized effort (including writing this book). I use it to write not just occam or pseudocode, but C, assembly, and even scripts. I use the folding editor **origami** but there are folding capabilities or add-ons for other editors including **vim** and **emacs**.

Some, but not all, of the usefulness of a folding editor can be provided by cut-and-paste. But a folding editor provides block moves, even from one file to another, with fewer complexities, and also offers the great convenience of being able to change indentation of a whole block with few keystrokes.

The most critical thing added by a real folding editor is what I call *codeface reduction*—the ability to reduce all the code you are contemplating to a page. It operates by reducing a whole block of code to a single comment WITH PROPER INDENTATION. The alternative, in a program file of any size, is microscopic font size (which is only readable by the very young), scrolling madness, or even keyword searches.

When the code can't be folded so that what you are contemplating takes up a page, or a little more, it's a sign that you are straying from good code organization. Of course the editor provides you with tools to "drill down" into any particular block. And **origami**, at least, permits this to be either with or without context—both being convenient at times. A search will penetrate into folds and open them.

Folding is normally implemented by special comments, which traditionally use triple-curly-brackets in some form, {{{ to open a fold and }}} to close a fold. The formats are of course different for different languages with their different comment conventions. They are also slightly different between folding editors, which means you cannot switch from one to another, though careful editing with a non-folding editor can produce code that looks right when folded.

However, it's better to operate on folding code with a folding editor when possible. This is because if folding comments are slightly changed (e.g. indentation) the file can become unreadable, or the fold disappear, in the folding editor view. In that case, careful work in a non-folding editor is needed to recover.

More about folds will become clear when we examine Connel code.

3.4 Introduction to Connel

The Connel library sets up macros (including constant, function-like, and code-block macros) and functions that permit C programs easily to be structured as communicating Wide processes. Connel does not deal with lightweight threading, but with separate programs that communicate with one another. It is designed to run under both Linux and Windows. In fact, the task of getting it to run both under Linux and Windows was a tremendous education in practical Wide programming. Just examining the Connel source will provide this education.

Here, we consider the basics through which Connel causes programs running under either OS to function in Wide fashion. The center is in named or physical communication channels, though timer and now graphics events are also supported. Synchronizing is mainly done on inputs or events. Although synchronizing on outputs also exists, it is generally less useful for three reasons: (1) Connel allows buffered channels which often means output is near-instantaneous; (2) due to hardware-software equivalence, we are sticking with the input/event select() model, and not implementing output ALTs; (3) if synchrony at output is needed, a single-word input can be programmed in, and this is necessary if buffering is to be avoided.

Connel, like occam, primarily does blocking communications, although the buffering can disguise this. Non-blocking communication often uses busy loops, hides timing, or overwrites shared memory, all undesirable. *All Connel coding should be accompanied by occam-like Wide pseudocoding.* This will lead you to state machine design and Boolean variables. The data is accessible to spies and testers as it passes.

Connel uses the operating system's tools to implement multitasking and communications. This means it does not have to deal with interrupt programming, but it suffers OS overhead, and where this is onerous, user programming should be designed to mitigate it. Typically, for instance, a single-word ALT shows which communication partner is ready to talk first, and then another communication or swap of shared buffers happens that moves the bulk of the data without blocking and very quickly. The reason it is without blocking is that the short ALT communication enforced synchrony.

Connel is perfectly capable of programming the Linux or Windows side of a communication that connects directly, via cable, USB, or Bluetooth, with an embedded board. In this case, the embedded board is made to drive the wires according to a standard serial protocol (most embedded chips have this capability programmed in for some of their pins). A pure blocking, binary character-mode serial connection is supported in both directions by Connel, and after baud rate agreement is settled and junk characters are flushed from the lines, embedded IO happens **at full speed.**

3.4.1 Static organization of Connel structs

Connel is intended for connectivity using a static set of connector links and an indexed set of state machines that are capable of doing select() and other IO or event operations. What connects on the connector links (connels) is not necessarily static (see the example of Table 3.2), but highly dynamic design is avoided. This is because Connel never uses **malloc** and other OS-based dynamic resource allocation, with their unavoidable hiding and unpredictable exhaustion of resources.

The set of connels (`connel_t` type) is an array of maximum length `CONNEL_MAX`, usually 32. Similarly, the set of selectable state machines (`connel_machine_t` type) is an array of maximum length `CONNEL_SET_MAX`, usually also 32. This permits quick bit tests to be used in the Connel algorithms. Its limitation on the number of communication channels should not be onerous in a good-quality program, because select() or any other form of ALT becomes inefficient between very large numbers of channels. A fan design (compare Chapter 2 orchard sensors) is the right way to deal with a massively complex IO network where top-known connectivity is wanted. This leads to clean scientific and robotic designs.

Each connel is capable of supporting up to three machines: input, output, and out-of-band (OOB), sometimes called error. As yet we have only implemented input. A set of machines (`connel_set_t` type) is what is made available to `connel_select`, the ALT capability. In actual use it is found that this list hardly ever needs to change; all the ALTs are called with nearly the same set. There are occasional variants due to full buffers and the like, and for this I put in `connel_machine_deafen` to stop listening and `connel_machine_listen` to start listening on a given machine.

You will notice the difference in setup with occam. In occam, the ALT stands on its own, each one possibly with different channels and with different Booleans if these are needed. In Connel, it is assumed that the select() is in a big loop, its list of channels more or less fixed, and Booleans not changing often, so that a deafen or listen call makes sense on those branches. It's possible, but rather bulky, to emulate the more episodic occam setup using Connel. In practice, the loop is what is done, even in classic occam.

3.4.2 Connel structs

Here we describe the structs used by connel (all typedefs). There are also a few bit values and indices in macros.

```
#define CONNEL_READ_BIT 1
#define CONNEL_WRITE_BIT 2
#define CONNEL_CONNECT_BIT 4
#define CONNEL_CREATE_BIT 8 /* use on c_capability */
#define CONNEL_STATE_SERVER_DISCONNECTED_BIT 8 /* use on c_state */
#define CONNEL_OOB_BIT 16
#define CONNEL_RET_FAILED 1
#define CONNEL_RET_PENDING 2
#define CONNEL_RET_COMPLETED 3
#define CONNEL_TEST_PENDING 2 /* use if forceready */
#define CONNEL_TEST_DONE 1 /* use if NOT forceready */

typedef enum {
  CONNEL_STD,
  CONNEL_SERIAL,
  CONNEL_NAMED_PIPE,
  CONNEL_SOCKET
} CONNEL_TYPE;
```

The macros whose names end in _BIT are to be ANDed with the c_capability through c_state members of the connel_t struct. The others are used internally in the connel functions.

The enum refers to the types of connector links that are currently explicitly supported.

What follows in the next few pages are the structs that Connel uses to store information necessary for its functions. Note that they contain members special to both Linux and Windows. In many cases, even the types of the members are special to one or the other.

```
/* connel_timeout_t is timeout input to WaitForMultipleObjects or
 * select, with a distinction having to be made about an ampersand.
 * Note that if CONNEL_LINUX we have defined INFINITE to equal (-1).
 * This is apparently the standard Windows definition too.
 */
typedef struct {
  long int ct_seconds;
  long int ct_microseconds;
} connel_timeout_t;
```

This struct can denote either an absolute time or a difference. The ct_microseconds value is always between 0 and 999999, even if ct_seconds is negative.

```
typedef struct connel_machine connel_machine_t;

/* connel_t is a connector link
 * For full duplex, requirement of disconnecting is shown by
 * !(connector_state&CONNEL_CONNECT_BIT) and
 * connector_state&(CONNEL_READ_BIT|CONNEL_WRITE_BIT|CONNEL_OOB_BIT).
 */
typedef struct {
  int c_index; /* in connel_list_t or -1 if invalid */
  CONNEL_TYPE c_type;  /* CONNEL_STD, CONNEL_NAMED_PIPE, etc */
  int c_machine_rwebits; /* 1 read, 2 write, 4 OOB (see machine) */
  /*  The bits of c_pending thru c_state are not indexed by cm_rwe.
   *  Some of the indices are:
   *  0    read
   *  1    write
   *  2    connect
   *  3    create [c_capability only]
   *  >3   control bits (OOB or states like CTS in serial port)
   */
  int c_capability; /* read (1), write (2), connect (4), ... */
  int c_pending; /* bitwise: TRUE if pending, FALSE if done */
  int c_laststart; /* bitwise: like pending but stays on longer */
  int c_state; /* same bits as c_pending plus possibly others */
#ifdef CONNEL_WINDOWS
  HANDLE c_handle;
  DWORD c_fdwOldMode; /* console save mode */
#else  /* CONNEL_LINUX */
  int c_fd;
  int c_listener_fd; /* used for socket server listen/accept */
  connel_machine_t *c_listener_cm; /* required unique for servers */
  struct termios c_settingsOld;
#endif
} connel_t;
```

This is the struct for a generic connector link, whether in Linux or in Windows. In Linux there is a file descriptor (in fact two file descriptors in the case of a SOCKLOCAL server), while in Windows there is a HANDLE. Special space is made to save old console settings.

The shared members are an index in the list (see below), the type of connel, the usable rwebits, and four state bitmaps. The different bits refer to different machines that are possible for this connel.

```
/* connel_list_t is a list maintained of all valid connector links */
typedef struct {
  int cl_nvalid; /* > 0 if any connels have been registered */
  connel_t *cl_entry[CONNEL_MAX];
} connel_list_t;
```

This is a simple current array of connels.

```
/* connel_machine_t is ENDURING state structure for a kind of event
 * triggering WaitForMultipleObjects or select
 */
struct connel_machine {
  connel_t *cm_c; /* One connel can have more than 1 event (full dup) */
  int cm_rwe; /* -1=invalid, 0=read or connect, 1=write, 2=OOB */
  connel_set_t *cm_cs; /* current connel_set if actively selecting */
  int cm_cs_index; /* current index in above connel_set */
  int cm_index_responding; /* index in OS-dependent set or -1 if deaf */
  int cm_nbytes; /* for reads or writes, requirement for completion */
  int cm_ndone; /* for reads or writes, number done */
#ifdef CONNEL_WINDOWS
  BYTE *cm_data; /* for either read or write */
  OVERLAPPED cm_ol; /* needed by SOME synchronization handles */
  int cm_repeatcount; /* for Windows console input */
  char cm_repeatchar; /* for Windows console input */
#else
  char *cm_data; /* for either read or write */
#endif
};
```

This contains information needed for a select() or WaitForMultipleObjects() call and for checks that follow it. It must include a data pointer **cm_data** because Windows works through asynchronous IO. It has back-pointers to the connel of which this is a machine, and to the set if ALTing.

```
/* connel_set_t is non-timeout input(s) to WaitForMultipleObjects or
 * select. This doubles up with the indexed set of cs_cm which feeds
 * into the bitmap of cs_responding to indicate whether a given
 * machine is currently mapped into the select, and into the bitmap of
 * cs_ready for a quick test of already ready stuff.
 */
typedef struct {
  unsigned long int cs_responding;
  unsigned long int cs_ready;
  int cs_ncm;
  connel_machine_t *cs_cm[CONNEL_SET_MAX];
#ifdef CONNEL_WINDOWS
  int cs_handle_index[CONNEL_SET_MAX];
  DWORD cs_ncount;
  HANDLE cs_handle[CONNEL_SET_MAX];
#else  /* CONNEL_LINUX */
  int cs_fdmaxp;
  struct {
    int cs_nvalid;
    fd_set cs_set;
  } fp1[3]; /* 0 input, 1 output, 2 error */
#ifdef CONNEL_GRFX
  int xcbfd;
  int xcbisset;
#endif
#endif
} connel_set_t;
```

This is the thing that is actually fed into **connel_select**. It points to all the machines active in the select. The **CONNEL_GRFX** #ifdef is some special information due to the fact that, in the Linux XCB graphics case, an extra file descriptor is used for graphics events. (In Windows, a special ALTing routine, MsgWaitForMultipleObjects(), detects graphics as a separate category of event.) The top two members are bitmaps, the third a count.

```
#ifdef CONNEL_GRFX
typedef struct {
#ifdef CONNEL_WINDOWS
  HINSTANCE hInstance;
  int nCmdShow;
  HWND hwnd;
  UINT msg;
  WPARAM wParam;
  LPARAM lParam;
  LRESULT ret;
  WNDPROC wproc;
  LPCTSTR classname;
  FILE *fpInput;
  FILE *fpOutput;
  FILE *fpError;
  HANDLE hStdin;
  HDC hDC;
  HDC hMemDC;
  HGDIOBJ hOld;
  HBITMAP hBitmap;
#else /* CONNEL_LINUX */
  xcb_connection_t *c;
  int xcbfd;
  xcb_generic_event_t *e;
  xcb_screen_t *s;
  xcb_window_t w;
  xcb_pixmap_t pmap;
  xcb_gcontext_t gc;
  xcb_image_t *image;
#endif
  char *title;
  unsigned char *imagebits;
} connel_grfx_t;
#endif
```

This struct, which is not actually used in the `connel.c` function code, supports graphics, which uses the separate library code `connel_g.c`. Notice that it is almost completely different between Windows and Linux. Windows uses a special message event approach with callbacks, always supported, whereas Linux uses the X Windows library and the XCB library on top of that, and these operate through a standard file descriptor.

However, both Linux and Windows support `unsigned char *imagebits`—and that is really important. It allows color graphics buffers to be constructed bit-for-bit the same for both Windows and Linux.

3.5 Connel library calls

These are Connel calls, used in user programs, including macros. The only other Connel contents that should be used in user programs are the constant macros.

IMPORTANT: No structs are dynamically declared in Connel. There are no constructors or destructors, and dynamic memory allocation is completely avoided in `connel.c`, though of course it may be used in programs that call the library. Every call that manipulates struct data, **including init, create, and open calls,** must point to an already declared, existing structure.

3.5.1 Callable macros

These are callable macros, either the function type or the type that does not return a value.

```
#define CONNEL_IS_SERVER_CONNECTED(c) \
  (((c)->c_state)&(~CONNEL_STATE_SERVER_DISCONNECTED_BIT))
```

Argument: `connel_t c` where `c` is a SOCKLOCAL server
Returns: Nonzero if server `c` is connected.

```
#define CONNEL_SERVER_DISCONNECT(c)\
...
```

Argument: `connel_t c` where `c` is a SOCKLOCAL server
Returns: Does not return a value

Call this to disconnect a SOCKLOCAL server's pipe. It uses Disconnect-NamedPipe() in Windows and close() on the data-transmitting file descriptor member `c_fd` in Linux. Returns the server to listening state, awaiting a connect.

```
#define CONNEL_FINISH(cs, index, longscratch) do {\
  int ncm = (cs)->cs_ncm;\
  (longscratch) = ((index) < 0) ? 0 :\
    (((index) < ncm) ? (((unsigned long)1)<<(index)) : 0);\
  if ((longscratch)&(cs)->cs_ready) {\
    (cs)->cs_ready &= ~(longscratch);\
  } else {\
    (longscratch) = 0;\
  }\
} while(0)
```

Arguments:

`connel_set_t *cs`

`int index`

`unsigned long longscratch` CHANGED

Returns: Does not return a value

Note that `longscratch` must be a long. This returns `longscratch = (cs)->cs_ready&(1<<(index))`. If nonzero, erases that bit from `(cs)->cs_ready`. This checks whether the `connel_select()` involving `cs` is finished, and if so, it marks it as ready to start anew.

```
#define CONNEL_MAKENAME(type, lenno, namein, nameout, pnameout) do {\
  ...
```

Arguments:

`CONNEL_TYPE type`

`int lenno`

`const char[] namein`

`char[] nameout` CHANGED

`char *pnameout` CHANGED

Returns: Does not return a value

Note that type must be CONNEL_TYPE such as CONNEL_SOCKET etc, and namein and nameout must be char arrays with something in namein and lots of room (lenno) in nameout. pnameout must be a char * so that it can be filled with NULL in some cases.

This makes a name for a serial (number or name) or for a SOCKLOCAL (name), appropriate to Windows or Linux. In Windows, it puts the serial in `\\.\COM` followed by the number or name, and the SOCKLOCAL in `\\.\pipe\`. In Linux it puts the serial in `/dev/ttyS` followed by the number, or `/dev/` followed by the name, and the SOCKLOCAL in `/tmp/`.

```
#define CONNEL_DALERT(...)\
...
#define CONNEL_DWARN(...)\
...
#define CONNEL_DINFO(...)\
...
```

These all take arguments like printf. They return no value.
CONNEL_DALERT always outputs to stderr.
CONNEL_DINFO outputs to stderr if compile parameter CONNEL_QUIET is not defined, otherwise it does nothing.
CONNEL_DWARN outputs to stderr if compile parameter CONNEL_QUIET is not defined or is ≤ 1, otherwise it does nothing.

3.5.2 Time functions

These are time-related Connel functions. Please note that one other Connel function uses the **connel_timeout_t** struct: **connel_select**, which always uses a timeout, which can be immediate, finite, or infinite (or NULL). An infinite timeout never expires.

```
int connel_timeout_init(connel_timeout_t *ct);

/* Returns -1 if ct is NULL. Otherwise, outputs current time base in
 * ct, and returns 1.
 */
int connel_timebase(connel_timeout_t *ct);

/* Returns 0 and changes nothing if either is INFINITE.
 * Returns -1 if either is NULL.
 * Returns 1 and increments ct by ctdel if successful.
 */
int connel_timeadd(connel_timeout_t *ct, const connel_timeout_t *ctdel);

/* Returns 0 and changes nothing if either is INFINITE.
 * Returns -1 if either is NULL.
 */
int connel_timesub(connel_timeout_t *ct, const connel_timeout_t *ctsub);

/* Returns -1 if ct is NULL. Otherwise, sleeps for max(ct,0). No
 * special case for INFINITE, though a long time interval can be
 * set.
 */
int connel_sleep(const connel_timeout_t *ct);
```

connel_timeout_init initializes a connel_timeout_t struct to an infinite (never expiring) value, and connel_timebase sets it to the current value of the operating system timer. connel_sleep makes the system sleep for the required time step. The other two routines increment or decrement the first formal parameter by the second.

In all of these, the first member, ct_seconds, of the struct shows the sign of the time interval, because the second member, ct_microseconds, is always nonnegative and less than a second.

3.5.3 Connector link functions

These are Connel functions that are related to the connector links (the links that are defined on the OS level or as hardware). They include synchronous read and write.

```
/* Call this once, before any other connel routines. Does
 * one-time initialization (in Linux, it sets up SIGPIPE
 * to be ignored).
 */
int connel_list_init(connel_list_t *cl);

int connel_begin(connel_list_t *cl, connel_t *c);

/* returns -1 to -3 if bad data;
 * returns -4 if (NOT force) and c->c_machine_rwebits shows some
 * machine is still active;
 * if (force) then it removes it anyway and returns 0.
 * Returns 0 if successful.
 */
int connel_end(connel_list_t *cl, connel_t *c, int force);
```

These are the calls that deal with the master list of connels. Note that connel_list_init is NOT A CONSTRUCTOR; it initializes an *already existing* list to "all invalid". The other two calls add or remove an *already existing* connel to or from the list. No connel should be used until it is attached to the master list.

The force formal, if set to true, disconnects the connel even if still open or communicating.

```
/* Returns 0 if this cannot be created but must pre-exist.
 * Returns -1 if input is illegal or not yet supported.
 * Returns -2 if the OS-dependent call failed.
 * Returns -3 if the link is already created or open.
 *
 * Important: Direction is IGNORED except where needed, e.g.
 * Linux (not Windows) named pipes. If it is needed, it MUST
 * take one of the two values CONNEL_READ_BIT or CONNEL_WRITE_BIT.
 */
int connel_create(const CONNEL_TYPE type, const char name[],
  const int direction, connel_t *c);
```

This call creates the entity to which the connel refers. It is only possible with those types of connels (as yet, named pipes or sockets) for which such OS-based creation is possible. It must be called after **connel_begin**.

```
/* This is used for a client call in create type links.
 * Returns positive if successful.
 * Returns -1 if input is illegal or not yet supported.
 * Returns -2 if the OS-dependent call failed.
 * Returns -3 if the link is already created or open.
 *
 * Important: Direction is IGNORED except where needed, e.g.
 * Linux (not Windows) named pipes or STD. If it is needed, it
 * MUST take one of the two values CONNEL_READ_BIT or
 * CONNEL_WRITE_BIT.
 */
int connel_open(const CONNEL_TYPE type, const char name[],
  const int direction, connel_t *c);
```

This call opens the entity to which the connel refers. It is only possible if this entity pre-exists the call (is already in the OS, or has been created by another program, *not this one*). It must be called after **connel_begin**. It is used for example for keyboard or serial, or for client-side access to named pipe or socket. Either **connel_create** or **connel_open** must be called for a particular entity, not both.

```
/* This closes but does not delete the name.
 * Returns positive if successful.
 * Returns 0 if it was already closed (if c_capability = 0 or 8).
 * Returns -1 if input is illegal or not yet supported.
 * Returns -2 if the OS-dependent call failed.
 */
int connel_close(connel_t *c);
```

This call closes the connection to the entity that underlies the connel. It must be called after all communication is done and before connel_end.

```
/* returns -1 for bad data
 * returns -2 if the completed write fails.
 * Check for -2 (disconnect) if you are running a server.
 */
int connel_write(connel_t *c, char *buffer, int nbytes);
```

```
/* returns < 0 if the completed read fails, or 0 if EOF or
 * disconnection.
 * Check for 0 or -2 (disconnect) if you are running a server.
 * Note that a read of stdin in Windows after asynchronous
 * reading can miss some of a set of repeated characters due to
 * holding a key down.
 */
int connel_read(connel_t *c, char *buffer, int nbytes);
```

These calls are synchronous blocking IO calls. They may be called after connel_begin and either connel_create or connel_open, and before connel_close and connel_end. For asynchronous IO, use the corresponding calls in the select section.

3.5.4 select()-related functions

These are Connel functions related to select and to asynchronous IO, including the definitions of the machine sets. Where a connel is an entity determined by the OS or the hardware, existing either physically or in the file system, a machine (meaning state machine) is a function of a connel. *A machine moves data in only one direction.* It can be input, output, or out-of-band (input), the last sometimes called "error." As yet, Connel only supports input in connel_select.

```
/* Windows:
 * It also calls CreateEvent if necessary, and returns
 * cm->cm_ol.hEvent to be the one that should be pointed to by
 * the handle array for WaitForMultipleObjects.
 */
int connel_machine_begin(connel_t *c, connel_machine_t *cm, int rwe);

int connel_machine_end(connel_machine_t *cm, int force);
```

These calls begin and end the machine that is dependent on a pre-existing connel. They must be called after **connel_create** or **connel_open**, and before **connel_close**. The "**force**" formal, if set true, shuts things down even if a communication is under way, or if the machine has already been shut down.

```
#ifdef CONNEL_GRFX
int connel_set_init(connel_set_t *cs, int xcbfd);
#else
int connel_set_init(connel_set_t *cs);
#endif

int connel_machine_add(connel_set_t *cs, connel_machine_t *cm);
```

These are the calls representing the master set of machines to be used in **connel_select**. The **connel_set_init** call sets it to empty, unless **CONNEL_GRFX** is defined in Linux, in which case it connects the "invisible" file descriptor that handles XCB.

The **connel_machine_add** call, which must follow **connel_set_init** and **connel_machine_begin** for this machine, adds the machine to the set to which select() is to be sensitive. There is no corresponding remove call, since the select() can be made insensitive temporarily or permanently by **connel_machine_deafen**. In fact, the newly added machine defaults to deaf, and **connel_machine_listen** must be called before a select() will listen to it.

```
/* This amounts to turning on the Boolean guard for this cm.
 * It does NOT turn on the c_pending which must be dealt with
 * afterward. It places it in the OS-dependent list of channels
 * responding to the select. If (force) then if already
 * listening it returns 0, else -5
 */
int connel_machine_listen(connel_machine_t *cm, int force);


/* This amounts to turning off the Boolean guard for this cm.
 * All the pendings corresponding to this cm must be off before
 * calling this. It removes it from cs_responding and from the
 * OS-dependent list of channels in the select. If (force) then
 * if already not listening it returns 0, else -5
 */
int connel_machine_deafen(connel_machine_t *cm, int force);
```

These are the Boolean guards, referred to above. A newly added machine defaults to deaf, and **connel_machine_listen** must be called before a select() will listen to it. The select() can then be made insensitive temporarily or permanently by **connel_machine_deafen**. This cycle can be repeated as many times as desired.

```
/* This should be called only for servers. Returns >0 if
 * applicable. Returns 0 and does nothing if it is a non-server
 * OR if CONNEL_CONNECT_STATE(cm->cm_c) is nonzero coming in.
 * All connel start routines require pending and ready be down
 * and, if forceready, that responding be up.
 * Note: cm must be in listening state if (forceready), while it
 * must not be in listening state if NOT forceready. If NOT
 * forceready and Pending is returned, listening must be turned
 * on afterward.
 *
 * Possible outputs ((p,s)=(c_pending,c_state)&CONNEL_CONNECT_BIT
 * and r = cm_ready&testresponding)
 * Failed: p==FALSE, s==FALSE if not forceready
 *         p==TRUE, s==FALSE, r=TRUE if forceready
 * Pending: p==TRUE, s==TRUE
 * Completed: p==FALSE, s==TRUE if not forceready
 *             p==TRUE, s==TRUE, r==TRUE if forceready
 * Returns:
 * <0 bad data or structs
 *  0 if not applicable (no action) or machine not reader or
 *    quiescent
 *  1 Failed
 *  2 Pending
 *  3 Completed
 */
int connel_connect_start(connel_machine_t *cm, int forceready);
```

IN PRACTICE, forceready IS ALWAYS SET TO TRUE. This means the machine must be in listening state.

This sets a SOCKLOCAL server to the state of being sensitive to connection by a client. It is applicable only to SOCKLOCAL servers: Windows named pipes and Linux sockets. Before using this, the server must either be in a "virgin" state, never having been connected, or the macro CONNEL_SERVER_DISCONNECT must have been called to disconnect an earlier client. Multiple clients are not allowed.

```
/* returns < 0 if the completed read fails, or 0 if EOF or
 * disconnection.
 * All connel start routines require pending and ready be down
 * and, if forceready, that responding be up.
 * Note: cm must be in listening state if (forceready), while it
 * must not be in listening state if NOT forceready. If NOT
 * forceready and Pending is returned, listening must be turned
 * on afterward.
 *
 * Possible outputs ((p,s)=(c_pending,c_state)&CONNEL_CONNECT_BIT
 * and r = cm_ready&testresponding)
 * Failed: p==FALSE, s==FALSE if not forceready
 *         p==TRUE, s==FALSE, r=TRUE if forceready
 * Pending: p==TRUE, s==TRUE
 * Completed: p==FALSE, s==TRUE if not forceready
 *            p==TRUE, s==TRUE, r==TRUE if forceready
 * Returns:
 * <0 bad data or structs
 *  0 if not applicable (no action) or machine not reader or
 *    quiescent
 *  1 Failed
 *  2 Pending
 *  3 Completed
 */
int connel_read_start(connel_machine_t *cm, char *buffer,
  int nbytes, int forceready);
```

IN PRACTICE, **forceready** IS ALWAYS SET TO TRUE. This means the machine must be in listening state. If it is a SOCKLOCAL server, it must also be connected to a client.

This commits to an asynchronous read. (In the case of Linux, it actually does nothing but set some state.) Connel requires the commitment to this read to precede **connel_select**. Once the select() is done, and this machine wins the select, the read will either be done, or it will be pending and the macro **CONNEL_FINISH** must be called to check when it is done. This is because, especially with kbd and serial, it is possible for the data transmission to be subdivided.

```
/* Returns negative if error, 0 if timeout, otherwise count+1
 * including those of cs_ready. If count > 0, and newready != NULL,
 * it depicts the ones of cs_responding&(~cs_ready) that have come
 * ready. The non-timeout count=0 case is possible because of a
 * Windows keystroke returning no output, or other incomplete data
 * transmission.
 *
 * If it returns -99, it means there is nothing ready, nothing to
 * respond to, and the timeout is infinite.
 */
int connel_select(connel_set_t *cs, connel_timeout_t *ct,
  unsigned long int *newready);
```

This is the ALT or select() capability, the heart of Connel. Unlike occam ALT, but like Linux select() and Windows WaitForMultipleObjects(), it can allow more than one thing to come ready. Each thing that comes ready should have a `CONNEL_FINISH` macro call succeed before its data is used. The optional `*newready` will contain bits corresponding to machines that have newly come ready.

If the timeout is infinite or NULL, it will wait as long as necessary for another input to become ready. If the timeout is zero, it will return immediately, and show all inputs that are currently ready. (This behavior is like ALT and select().) If the timeout is finite and positive, it will prefer input ready to timing out, if that input comes in time.

In the case of graphics (defined macro `CONNEL_GRFX`), a check for zero or more graphics events should always be made when `connel_select` returns successfully. These should always be flushed completely before another `connel_select` call.

3.6 Sample program using Connel

This is a sample program showing many of the operations of Connel in action. It supports a bidirectional serial IO stream. The input from the serial connection is output to the screen or redirected in one of three formats, and the input from the keyboard is output to the serial connection.

Because the serial connel is not SOCKLOCAL, the server/client distinction and connect capability are not used. No timers are used. Most of the other capabilities of Connel are demonstrated here.

```
#ifndef CONNEL_LINUX
#define CONNEL_WINDOWS
#else
#undef CONNEL_WINDOWS
#endif
#ifdef CONNEL_WINDOWS
#include "..\LAZM\connel.h"
#else
#include "../LAZM/connel.h"
#endif
#define LNAMEOUT 200
int notInterrupted = 1;
#ifdef CONNEL_LINUX
void ctrlc(int sig) {
  notInterrupted = 0;
}
#endif
char legalize(char c) {
  if (('\a' <= c && c <= '\r') || (' ' <= c && c <= '~'))
    return c;
  return '?';
}
int main(int argc, char *argv[])
{
  char *remargv[10];
  int remargc = 0;
  char nameout[LNAMEOUT];
  char *pname;
  char exitchar = 'x';
  int noexitchar = 1; /* if set, then must use Ctrl-C to stop */
  int isbinary = 0; /* if set, treat input as binary */
  int notQuiet = 1;
  int yesdrop = 1; /* standard behavior: close connel. LJD 11/14/11 */
  int ret;
  ...  declare connel structs and their pointers
  ...  introduce test program self, get name
  ...  REAL CODE BEGINS
  ...  DO THE ACTION
  ...  END
  return 0;
}
}}}
```

Table 3.4: Toplevel view of sercomio.c in origami (top comments removed)

```
{{{ declare connel structs and their pointers
connel_list_t scl;
connel_list_t *cl = &scl;
connel_set_t scs;
connel_set_t *cs = &scs;
connel_t sckbd, scscr, scserial;
connel_t *ckbd = &sckbd;
connel_t *cscr = &scscr;
connel_t *cserial = &scserial;
connel_machine_t scmkbd, scmserinp;
connel_machine_t *cmkbd = &scmkbd;
connel_machine_t *cmserinp = &scmserinp;
}}}
```

Table 3.5: First fold view in origami

3.6.1 Entrance into the program

A fixed list of Connel structs is declared, after declarations particular to the main program, and standard C program initialization is carried out.

In the Connel declarations, the customary prefix s refers to the actual struct, to which a pointer without the prefix is also defined. Usually it is the pointer that is used in the calls. Note that even though keyboard ckbd and screen (stdout) cscr are by nature unidirectional, ckbd still has a machine separately defined for use in connel_select.

By convention, the double dash is used on expected program arguments, with up to 10 others being collected in remargv. The only one of those used is a number or name that will be expanded to a serial port name by CONNEL_MAKENAME.

The expected arguments can include --q to minimize chatter, --exitchar or --noexitchar to determine if a special kill character (other than Ctrl-C) is watched for, --binary to specify a special, terse hex format for output, and --nodrop to prevent the closing of the serial connection when the program quits. The last is useful when another program is waiting to pick up the serial connection after this one goes down.

3.6.2 Setting up Connel

The code of Table 3.6 is a fold containing all the initial setup calls of the Connel structs and their state. All programs using Connel should contain a section like this. Usually, a section from an old or a sample program is picked up, transplanted, and then modified as needed.

```
{{{  introduce test program self, get name
#ifdef CONNEL_LINUX
printf("Linux test case\n");
signal(SIGINT, ctrlc);
#else
printf("Windows test case\n");
#endif
CONNEL_DINFO("sizeof(connel_t) is %d.\n", sizeof(connel_t));
CONNEL_DINFO("sizeof(connel_list_t) is %d.\n", sizeof(connel_list_t));
CONNEL_DINFO("sizeof(connel_machine_t) is %d.\n", sizeof(connel_machine_t));
CONNEL_DINFO("sizeof(connel_set_t) is %d.\n", sizeof(connel_set_t));
CONNEL_DINFO("sizeof(connel_timeout_t) is %d.\n", sizeof(connel_timeout_t));
remargv[0] = argv[0];
remargc = 1;
for (ret=1; ret<argc; ret++) {
  if ((strncmp(argv[ret], "--", 2)&&(remargc < 10))) {
    remargv[remargc] = argv[ret];
    remargc++;
  } else if (!strncmp(argv[ret], "--q", 3)) {
    notQuiet = 0;
  } else if (!strncmp(argv[ret], "--noexitchar", 5)) {
    noexitchar = 1;
  } else if (!strncmp(argv[ret], "--nodrop", 8)) {
    yesdrop = 0;
  } else if (!strncmp(argv[ret], "--exitchar=", 11)) {
    char thechar = argv[ret][11];
    if (thechar) {
      noexitchar = 0;
      exitchar = thechar;
    }
  } else if (!strncmp(argv[ret], "--exitchar", 10)) {
    noexitchar = 0;
    exitchar = 'x';
  } else if (!strncmp(argv[ret], "--binary", 4)) {
    isbinary = 1;
  }
}
if (remargc < 2) {
  CONNEL_DINFO("Syntax: sercomio <com port number>\n");
  exit(1);
}
CONNEL_MAKENAME(CONNEL_SERIAL, LNAMEOUT, remargv[1], nameout, pname);
if (pname) CONNEL_DINFO("Concocted name: %s\n", pname);
}}}
```

Table 3.6: Second fold view in origami

```
{{{  REAL CODE BEGINS
...  init list and set
...  kbd begin, open, machine begin, add
...  serial begin, open, serinp machine begin, add
...  scr begin and open
}}}
```

Table 3.7: Third fold view in origami

```
{{{  init list and set
ret = connel_list_init(cl);
CONNEL_DINFO("connel_list_init returned %d\n", ret);
ret = connel_set_init(cs);
CONNEL_DINFO("connel_set_init returned %d\n", ret);
}}}
```

Table 3.8: First subfold view in third fold

```
{{{  kbd begin, open, machine begin, add
ret = connel_begin(cl, ckbd);
CONNEL_DINFO("connel_begin(cl, ckbd) returned %d\n", ret);
ret = connel_open(CONNEL_STD, NULL, CONNEL_READ_BIT, ckbd);
CONNEL_DINFO("connel_open(%d, NULL, %d, ckbd) returned %d\n",
  CONNEL_STD, CONNEL_READ_BIT, ret);
ret = connel_machine_begin(ckbd, cmkbd, 0);
CONNEL_DINFO("connel_machine_begin(ckbd, cmkbd, 0) returned %d\n", ret);
ret = connel_machine_add(cs, cmkbd);
CONNEL_DINFO("connel_machine_add(cs, cmkbd) returned %d\n", ret);
}}}
```

Table 3.9: Second subfold view in third fold

When opened in the fold editor, the code of Table 3.7 presents itself as a collection of subsections which can be opened in turn.

The master list for the connels, and the master set for the machines to be used in the select loop, are set up in Table 3.8. Verbose commentary is available to guide the coder or user in debugging the code. A compile option can activate it or shut it off.

Table 3.9 does everything necessary for the keyboard and its associated machine. It also opens the keyboard using CONNEL_STD as description of the connel and CONNEL_READ_BIT to define its only direction. Note that the keyboard must be opened before its machine can be begun.

Table 3.10 does everything necessary for the serial and its associated input

```
{{{ serial begin, open, serinp machine begin, add
ret = connel_begin(cl, cserial);
CONNEL_DINFO("connel_begin(cl, cserial) returned %d\n", ret);
ret = connel_open(CONNEL_SERIAL, pname,
  CONNEL_READ_BIT|CONNEL_WRITE_BIT, cserial);
CONNEL_DINFO("connel_open(%d, %s, %d, cserial) returned %d\n",
  CONNEL_SERIAL, pname, CONNEL_READ_BIT|CONNEL_WRITE_BIT, ret);
ret = connel_machine_begin(cserial, cmserinp, 0);
CONNEL_DINFO("connel_machine_begin(cserial, cmserinp, 0) returned %d\n", ret);
ret = connel_machine_add(cs, cmserinp);
CONNEL_DINFO("connel_machine_add(cs, cmserinp) returned %d\n", ret);
}}}
```

Table 3.10: Third subfold view in third fold

```
{{{ scr begin and open
ret = connel_begin(cl, cscr);
CONNEL_DINFO("connel_begin(cl, cscr) returned %d\n", ret);
ret = connel_open(CONNEL_STD, NULL, CONNEL_WRITE_BIT, cscr);
CONNEL_DINFO("connel_open(%d, NULL, %d, cscr) returned %d\n",
  CONNEL_STD, CONNEL_WRITE_BIT, ret);
}}}
```

Table 3.11: Fourth subfold view in third fold

machine. Note that the open is bidirectional, and happens before the input-only machine is begun.

Table 3.11 does what is needed for the screen (stdout). Notice that the unidirectional connel is also type CONNEL_STD but in the opposite direction. No machine is defined because we are using input-only select. This works for programs that are output-ready when output is called, otherwise it may result in blocking that delays an input.

3.6.3 Active program loop

This is the active loop, together with the listen part of its setup, and a deafen step in its shutdown. The listen is always necessary, but not the final deafen, though it can provide valuable status if used.

The view of Table 3.12 is that of the general program, corresponding to the pseudocode. Critical is the boolean **notdone** which is an occam device to avoid early exits. A search on it reveals what can cause the loop to end.

First, the two machines are made to listen, then an asynchronous read is started for each. (This is Windows style, but does not harm Linux.) In the

```
{{{  DO THE ACTION
{
  char thechar = '#';
  char thechar2 = '&';
  int notdone;
  ...  kbd and serial listen
  notdone = (ret > 0)&&(notInterrupted > 0);
  if (notdone) {
    int ret2;
    ...  kbd and serial read_start
    notdone = (ret > 0)||(ret2 > 0);
  }
  while (notdone) {
    unsigned long newready = 0;
    ret = connel_select(cs, NULL, &newready);
    if (notQuiet) {
      CONNEL_DINFO(
        "connel_select(cs, NULL, &newready) output %ld, returned %d\n",
        newready, ret);
    }
    newready |= cs->cs_ready;
    if (ret > 0) {
      ...  kbd response
      ...  serial response
    } else if (ret == -10) {
      notdone = 0;
    }
  }
  ...  kbd and serial deafen
}
}}}
```

Table 3.12: Fourth fold view in origami

loop, the select is called, always with **forceready** TRUE, with **newready** bits showing what fired. A failure of Linux select (which can happen because the file descriptor becomes invalid) will cause -10 to be returned, and that branch exits to avoid a busy spin. There is no timeout.

When the loop is done, the machines may be deafened.

Table 3.13 is the detail of the listen step. Each listen is retried with **force** TRUE if necessary, in case it came in in an unexpected state; that approach is used with the deafen below too.

Table 3.14 is the detail of the first asynchronous trigger of both inputs.

Table 3.15 is the detail of the keyboard response. Note $1 = 2^0$ to relate the bit test of **newready** with the second parameter of CONNEL_FINISH. Success

```
{{{  kbd and serial listen
ret = connel_machine_listen(cmkbd, 0);
CONNEL_DINFO("connel_machine_listen(cmkbd, 0) returned %d\n", ret);
if (ret<1) {
  ret = connel_machine_listen(cmkbd, 1);
  CONNEL_DINFO("connel_machine_listen(cmkbd, 1) returned %d\n", ret);
}
ret = connel_machine_listen(cmserinp, 0);
if (ret > 0) {
  CONNEL_DINFO("connel_machine_listen(cmserinp, 0) returned %d\n", ret);
  if (ret<1) {
    ret = connel_machine_listen(cmserinp, 1);
    CONNEL_DINFO("connel_machine_listen(cmserinp, 1) returned %d\n", ret);
  }
}
}}}
```

Table 3.13: First subfold view in fourth fold

```
{{{  kbd and serial read_start
ret = connel_read_start(cmkbd, &thechar, 1, 1);
if (notQuiet) {
  CONNEL_DINFO(
    "connel_read_start(cmkbd, &thechar, 1, 1) returned %d\n", ret);
  CONNEL_DINFO("nbytes %d ndone %d\n",
    cmkbd->cm_nbytes, cmkbd->cm_ndone);
}
ret2 = connel_read_start(cmserinp, &thechar2, 1, 1);
if (notQuiet) {
  CONNEL_DINFO(
    "connel_read_start(cmserinp, &thechar2, 1, 1) returned %d\n", ret2);
  CONNEL_DINFO("nbytes %d ndone %d\n",
    cmserinp->cm_nbytes, cmserinp->cm_ndone);
}
}}}
```

Table 3.14: Second subfold view in fourth fold

```
{{{ kbd response
if (newready&1) {
  unsigned long finish = 0;
  notdone = 0;
  CONNEL_FINISH(cs, 0, finish);
  if (notQuiet) {
    CONNEL_DINFO(
      "CONNEL_FINISH(cs, 0, finish) returned finish = 0x%lX\n",
      finish);
  }
  if (finish) {
    if (notQuiet) {
      CONNEL_DINFO("============= KEY byte: 0x%02X %c\n",
        (int)thechar, thechar);
    }
    connel_write(cserial, &thechar, 1);
    if (notQuiet) {
      CONNEL_DINFO("SERIAL output KEY byte.\n");
    } else {
      CONNEL_DWARN("Sent byte: 0x%02X \'%c\'\n", (int)thechar, thechar);
    }
    notdone = noexitchar||(thechar != exitchar);
    notdone = notdone&&(notInterrupted > 0);
    if (notdone) {
      ret = connel_read_start(cmkbd, &thechar, 1, 1);
      if (notQuiet) {
        CONNEL_DINFO(
          "connel_read_start(cmkbd, &thechar, 1, 1) returned %d\n", ret);
      }
    }
  }
}
}}}
```

Table 3.15: Third subfold view in fourth fold

```
{{{ serial response
if (newready&2) {
  unsigned long finish = 0;
  notdone = 0;
  CONNEL_FINISH(cs, 1, finish);
  if (notQuiet) {
    CONNEL_DINFO(
      "CONNEL_FINISH(cs, 1, finish) returned finish = 0x%1X\n",
      finish);
  }
  if (finish) {
    if ((cs->cs_cm[1]->cm_c->c_state)==0) {
      CONNEL_DWARN(" State of SERIAL is 0 (failed).\n");
      notInterrupted = 0;
    } else if (isbinary) {
      CONNEL_DWARN("%02X\n", (int)((unsigned char)thechar2));
    } else if (notQuiet) {
      CONNEL_DINFO("========== SERIAL byte: 0x%02X %c\n",
        (int)(unsigned char)thechar2, legalize(thechar2));
    } else {
      CONNEL_DWARN(" Got byte: 0x%02X    \'%c\'\n",
        (int)(unsigned char)thechar2, legalize(thechar2));
    }
    notdone = noexitchar||(thechar2 != exitchar);
    notdone = notdone&&(notInterrupted > 0);
    if (notdone) {
      ret = connel_read_start(cmserinp, &thechar2, 1, 1);
      if (notQuiet) {
        CONNEL_DINFO(
          "connel_read_start(cmserinp, &thechar2, 1, 1) returned %d\n", ret);
      }
    }
  }
}
}}}
```

Table 3.16: Fourth subfold view in fourth fold

causes an unconditional write of the input byte to the serial connection. Either a Ctrl-C or an exit character can cause the loop to end, otherwise a new asynchronous keyboard read is started.

Table 3.16 is the detail of the serial input response. Note $2 = 2^1$ to relate the bit test of newready with the second parameter of CONNEL_FINISH. Success causes an unconditional write of a response to the input byte via CONNEL_DWARN or CONNEL_DINFO. The stdout connel cscr is actually not used. Either a Ctrl-C or an exit character can cause the loop to end, otherwise a new asynchronous

```
{{{ kbd and serial deafen
if (yesdrop) {
  ret = connel_machine_deafen(cmserinp, 0);
  CONNEL_DINFO("connel_machine_deafen(cmserinp, 0) returned %d\n", ret);
  if (ret<1) {
    ret = connel_machine_deafen(cmserinp, 1);
    CONNEL_DINFO("connel_machine_deafen(cmserinp, 1) returned %d\n", ret);
  }
}
ret = connel_machine_deafen(cmkbd, 0);
CONNEL_DINFO("connel_machine_deafen(cmkbd, 0) returned %d\n", ret);
if (ret<1) {
  ret = connel_machine_deafen(cmkbd, 1);
  CONNEL_DINFO("connel_machine_deafen(cmkbd, 1) returned %d\n", ret);
}
}}}
```

Table 3.17: Fifth subfold view in fourth fold

```
{{{ END
ret = connel_close(cscr);
CONNEL_DINFO("connel_close(cscr) returned %d\n", ret);
if (yesdrop) {
  ret = connel_close(cserial);
  CONNEL_DINFO("connel_close(cserial) returned %d\n", ret);
}
ret = connel_close(ckbd);
CONNEL_DINFO("connel_close(ckbd) returned %d\n", ret);
}}}
```

Table 3.18: Fifth fold view in origami

serial read is started.

After the end of the loop, the inputs are deafened, except that in the case of -nodrop, the serial is NOT deafened (Table 3.17).

3.6.4 Closing Connel

All Table 3.18 does is to close the connels. Machines do not close, though it is sometimes useful to deafen them as a final step, as above. In the case of -nodrop, the serial is NOT closed, leaving it for another program to pick up. -

3.7 Standard third party tools

We have already covered one of the tools needed for creating and running Wide code: an editor, preferably a folding editor. The output of an editor is a file of ASCII text in a file system on a computer running a desktop OS or something similar (like a tablet OS). The ultimate goal is to run our code in the real world. That requires several other tools, but the good news is that these tools, in the case of C programs, are standard tools available from third parties—usually several competing third parties, so you can pick ones that best fit your needs.

In this section, I will work through software tools for both OS-based and embedded coding. Hardware design and creation uses a set of different but related tools, which will be dealt with in a later chapter.

3.7.1 Detailed description of steps

The route from text editor to run for a C program has several components, which you need to understand so that you won't be trapped by the "magic" of pushing a button on a screen. It's not really all that deep, and every part of it makes sense if you think about it.

ACTION	TOOL	ALSO NEEDED
Compile	Compiler	Header files
Link	Linker	System routines
Load	Loader	Physical connection to target
Run	UI or power switch	Triggering mechanism
Debug	Debugger	Code disassembler and bidirectional JTAG or similar

Table 3.19: Needs and tools in sequence

It is necessary to turn the text code into a form of machine-readable code that can drive the hardware. This is done in two steps: translation of the text into a form of machine instructions, and packaging these machine instructions into a set of instructions that will actually drive the hardware. The important thing is to understand the hidden parts of the two steps.

3.7.1.1   Stage 1: compiling

The first step (the translation) is called COMPILING. The text satisfies certain restrictions that make it uniquely clear to a program, the *compiler,* exactly what machine commands are implied by it. The compiler is also capable of rejecting code that does not fit these restrictions, and does so in a helpful way, allowing the coder to correct the errors. (Unfortunately, there is no way it can catch code that is correctly phrased but does not do what the coder intends.)

Almost all code refers to functionality outside itself, the so-called *externals.* Because of this, outside information, different from what the coder has created, is needed by the compiler to tell if the external references are correct. These are *header files* which are present in some form. C has the virtue of explicitly mentioning them. Often much work must be done to trace the external references, since header files can `#include` other header files. So it is in the sercomio.c example: `connel.h` proves to reference a large number of system header files.

So by consulting the header files, the compiler is able to see if the external references (at least the ones known to the header files) are syntactically correct. There can be other external references too, not in the header files: all the compiler can do in this case is check for consistency. All external references result in a "mark" being placed in the compiled code that says "I'm not correctly filled in yet!"

3.7.1.2   Stage 2: linking

As implied by the last paragraph, the output machine-type code produced by the compiler is usually incomplete in two ways: known external references (fitting header files), and unknown external references. The LINKING operation supplies other machine-type code that satisfies all these references correctly, and produces a code file that is sufficient to run the hardware.

Some prefer to eliminate the distinction between compiling and linking, especially for embedded code, where the entire source text is often explicitly available. This is a judgement call, but in my opinion, it is better to subdivide the program into manageable parts for compiling, for two reasons: (1) If well-defined, each such part is easier to handle and maintain; and (2) defining the relations between the parts is a great aid in defining and documenting the program as a whole. This is modular coding. Even in embedded code, one massive part of the code may deal mostly with mathematics while another massive part may deal mostly with interrupts, for example.

The *linker,* which is often as a program call seen as part of the compiler, must access all the real code that corresponds to the external references, whether or not they had a header file. It's quite possible for all the parts (*object files*) to have compiled correctly and yet they fail to link. This can be for two reasons: (A) some external does not match any real code; or (B) the descriptions of the externals (variables, calls, etc) do not match each other or the real code. Another cause of failure is now more common in embedded code: (C) the resulting *image file* is too big to fit in the code space of its chip, or exceeds the maximum allowed by the (free or low-priced) linker.

The combination of the compiler and the linker yields code that is sufficient to drive the hardware.

3.7.1.3   Stage 3: loading

After the image file has been created, LOADING places it in the correct memory so that it can drive its hardware. This is a more complex problem than it seems. In many architectures, such as "Harvard architecture," the memory out of which code runs is actually different in kind from the memory where data variables live. In other architectures, especially embedded ones or ones meant for computer security, code memory cannot normally be written; so a special state must be used for code to be written at all. In these one speaks of "burning" new code into the chip's program memory.

In standard OS-based systems, the usual approach is "load and run" in one operation, usually either by keying in or scripting a call to the program in a command line, or by making a selection in a GUI. There are other more abstruse possibilities, like another program that does an "exec" call to this one.

It is usually true that the loading process is complex, because the image file calls for more than one kind of resource. Not only does it need space for its machine code commands, but normally it requires allocation of data memory and other resources. Usually (but not always, in the case of interpreted C) there is a move from mass storage (e.g. disk) to processor memory, perhaps more than one kind of processor memory.

The loading process is of interest as the way malware gains the ability to run a computer. In the case of embedded chips, code is loaded only rarely, by "burning a PROM" or by "upgrading the firmware" as a total body. Special states and cabling, and often jumpers, are needed to do this.

3.7.1.4 Stage 4: running

The next step is RUNNING or, more precisely, triggering a run. The casual user may be deceived into thinking that this is a trivial process, since it happens automatically in an OS and is usually caused by power-on or reset in an embedded CPU. But it always involves at least two things: (a) preparation of the CPU state to do the run (either a reset or an allocation of runtime resources, both usually rather involved); and (b) a so-called "jump" or transfer of control of at least one CPU core to an instruction within the program. Not surprisingly, both these steps are also of great interest to writers and fighters of malware.

Load and run go together only in OS-type code running on a main CPU. Embedded code may have been loaded to ROM and/or flash memory a long time ago, and a run merely branches to the start instruction. This makes a big difference in global variable definitions like

```
int loopcount = 20;
```

because merely setting the memory variable `loopcount` to the initial value 20 at load time does not suffice for embedded code. When restarted, it can have random data in it. This is why occam disallows definitions like this; you have to say

```
INT loopcount :
SEQ
  loopcount := 20
```

which establishes the clear separation. C compilers for embedded CPUs typically cobble together a special initialization routine, run "before starting," that does all the initializations for all the toplevel definitions of this sort.

3.7.1.5 Stage 5: debugging

Perhaps I'm being cynical, but I here include in DEBUGGING all actions of the program after its startup. If you write perfect code, it will of course just be a normal run! In every case, it will be slavish, legalistic following of every instruction encountered, until either normal termination (a "jump" outside the program, usually to a higher level program or to an OS), an interrupt or nested program that never returns, or power-off or other hardware failure.

Consider the case when something abnormal is happening in the program, and concerted debugging is done. There are two kinds of debugging: *post-mortem* debugging, and *monitoring*. Both of them require the cooperation of the OS and/or the hardware, as well as special debugging programs.

In post-mortem debugging, a correctly designed CPU and OS can take advantage of the fact that the default behavior of most computer resources after a program using them has terminated (or been killed) is to do nothing. Then a properly designed program *operating out of different resources* can examine the state left by the terminated program and draw conclusions about its behavior or misbehavior. Shared resources (e.g. cache) militate against this, and multicore systems are friendly to it. One core may be able to trickle the state off another and store it for later examination (an old Transputer trick).

In monitoring, the core under examination, or an emulator of it, not only does what it is instructed to do but also reports ongoing state to an observer. In addition, it may allow "poking" like single-stepping or breakpointing through interfaces like JTAG. This creates a kind of Heisenberg uncertainty since this monitoring burdens the core (or cores) under observation, and can change their timing and behavior. Single-stepping in particular is hardly usable for timing-dependent problems.

A common form of monitoring is done without a debugger, by putting branches and special informative "diagnostics" into the code. Though this can cause a hiccup in program progress, the hope is that the syndrome is fully developed by that time and will reveal itself. In embedded chips an extra serial connection or other link is often useful for this purpose. Compiler options (such as were used in `sercomio` above) can be left in along with the diagnostics, though this clutters up the code.

3.7.2 Integrated Development Environments

Figure 3.1 shows a startup screen for Code Composer, an Integrated Development Environment (IDE) for the Texas Instruments MSP430 family of embedded CPUs.

IDEs are not only used for embedded cross-compiling (i.e. compiling for a target different from the CPU the compiler is running on). They are also available for OS-based compiling, as with Windows Visual Studio.

An IDE combines all the operations listed in the previous subsection, making them accessible through a GUI. The oldest of them, such as the Transputer Development System (TDS) of the 1980s, did not need a GUI but used the `ansi.sys` selection and control system on a text screen. The key here is the menu-driven functionality. All you do is make sure all your hardware is connected properly and powered up, and then open the IDE.

For example, the Energia IDE, which is an MSP430 variant of the famous Arduino IDE, can run on any of the common operating systems: Linux, Windows, or Mac. In the Kicksat project, we use a Zac Manchester variant of

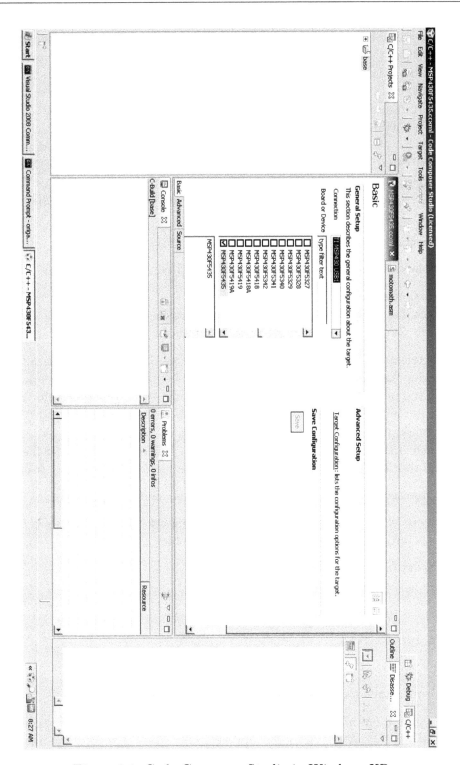

Figure 3.1: Code Composer Studio in Windows XP

Energia which has special system files needed to do satellite radio when you are the satellite. Pick MagGyro_Serial_OK_dbl_blink_w_LJD_Tempmods_R4 (it's really a .ino file, which is a variant on a C or C++ file, in a subdirectory of that name) or one of 37 other selections in my Sketchbook, press the go button (an arrow pointing to the right), and the code gets compiled, linked, loaded via USB to my Sprite, and a run is triggered.

This is, of course, magic, which is not good enough from the Wide Computing point of view. The best way to use an IDE is in tandem with non-IDE tools that access the same files. The first thing you have to do is find the files. That's different for every IDE and every OS. Opening a BSD command window on my Mac, I find

```
~/Documents/Energia/MagGyro_Serial_OK_dbl_blink_w_LJD_Tempmods_R4
```

to be the directory that contains my .ino file. I confirm by typing in

```
file ~/Documents/Energia/\
MagGyro_Serial_OK_dbl_blink_w_LJD_Tempmods_R4/\
MagGyro_Serial_OK_dbl_blink_w_LJD_Tempmods_R4.ino
```

and it tells me I have a C++ file. (Yes, backslash-Enter lets you fold lines in both Mac and Linux, not Windows, and I'm using it here so my command fits in the page. In real life, you do better using tab completion and let the command get as long as it wants.) I then look in the file and indeed it's the file I think it is.

Table 3.19 informs us that we are not done. Where are the header files and system routines? In the Mac we find them in a huge tree branching from

```
/Applications/Energia.app/Contents/Resources/Java/hardware/
```

But more yet is needed, as implied by finding such branches as **variants**. Settings imposed by the user are found in the file

```
~/Library/Energia/preferences.txt
```

Here's an example. After a long and fruitless search for the definition of **F_CPU**, I returned to **preferences.txt** and found the suggestive entry

```
board=lpcc430f5137
```

Then I went to the tree root given above, and ran the search

```
grep -rl "lpcc430f5137" *
```

which should list all the files containing that keyword. **msp430/boards.txt** was the only hit. A search for the keyword immediately yielded the line

```
lpcc430f5137.build.f_cpu=8000000L
```

along with other information, like `variant=Sprite`. Thus, our chip is not the advertised 16MHz speedster, but the energy-saving 8MHz variant. And some magic in Energia apparently creates the macro `F_CPU` out of the lowercased version in this file.

It's worth noting that most of these tools exist in BSD (Mac) and Linux, but Windows lacks some and offers others under different names (`FIND` instead of `grep`, for instance). However, modern systems offer an effective workaround. Install a virtual machine program, such as VMWare, on your native system (in my case, a Mac), and then it's easy to overlap it with virtual machines in the other OSs. By "overlap" I mean that you can arrange for them to share the same disk space, except for some system areas that each OS insists on having private to itself.

After doing this, make sure that as far as possible you force your IDEs to point to the shared disk space, not the private disk space. Then you can jump around from one OS to another, using the most effective tools from each. It's true that Windows will want to terminate lines with CRLF (hex 0D 0A) while Linux prefers nl (hex 0A) and the Mac sometimes uses CR (hex 0D), but except for the last, most tools will deal with any of the above.

3.7.3 Development toolsets

The other way to go, self-documenting and often cheaper and less restrictive, is to use the command line. For most targets, a small development toolset gets from source code to running program. Typically, the functions are packaged into two programs: a compiler (which with different options also functions as a linker and a disassembler), and a debugger. In the case of OS-based programs, loading and triggering of the run are usually done by a program command, using the name or icon of the image file. In the case of embedded code, they are usually a function of the debugger.

3.7.3.1 The command line

The command line has a major advantage over menus, once you can get it to work: its short command is a complete specification of what is to be done. It eliminates frantic sessions, picking one sequence of mouse selections after another, trying to get the exact one that actually made the thing work. And command line tools have evolved to lock on to this advantage.

People sometimes dread the command line, because it requires perfect spelling and ordering of program arguments, sometimes many dozens of characters long. Things are actually not that bad. The command line has come a long way since the IBM keyboard replaced punched cards. Key aids include:

(A) *Tab completion and history scrolling:* Both command name and filename typing can usually be helped by tab completion—type part of it, then <Tab>, and the OS will try to fill in for you. (It helps if the first few letters are unique; if not, it goes as far as it can.) And once you've got it to work, up-arrow history scrolling will let you rerun it, and a one-line editor lets you change it.

This works in all the OSs, and is convenient enough to be dangerous: rely on it too much, in a VM which saves state of multiple screens across sessions, and a crash that "forgets" some of it can lose you a lot of information! But the **history** command lets you transfer it to a file, at least in Linux and Mac; for Windows you have to use F7 and a cut and paste.

(B) *Scripts:* Runnable text files, **bash** scripts in Linux and BSD (Mac) and **.BAT** ("batch" or "PowerShell") scripts on the Windows command line, are key to doing any repeatable work. They consist of commands, sometimes glued together by control words which look like a coding language but are actually special commands carried out by the operating system command processor. The syntax is very similar between Linux and BSD but the Windows syntax is different and uses a lot of % signs.

The wise programmer (wiser than I've been lots of times) moves his history into a script rather frequently, and takes the trouble to put in parameters that let him vary it. Then everything is documented, for months and years in the future. Command-line functionality tends to be stable, not changing "out from under you" but at most, with new versions, adding capabilities.

(C) *Makefiles:* Finally, there is the Makefile, a kind of super-script run by the program **make** in Linux or BSD and by **NMAKE** in Windows. As its name indicates, this is a setup especially adapted to build programs. You can think of it as using a lot of clues (continually updated in your Makefile and checked in the file system, especially dates) to build a script on the fly, and then run it. Typically you do the whole job by typing in **make** or **NMAKE**—nothing more!

But you can do special jobs with keywords like

```
make clean
```

or

```
make debug
```

—in fact, anything you want. If you think it over, this is as useful as any IDE in ordinary use. It is completely self-documenting. It requires a little more effort to maintain, but is more flexible and completely under your control. The best way to learn Makefiles is to find a simple template program with a Makefile on the Internet, and then to vary it and its Makefile into something of your design.

3.7.3.2 Setup and serial

Setup is of critical importance and can take many forms. In every usual case there is electric power and some form of connection. All five tasks (compilation, linking, loading, triggering of run, and successful run or debugging) must be supported by the connection, though not necessarily the same connection, at some time. Usually if *loading* is supported then the connection is complete and all the rest is also supported.

In the case of pure OS-based programming, the minimum is usually mass storage (disk), keyboard, screen, and OS CPU (and memory), with their interconnections. Embedded cross-compiling work requires more, a second (embedded) CPU/memory with at least a serial connection or other link with the first, and usually with yet more connections related to its purpose. However, past the loading stage, the OS components may fall away. And it's possible, though not usual, that compiling and linking may be done without the embedded CPU present, and loading with only a bare connection to a powered embedded CPU.

The reason this is not usual is that testing of new code is usually required, and it is more convenient to have the whole setup ready than to pause and redo the physical configuration between the phases of the work. I've done it though, with Kicksat work, when I'm not the one with our group's Flying Sprite prototype.

When setting up OS machines, it's convenient to use a virtual machine program like VMWare to get several machines for the price of one. Then the question immediately arises how to get them communicating. The simplest Wide approach is a serial connection, which in this case is a virtual serial connection between two virtual machines. It is set up by adding a few lines to the configuration files that describe the VMs.

In [5] it describes where these files are, at least in Mac VMWare Fusion. (Other systems will have similar paths.) After setting up my Ubuntu 9.04 under the name "Ubuntu" I found the virtual serial in

```
~/Documents/Virtual Machines.localized/Ubuntu.vmwarevm/Ubuntu.vmx
```

and, following the instructions in [6], added these lines:

```
serial1.present = "TRUE"
serial1.fileType = "pipe"
serial1.yieldOnMsrRead = "TRUE"
serial1.startConnected = "TRUE"
serial1.fileName = "/tmp/dev_com"
```

They follow immediately after **serial0** which was found already defined for fileType **thinprint**. In the similarly named **vmx** file in the Windows XP **vmwarevm** directory, I added

```
serial1.present = "TRUE"
serial1.fileType = "pipe"
serial1.yieldOnMsrRead = "TRUE"
serial1.startConnected = "TRUE"
serial1.fileName = "/tmp/dev_com"
serial1.pipe.endPoint = "client"
```

because it too was using **serial0** for **thinprint**.

This activated **/dev/ttyS1** and **COM2** respectively, just as if they were physical connections. They connect with each other because the **fileName** is the same.

Like real serial connections, they still will not talk properly unless their baud rate, data bits, stop bits, and parity settings are the same. In Linux, use **stty** both to find and change these.

```
stty -F /dev/ttyS1 -a
```

should show the right baud rate, no parity (**-parenb**), 8 data bits (**cs8**), one stop bit (**-cstopb**). A baud rate change, for example, would be

```
stty -F /dev/ttyS1 9600
```

(see man file for more). In Windows, use **MODE** for the same:

```
MODE COM2
```

gives the information and

```
MODE COM2:9600,N,8,1
```

makes the settings. (Many other baud rates are possible, up to 115200. Bytes per second is typically baud rate divided by 10.)

To test this, run **sercomio** on both sides, using standard (not QUIET) compiled version. In the example given, it would be

```
./sercomio 1
```

(for /dev/ttyS1) on the Linux side and

```
sercomio 2
```

(for COM2) on the Windows side. Then key in some characters from both sides. They should be echoed on the other. To end, use Ctrl-C.

3.7.3.3 From compilers to debuggers

Once the machines for which code is to be written have been set up with proper connectivity, it is also necessary to connect them to machines which will compile, link, load, trigger and debug the code. Even if these are the same machines, the connections are not necessarily the same. Typically, Universal Serial Bus (USB) is the great connector through which code is loaded and, often, through which embedded devices are powered. Extra cables may be needed for JTAG debugging too.

Here is where Wide Computing techniques come into their own. The laying of the foundation, the initial job, under the Wide scheme is **to get all these parts talking properly.** As in our previous exercise with `sercomio`, they do not have to say much. All we need is little programs, running and communicating on all our real CPUs and virtual machines. What they communicate does not have to have much resemblance to the final goal; it just has to operate the same "chat lines."

Before the prospective coder draws back in consternation from this front-loaded task, let me mention the mighty friend that makes it all pretty easy: THE INTERNET. Every single component in the setup is a product that somebody has to sell (or, in the case of free software, give away). They all want their stuff to be used! Therefore the Internet is full of descriptions, apnotes, and worked-through examples (complete with pictures) that you can find with a simple Google search. Just enter every specifying term, correctly spelled, in no particular order, and put quotes around terms that belong together. Examples:

```
dos "serial port" status
```

or

```
windows msp430 jtag debugger
```

(it is case-insensitive). The more necessarily relevant stuff you can give Google, the better it can narrow it down.

I do this all the time. It has worked for me for the last ten years.

You will almost always find your way to details that are poorly explained or simply omitted, so don't be discouraged if your experimental runs fail at first. *You are doing the most critical and valuable part of your project.* Just persist, search FAQs and user group commentary, and even join the user group if you need to post a question. In the end, it will either work or you will be lionized as the one who forced a redesign of the whole product! (Don't worry. The latter case is pretty rare. It's just that you sometimes have to do weird, unintuitive stuff to make it work.)

Here's an example from embedded coding:

```
mspdebug olimex --fet-force-id msp430f5418
```

Here **mspdebug** is an open-source debugger for the Texas Instruments MSP430 family, and the Olimex is a good JTAG connector that lets you load and debug code. The chip we used was NOT the MSP430F5418, and was not offered as one of the possible options! But some research found that this was a common problem, and if chips were similar enough (for example, just differing in amount of program memory) you could get away with specifying a different chip using the **--fet-force-id** option.

Less difficult are the typical compile and link commands used by programs in an OS. Here, from the Makefile, is the Linux sequence for **sercomio**:

```
tjoccam@ubuntu:/mnt/hgfs/tjoccam/SpcTime/LAZM$ make -n sercomio
gcc -DCONNEL_LINUX -c sercomio.c
gcc -DCONNEL_LINUX -c connel.c
gcc -o sercomio sercomio.o connel.o
```

And here is the Windows sequence, which must be run from within a Visual Studio Command Prompt window:

```
Y:\tjoccam\SpcTime\LAZM>NMAKE /N sercomio.exe

Microsoft (R) Program Maintenance Utility Version 9.00.30729.01
Copyright (C) Microsoft Corporation.  All rights reserved.

        cl /c sercomio.c
        cl /c connel.c
        cl sercomio.obj connel.obj User32.lib
```

Note the use of the makefile and the special display-only option of **make** or **NMAKE** to show what is called. To make this display work, you may have to temporarily rename the object files to fool **make** into thinking it has to redo the whole thing.

Finally, here is a variant of embedded calls that do a cross-compile for the MSP430:

```
msp430-gcc -mmcu=msp430f5418 -g -Wall -c -MMD -o\
 m-asm.lo mmbase.S -Xassembler -al |\
 sed -e's/\/tmp\/........[.][os]//g' > asmlisting
msp430-gcc -mmcu=msp430f5418 -g -Wall -c -MMD -o\
 m-c.lo m.c -Xassembler -al |\
 sed -e's/\/tmp\/........[.][os]//g' > clisting
```

This assembles **mmbase.S** and compiles **m.c**, using **-al** to generate disassembled listings, and the sed scripts to remove clutter.

```
msp430-gcc -mmcu=msp430f5418 -g -Wimplicit -Os\
 -o basem base-driver.o base-core.o ../base/m/m.o\
 -Xlinker --print-map | sed -e's/\/tmp\/........[.][os]//g' > map
```

This (after more work) is the linking, using **--print-map** to generate a dis-assembled map, and sed script to remove clutter. (The listings are extremely useful during debugging, since they give exact addresses in the code.) Simpler forms are found in Makefiles, and **basem** is able to be loaded to the embedded CPU called "base".

Note that in these command-line calls, unlike Google search, the arguments are NOT case-insensitive. Also, dashes and underscores are not equivalent, a frequent point of confusion for a beginner. If there are embedded spaces in an argument, it is usually OK to enclose it in quotes, e.g.

```
confundus --file "big ugly"
```

and the command interpreter strips away the quotes and treats what is inside them as only one argument, not two. There are other tricks (like using \" if the quote is really part of the argument) that you will pick up as you go along.

Once you have discovered these secrets, don't forget them! Enshrine them in a script or Makefile, or write yourself a little apnote.

3.7.4 Vanishing code and other oddities

Whether an IDE or a toolset is used, fantastic behavior is sometimes encountered that comes, not from the program code, but from the tool. The ultimate cause of most of this is the Deep Programming monoculture and some of the odd decisions that have been made to band-aid its problems. However, Deep or Wide, these can bite you, and I'll warn you here of some that I have encountered. This may save you days of wasted debugging effort.

3.7.4.1 The vanishing code codicil

Many perfectly sane and logical usages in C and other languages produce, according to the language definition, "undefined" results. This usually means (and probably originally was intended to mean) different results depending on implementation, e.g. big-endian versus little-endian. The normal toolmaker's response in such a case would be to make a best effort and, perhaps, issue a warning. Some compilers, typically Windows compilers, do this.

Other much-used and even unavoidable compilers, such as `gcc`, follow a so-called *language lawyer* approach. This means doing the strict minimum that the definition allows. In many cases this means—**no code output!** And no errors or warnings either. Your code simply vanishes, and the only way to tell this is to use a disassembler and look at the machine code output.

A common example of this is STRICT ALIASING, which says that after casting a pointer to a pointer of a different type, every dereference is undefined. Example:

```
{
  double x;
  unsigned char *xbytes = (unsigned char *)&x;
  /* perform byte-by-byte operations on the 8-byte
   * double-precision floating-point variable x
   */
}
```

In some compilers, like `gcc` at higher optimization levels, the code you put here will simply vanish, even though you know the target and have researched how the bytes of a double are dealt with in your target architecture. See [3]. An exception is made for `memcpy`, since otherwise hardly any code would work, and `char` will sometimes work where `unsigned char` will not.

You just work around absurdities like this—for instance, by using a union—although strictly speaking *unions are illegal too!* (They just haven't dared to crush them.) Only Linus Torvalds ([4]) can actually fight it. He made them include a compiler option

```
-fno-strict-aliasing
```

but they struck back by not documenting it.

3.7.4.2 Mixed ordering

It might seem logical for the compiler to try to order the memory assigned to the variables in the same order the variables are declared. Windows compilers tend to do this (although they pack variables smaller than a word in a way that will save space). But `gcc` apparently randomizes the placement of the variables. Never expect there to be any memory coherency on a scale bigger than that of the actual variables declared.

Even code location can be swapped around, especially by an optimizing compiler. Loops can be unwrapped or partially unwrapped. And, of course, variables can disappear entirely or be reduced to registers, especially if nothing accesses a pointer to the variable. Always declare a variable `volatile` if anything outside the code being compiled can affect its value, or even tacitly read its value.

3.7.4.3 State machines

Though not strictly speaking the compiler's fault, unintuitive state machines can wreak havoc. If interrupts or multitasking are sharing a resource, such as a state variable, it can change its value between being set and what appears to be an *immediately following* test. A FIFO can become empty or full between one instruction and the next!

Always be sure you know under what conditions other code can interrupt or pre-empt your code stream. Wide Computing allows occam-like variables, which by design are usually immune to this kind of thing, to be mixed with C conveniences like global variables. The best thing is to use lots of comments and documentation to keep track of such dangerous exceptions.

3.8 References

[1] Inmos Limited: *Transputer Instruction Set, a compiler writer's guide* (Document Number 72 TRN 119 05). Prentice Hall, 1988. PDF found at `http://www.transputer.net/iset/iset.asp`

[2] Inmos Limited: *occam 2 Reference Manual* (Document Number 72 occ 45 01 or 72 occ 45 02). Prentice Hall, 1988. PDF found at `http://www.transputer.net/obooks/obooks.asp`

[3] stackoverflow: "What is the strict aliasing rule?" October 8, 2011. `http://stackoverflow.com/questions/98650/what-is-the-strict-aliasing-rule/99010#99010`

[4] Linus Torvalds: "Re: Invalid compilation without -fno-strict-aliasing" Wed, 26 Feb 2003 17:26:37 +0000 (UTC) `http://lkml.org/lkml/2003/2/26/158`

[5] VMWare files description for Fusion `http://communities.vmware.com/docs/DOC-1110`

[6] VMWare serial connections between virtual machines, Fusion `http://communities.vmware.com/message/748577#748577`

Second Wave: Pseudocode   4
The Hardware And The Data
Flow

Abstract

The purpose of this chapter is to detail the techniques of pseudocoding. These assume that the First Wave of project design is complete, so that the tasks to be done and major pieces to do them are known. The Second Wave defines a state machine that will actually work, down to each bit flipping at the right time. This operates on several levels. As examples of focused (low-level) pseudocoding we offer two FIFO designs, and as examples of data-flow (high-level) pseudocoding we proceed with the projects discussed in Chapter 2.

4.1   The step from design to pseudocode

The purpose of Second Wave Wide programming, or pseudocoding, is to define mechanism. The First Wave has proved plausibility of the project by tracking its tasks through its component pieces, using knowledge and published specs to make sure that you are not biting off more that you can chew. When the First Wave is done, it should be clear that each demand on the resources you have assembled is well within their ability to fulfill. But just showing that the door is big enough for the piano is not enough.

After all, your goal is a program—which means a set of "laws" (instructions) which, when followed with slavish, uncritical devotion, will reliably cause the results you want. That could mean thousands of lines of code, an intimidating prospect if you just mean to jump in. Wide Programming and Second Wave pseudocoding come to the rescue, because they have identified most of these lines of code as being in the "regular" (non-critical) parts, and permit the critical parts to be expressed in a clear formalism (see [1], Section 2).

My repeated metaphor of "waves" is based on experience. There ought to be a pause for reflection (and discussion) after each wave. Frequently, something does not work and an earlier wave has to be modified. Rushing forward is followed by backing off, but the tide comes in a little each time. This front-loaded effort does **NOT** fit the corporate accounting model of steady value-per-hour progress, but is more like poetry! That is why so many outsourced computing projects are such disasters.

This knowledge is literally worth hundreds of millions of dollars, as recent news of failing software projects should make clear. Unfortunately, this value can hardly ever be realized, since corporate and government planners, who control the money, will not budge from their assumptions. So don't be disappointed. Just keep plugging along successfully with your small self-funded projects, while enjoying your front-row seat at the demolition derby of the giants—including Nissan, Toyota, and GM at latest report ([13]).

Anyway, let's return from that digression to the question of regular versus critical. Pseudocode typically puts in a comment or unexpanded PROC call to represent regular code, while working out every detail of the critical code. And that leads to another consideration. [1] defines critical code as that which is outside the shared universal implication of the metaphoric construct, a definition which is aimed at language considerations. Here we are using a simple language, not an object-oriented one, so we can focus on *timing and state* variations outside the shared universal of the code. In other words, regular code is that which works the same independently of outside behavior, while critical code depends significantly on outside behavior.

An example of regular code would be a long math-crunching operation. As a low-priority "nice" process, it may be interrupted or swapped out by other processes, but that should not *significantly* affect its work. But what if it depends, say, on a web search that may be delayed or give an unexpected result? The math-crunching operation now looks like regular code when viewed at a distance, but a close-up view shows it has a complex structure that includes critical parts.

So pseudocode frequently has to be nested. Another block of pseudocode may be denoted by a comment, or by a procedure call or a fold. In many cases, commentary is enough to describe the real coding task that is demanded, thus avoiding doubling up the labor, e.g. coding a long CASE statement in occam that is just going to be recoded in a long switch statement in C. But beware! That escape should be used ONLY IF THE EXPANSION IS TRULY TRIVIAL. It's easy to "kid yourself" and gloss over some critical code that is really a hard nut to crack, or even a design flaw.

The general rule is that a CASE can be waved at, but not an ALT. If some of the branches involve state machine waits, then at least these should be pseudocoded in detail.

4.2 Focused pseudocoding of some FIFOs

The first examples will be of *focused pseudocoding*. This is very close to real occam programming, and is usually used to design low-level hardware or something very close to it. The idea is to imply a fully detailed state machine as a specification. Later implementations may not greatly resemble the pseudocode, since they can use combinatorial as well as sequential hardware design, but they are required to perform exactly as the pseudocode implies.

The example here is a common component of basic hardware: a First-In First-Out (FIFO) buffer. This is the same as a queue. In it, *up to a certain capacity,* packets can be stored and later output in the order of their reception. Contrast it with a stack, or Last-In First-Out (LIFO) buffer.

The size of a packet is usually fixed, but can be any value. Even one-bit packets can be queued in a "shift register." A shift register is usually synchronous, meaning every member of the queue moves one slot upon a clock signal. That, however, is too inflexible for most queue uses with packets of one byte or bigger. Usually an asynchronous design is desired, where the packet input and the packet output are under independent external timing controls.

4.2.1 Simple FIFO

The simplest asynchronous FIFO design is rawFIFO, a PAR of n identical members, specified in Table 4.1.

When considering the design of rawFIFO, remember the definition of a PAR in Chapter 3. The execution of members of the PAR can be ordered **in any way** that is consistent with points of synchronization (that is here communication on a channel). This includes interleaving, sequence, or true parallel.

In focused hardware pseudocoding, internal channels as well as programming and internal (local) variables are a convenience serving to define the device's behavior from the point of view of the outside world. Also usually convenient is a presumption that internal activity is "fast" compared with interactions with the outside world. These two considerations lead to the definition of a STABLE STATE as *a state that cannot change as long as the part of it that is shared with the outside world does not change.*

Now rawFIFO (with n=5) can be visualized as Figure 4.1, with the external channels `in` and `out` connecting to `buffer.d[4]` and `buffer.d[0]` respectively. (Here remember period in occam, like underscore in C, is part of names; and I am using `buffer.d[k]` to refer to that instance of `PROC buffer` that is called

111

```
-- This is a raw FIFO implemented in occam-like Crawl Space
-- pseudocode. It is the raw or theoretical FIFO of n parallel
-- buffers, each storing one PACKET and passing it on as soon as
-- possible. An actual implementation of a FIFO using this approach
-- is usually not practical, since it passes each packet a large
-- number of times internally, and a circular indexing system as in
-- "FIFO.occ" is preferred. However, this is the defining standard
-- against which any FIFO implementation (software or hardware) is
-- judged.
-- Global resources are:
-- CHAN OF PACKET in : for the input to the FIFO
-- CHAN OF PACKET out : for the output from the FIFO
-- The size of the FIFO is defined below. (The structure assumes
-- n >= 2.)
VAL INT n IS 32 :
VAL INT nm1 IS n - 1 :
VAL INT nm2 IS n - 2 :
-- this buffer code is repeated n times in parallel
PROC buffer(CHAN OF PACKET enterch, exitch, PACKET pkt)
  WHILE TRUE
    SEQ
      enterch ? pkt
      exitch ! pkt
:
-- this is the main program and its local resources
[n]PACKET pktall : -- for clarity; these could be local to the buffers
[nm1]CHAN OF PACKET ch : -- ch[n-1]=in and ch[-1]=out, conceptually
PAR
  buffer(ch[0], out, pktall[0])
  PAR i FROM 1 FOR nm2
    buffer(ch[i], ch[i-1], pktall[i])
  buffer(in, ch[nm2], pktall[nm1])
--END PAR
}}}
```

Table 4.1: Toplevel view of rawFIFO.occ in origami (irrelevant comments removed)

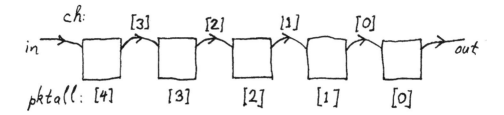

Figure 4.1: rawFIFO (n = 5)

with `pktall[k]`.) All the links operate only in one direction, which means that information is transmitted "backwards" (toward **in**) only by blocking.

Since this is a FIFO that is being designed, internal FIFOs in the channels would be superfluous. An output transmission (!) by `buffer.d[k]` is therefore simultaneous with an input reception (?) by `buffer.d[k-1]` to its right. Branching, looping and communicating are clearly not stable states, since they proceed to completion. Therefore the only stable state candidates for each member of the PAR are just before the input and just before the output, which can be points of blocking. They will be denoted ? and ! respectively, resulting in an n-letter word made of these characters.

It is immediately obvious that !? anywhere in this word is not stable, since a communication can and will begin immediately. Therefore all the ! must be to the right of all the ?. It follows that the only stable states are denoted by the count of ! (waits on output):

$$
\begin{array}{ll}
\text{????? } & 0 \\
\text{????! } & 1 \\
\text{???!! } & 2 \\
\text{??!!! } & 3 \\
\text{?!!!! } & 4 \\
\text{!!!!! } & 5 \\
\end{array}
$$

Closer examination shows that each member of the PAR begins at an input, so that stable state 0 is the initial state. An internal packet communication means a !? changes to a ?! in the word, but a packet coming in on **in** causes the leftmost ? to change to !, and a packet leaving on **out** causes the rightmost ! to change to ?. Therefore the first state change from stable state 0 has to be a packet input on **in**.

Figure 4.2: Unstable after `in`

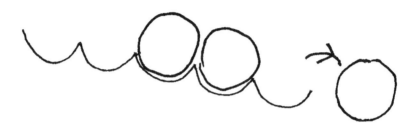

Figure 4.3: Unstable after `out`

The key insight is that information flows to the right. Therefore even though after !? changes to ?! the packet still remains in the left member (it's a *copy* not a *move*), it can be treated as a move, and the left copy of the packet can be ignored. It will be overwritten as soon as new information enters from `in`. A member's buffer is **full** if it has received data that it has not re-transmitted, and **empty** if either it has never received data, or if the data it currently contains has been re-transmitted. This means that (whether stable or unstable) ! always means full, and ? always means empty.

Figure 4.2 is an unstable state with two packets ready to output, and a new packet just input. It corresponds to !??!!. Figure 4.3 is an unstable state that came from a stable state of three packets queued, but the rightmost packet was just output. It corresponds to ??!!?. It is easy to see how these will "fix" themselves (if they are given time) and reach the stable states ??!!! and ???!! respectively.

Inspection shows that, if the code is strictly followed, Figure 4.4 cannot happen. The transmission from [2] to [1] cannot be at the same time as that from [1] to [0], because of the sequence in [1]. If `PROC buffer` were made into a

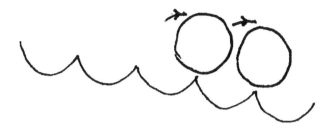

Figure 4.4: Simultaneous move ?

loop on PAR, that would not solve this problem, since the shared buffer would be illegal. And yet it seems that the simultaneous communications would be the most time-efficient way to do the move.

Not quite. The communication into [1] must lag a little behind that out of [1], otherwise the value transmitted out will be uncertain. Careful hardware can make this lag much less than a packet, thus improving on the efficiency of the strict occam `rawFIFO`. Given that the pseudocode is intended to define the function of the FIFO (its behavior to the outside world), this is perfectly OK.

4.2.2 Circular indexed FIFO

In any case, there is an inefficiency with `rawFIFO`, in that every packet must be transmitted n-1 times internally. One can imagine the FIFO as a circular buffer, with rotating input and output access, where input can fire whenever the buffer is not full and output can fire whenever it is not empty. "Rotating input and output access" can be modeled by two indices. But the necessary race presents a difficulty. It would be most simply represented by an ALT on both input and output. And, like the occam language, I have settled on input-only ALTs.

Why? The reason is that for a pure CSP communication, both sides have to act independently, not under control of an all-knowing supervisor. That is critical to the goal of simplifying design by dividing it into multiple independently maintained entities. Therefore, to avoid an infinite regress, that means one side of each communication has to commit unconditionally to communicating. In the occam tradition, it is the output side.

This is actually expressed in Transputer design. At one point I said that Transputer occam communication is *almost* unbuffered. This is because when two Transputers are connected by a wired link, the outputting side always

```
-- This is a FIFO implemented in occam-like Crawl Space pseudocode.
-- On a fast system it is equivalent to n parallel buffers, each
-- storing one PACKET and passing it on as soon as possible.
-- Global resources are:
-- CHAN OF PACKET in : for the input to the FIFO
-- CHAN OF PACKET out : for the output from the FIFO
-- The size of the FIFO is defined below.
VAL INT n IS 32 :
...   PROC shelf(CHAN OF PACKET out, fromstore, CHAN OF BOOL need, PACKET pkt)
...   PROC store(CHAN OF PACKET in, toshelf, CHAN OF BOOL need, []PACKET pkt)
...   main program with local resources
}}}
```

Table 4.2: Toplevel view of FIFO.occ in origami (irrelevant comments removed)

starts the communication by sending one byte across the link. That byte is committed, though if the receiver never sends an ACK, then the communication is deemed not to be complete. There can be an ALT on the receiving side, and the link may not be the winner. Every point-to-point communication between independent hardware entities must deal with this problem in a similar way.

It would be possible to reverse this, and have the receiver send a REQ before the transmitter sends a byte, but you cannot have it both ways on the same communication. It would even be possible to have a FIFO that did ACK-type communication on its input end and REQ-type communication on its output end, and then the input and output ALT FIFO would be possible. But this has strange and nonstandard implications, and we can save the standard communication order with a special member of the PAR. Table 4.2 shows the solution.

In FIFO, the storage is divided into a one-packet shelf and an n-1-packet store. Here, shelf corresponds to pktall[0] in rawFIFO, the buffer just before the external output channel. The circular buffer store corresponds to all the other storage in rawFIFO. And a new, upstream internal channel is added, through which shelf can send an event (a timing-only communication, here represented by a BOOL) to store. The analogy is to a retail shelf and a backroom store.

Table 4.3 shows the programming of shelf. It is like buffer in rawFIFO except that, before inputting a new packet, it sends its ready signal to the upstream member. This allows the upstream member to handle the circular buffer with an input-only ALT.

Table 4.4 shows the coding for a circular buffer. Indexing takes the place of the internal communications of rawFIFO. Here a feature of the ALT implemen-

```
{{{  PROC shelf(CHAN OF PACKET out, fromstore, CHAN OF BOOL need, PACKET pkt)
PROC shelf(CHAN OF PACKET out, fromstore, CHAN OF BOOL need, PACKET pkt)
  WHILE TRUE
    SEQ
      -- When waiting on following instruction, shelf is EMPTY.
      need ! TRUE -- Because of the nature of the code of PROC store,
      fromstore ? pkt -- this input communication NEVER blocks.
      -- When waiting on following instruction, shelf is FULL.
      out ! pkt
:
}}}
```

Table 4.3: First fold view in origami

tation in [2] is of great importance. If `shelf` reaches the communication on channel `need` first, it must clearly block waiting for `store` to execute an ALT in which `need` wins. But if `store` gets there first, then `shelf` still has to block, because control has to go back to `store` to disable (adjudicate) the ALT and declare `need` the winner. Therefore, in every case, the first thing to happen after the event is that `store` will run its code to the point of outputting on `toshelf`. It must there block, because `shelf` hasn't had a chance to run yet, and `shelf` will then run and do the input on `fromstore` **without having to wait.** And even though `store` has to block momentarily while `shelf` is doing this, `shelf` will quickly run to block at output either on `out` or on `need`, and `store` will run back to the ALT.

Therefore the only possibilities for stable states in `shelf` are at the outputs, not the input. And the only possibility for a stable state in `store` is at the ALT. The state where `shelf` is at the output on `need` and `store` has $fl > 0$ is not stable because the ALT will immediately fire and a packet will be transmitted to `shelf`. Therefore `shelf` can be waiting at either `need` or `out` if $fl = 0$ but must be waiting at `out` if $fl > 0$. These correspond to queue length 0, 1, and $fl+1$, respectively.

Both `shelf` and `store` above are PROCs, exactly like void functions in C, and they must be called, their formals filled in, in a calling program (like `main`). Table 4.5 shows this. Each packet is communicated three times: input on `in`, internally on `passer`, and output on `out`. The upstream communication on `need` is done with a minimum of data transmission, and since the value of its BOOL is never checked, can be implemented by a timing-only event.

```
{{{  PROC store(CHAN OF PACKET in, toshelf, CHAN OF BOOL need, []PACKET pkt)
PROC store(CHAN OF PACKET in, toshelf, CHAN OF BOOL need, []PACKET pkt)
  VAL INT nm1 IS n - 1:
  VAL INT nm2 IS n - 2:
  INT fl, indin, indout :
  BOOL ready :
  SEQ
    indin := 0 -- input index
    indout := 0 -- output index
    fl := 0 -- number of packets (starts empty)
    WHILE TRUE
      PRI ALT
        -- If there is stuff in store, stocking the shelf takes priority
        (fl > 0) & need ? ready
          SEQ
            toshelf ! pkt[indout]
            IF
              indout < nm2
                indout := indout + 1
              TRUE
                indout := 0
            fl := fl - 1
        -- If the store is not full, new packets are input.
        -- Starvation of this line is not possible because output will
        -- soon lead to fl = 0, which deactivates the top alternative.
        (fl < nm1) & in ? pkt[indin]
          SEQ
            IF
              indin < nm2
                indin := indin + 1
              TRUE
                indin := 0
            fl := fl + 1
:
}}}
```

Table 4.4: Second fold view in origami

```
{{{  main program with local resources
[n]PACKET pktall :
CHAN OF PACKET passer :
CHAN OF BOOL need :
PAR
  store(in, passer, need, [pktall FROM 1 FOR n-1])
  shelf(out, passer, need, pktall[0])
--END PAR
}}}
```

Table 4.5: Third fold view in origami

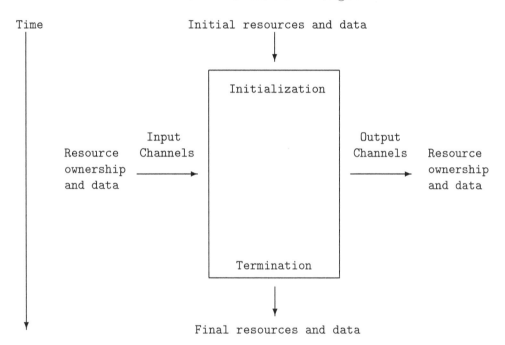

Figure 4.5: Box data and resource flow over time (strictly enforced)

4.2.3 Startup, shutdown, and nesting

Both programs described above are somewhat fragmentary, because they omit details of startup and shutdown. See Figure 4.5, which was taken from [1].

The structure both of rawFIFO.occ and FIFO.occ consists of some initialization, followed by outer PARs with members ending in a WHILE TRUE loop. This is like the "setup" and "loop" approach found in many embedded IDEs like Arduino and its variants.

It begs the question of shutdown completely, since a `WHILE TRUE` loop means "go on for all eternity." It really means "go on until an uncontrolled failure like a power-off." So strictly speaking, it is an invalid code design. What it really means is "the output of this code will cease to matter before hardware failure causes its behavior to become undefined." In many simple embedded uses this is OK, as long as everyone is aware of it. In the focused hardware design case, there will actually have to be some work done beyond this pseudocode to make sure the FIFO quits gracefully.

The code, as we have noted above, implies that there are data buffers but no valid packet data at startup. However, there are other things to note. In both programs, `n` is defined but the external channels are not. This would normally mean they are passed in by a PROC definition embracing all the code, or by nested PARs. The reason the outer code has to be PARs is that this code has to be the last to be executed in its sequence, if there is a sequence. Otherwise the `WHILE TRUE`, which never terminates, will make the following code inaccessible and definitely incorrect. What this means is that the FIFO is outermost with respect to Deep nesting, which is just what you would expect, since it is hardware or emulates hardware.

Given this PAR structure embracing our FIFO code, with `in` and `out` declared in some outdented high place, another interesting possibility follows. The kind of thing shown in Table 3.1 of Chapter 3 is possible, with the clients using the FIFO. Since it outlives these clients, there is nothing in the `WHILE TRUE` loop to stop its being nonempty between clients. This is a consequence of a lack of proper shutdown that is an actual problem using buffered IO such as serial. If a running program is deaf to the keyboard buffer, for example, you can actually type in another command during its run, and that will flash on the screen and be executed right after the old program ends.

When doing data-flow (higher level) pseudocode, it will pay to consider shutdown. In occam, a Boolean "notdone" variable may be turned off by anything capable of interrupting the program, which not only loops on `WHILE notdone`, but all significant actions are enclosed by an IF test checking this variable. Then you actually have to design to the time pad offered by your Uninterruptible Power Supply (UPS) and provide a graceful shutdown at each point.

4.3 Data-flow pseudocoding of the orchard sensor system

Careful examination of the orchard sensor design in Chapter 2 leads to the following initial try at the pseudocode for the "generic" sensor system.

4.3.1 Naive first attempt at generic sensor

In Table 4.6, the new concept of CHAN OF EVENT corresponds to the Transputer event pin, mentioned in [4] under "5.4 Peripheral interfacing." It is an edge-activated interrupt, modeled on the input side as an occam channel. Its utility to pseudocode comes from examining the behavior of an edge-activated interrupt, looking at the output side too.

The output side of an edge-activated interrupt is a PORT, an output with no acknowledge, which therefore cannot block a process. Usually, in embedded coding, this is represented by a mere write to a memory-mapped bit. In Wide pseudocoding we want to treat both output and input as a single entity, as it is in embedded coding using interrupts: one wire, with possible driver coding to mitigate "keyboard bounce." Therefore the input side of a CHAN OF EVENT is defined to be like a CHAN OF BOOL, a single-bit input of the "after" state which is as close as we can get to a no-bit input, and which will also suffice if our hardware happens to fire on both transitions. However, it generates no ACK. The output side of a CHAN OF EVENT is defined to be a PORT OF BOOL. Thus, input blocks but output does not, and communication is uncertain—the exact behavior of a standard embedded interrupt.

Table 4.6's first hack at the pseudocode does not reflect this uncertainty. But it shows the behavior of the sensor systems, except for the *leaf sensors* (the sensors that do not have branches below them). Each *mid-sensor* has a single connection to a master (uin and uout) and two connections to slaves (in[k] and out[k]). Remember that a separate channel has to be declared for each direction, like a machine in Connel. This is part of the design of a Bluetooth *scatternet*, where each low-energy Bluetooth node supports a *piconet* with at most three other nodes.

In addition, there is a per-slave return packet count inlen and a wait between slave triggerings wait. Referring back to Chapter 2 reveals that for level 1 mid-sensors (the ones connecting directly to leaves), inlen equals 1 and wait equals 1 minute 45 seconds, while for level 2 mid-sensors (the ones connecting directly to mission control), inlen equals 3 and wait equals 6 minutes 30 seconds.

121

```
-- This is a first attempt at the "mid" PROC pseudocode of the orchard
-- sensors. It uses CHAN OF EVENT which is a PORT OF BOOL on the
-- sending side and a rising-edge event on the receiving side.
PROC mid(CHAN OF EVENT uin, [2]CHAN OF EVENT out, CHAN OF PACKET uout,
  [2]CHAN OF PACKET in, VAL INT inlen, wait)
  TIMER clock :
  PORT OF EVENTS get : -- this represents triggering the sensors
  PORT OF PACKET back : -- this represents reading the sensors
  BOOL trigger :
  [7]PACKET dta :
  INT time :
  SEQ
    out[0] ! FALSE -- set up for events transmitted to children
    out[1] ! FALSE
    WHILE TRUE
      SEQ
        -- waits here until parent wakes up with a trigger event
        uin ? trigger -- rising edge signal wakes up
        clock ? time -- register current time
        out[0] ! TRUE -- trigger first child immediately
        get ! TRUE -- tell the sensors to register
        SEQ i FROM 0 FOR inlen -- get data from 1st child
          in[0] ? dta[i]
        out[0] ! FALSE -- reset the event line
        time := time PLUS wait -- define a sleep
        -- waits here until defined time after incoming trigger
        clock ? AFTER time
        out[1] ! TRUE -- trigger second child after wait
        PAR
          SEQ i FROM inlen FOR inlen -- get data from 2nd child
            in[1] ? dta[i]
          back ? dta[2*inlen] -- get the local data from sensors
        out[1] ! FALSE -- reset the event line
        time := time PLUS wait -- define a sleep
        -- waits here until 2 * defined time after incoming trigger
        clock ? AFTER time
        SEQ i FROM 0 FOR (2*inlen + 1)
          uout ! dta[i]
:
}}}
```

Table 4.6: Initial hack at PROC mid (irrelevant comments removed)

The `PORT OF EVENTS` is a minor innovation. The plural on `EVENTS` denotes vagueness, a pseudocode-only construct, and as mentioned above, `PORT` denotes no blocking. In the case of `get`, the pseudocode is referring to activating the sensors, so the single line of pseudocode is shorthand for "start taking temperature, start taking humidity, start whatever." Note that all PORT-type actions are given time before results (e.g. `back`) are expected, and this includes the `CHAN OF EVENT` output, which is really a PORT, and waits past a response before resetting.

The structure of Table 4.6's `mid` code now becomes clear. Its setup code consists merely in putting both its output event lines in the reset state, ready to communicate.

Each time around the loop, a trigger on `uin` is communicated by the master to wake the sensor up. (It should be in low-energy sleep mode until this trigger comes.) The sensor system notes the time at wakeup, wakes up its first slave, then commands its sensor array to take data. That is probably a complex action, merely symbolized by one pseudocode command, but should take little time. What does take time is the sequence of `inlen` packet communications from the awakened slave. Note that significant time may elapse before the first such communication. Presumably this sensor is in a reasonably efficient sleep state while waiting.

Having picked up the correct, fixed number of packets from the first slave, the sensor now goes to sleep in such a way that it awakes time `wait` after its master-triggered awakening. Notice that the actual time asleep after the last packet was received may be much less than `wait`. Then it performs the same actions for the second slave as it did for the first, with one exception. It has to pick up data from its own local sensors. There has been plenty of time for them to register. Since no resources are shared between this data pickup (using `back`) and the input from the slave, these can (at least in principle) be done simultaneously, by a PAR.

After a second exact wait, the mid-sensor performs its last duty. It pumps out the packets of information from both slaves and its own local sensors to its master. In the case of a level 1 mid-sensor, that master is a level 2 mid-sensor, while in the case of a level 2 mid-sensor, that master is mission control.

The final thing this code does is loop to the `WHILE TRUE` and block at the `uin ? trigger` instruction, awaiting the next trigger from the master.

4.3.2 Naive parallel nesting, mission control, and leaf

Now we can continue with leaf and mission control, and then show the full PAR structure of the naive orchard sensor array.

```
-- This is an initial hack at the 21-sensor orchard system described
-- in the Crawl Space book.
...  PROC mid(CHAN OF EVENT uin, [2]CHAN OF EVENT out, CHAN OF PACKET uout,
...  PROC leaf(CHAN OF EVENT uin, CHAN OF PACKET uout, VAL INT getwait, wait)
...  PROC MC([3]CHAN OF EVENT out, [3]CHAN OF PACKET in, VAL INT inlen, wait)
...  main program with local resources
}}}
```

Table 4.7: Structure of full orchard hack (irrelevant comments removed)

In the pseudocode file of Table 4.7, the fold labeled PROC mid... is Table 4.6. The leaf is essentially mid without the slave communications, and the mission control (MC) lacks the master communications, and replaces the trigger with a timed start, and the output with a (missing) hourly.output routine. (The period in an occam name is just another letter, like underscore in C, not like period in C.)

Here, there is a special short wait getwait, defined so that the full wait wait is enough both to register the sensor values, and to copy the sensor values into the packet. In the call we will set getwait to 30 seconds and wait to 45 seconds, thus leaving 15 seconds to copy and convert all data in the sensors.

The main assumption here is that hourly.output takes less time than that imposed by wait, which in the call is 20 minutes. In real life, there will be many outputs of one sort or another, and in this crude pseudocode their channels are not shown (i.e. they are assumed to be in global variables accessed by hourly.output). This is OK as a first approximation when the output is handled by standard OS features like file system and internet. For a full hour allowance, it would make sense to transmit dta to a dedicated outputter running in parallel.

Here a major and very friendly feature of occam is used in pseudocode. In occam, in multidimensional arrays, an index to the left is coarser, but the indices are placed to the left of the type in declaration and to the right of the name in use. As counterintuitive as this seems, it makes it possible to gather one or more right indices onto the type and decree that a compound type, and causes it to make sense. For example,

[3][2][2]CHAN OF EVENT to0 :

can be considered equivalent to

[3]TYPE2DCHAN to0 :

where TYPE2DCHAN is equivalent to [2][2]CHAN OF EVENT, and thus to0[1] is equivalent to the collection of to0[1][j][i] for all i and j. This works

```
{{{ PROC leaf(CHAN OF EVENT uin, CHAN OF PACKET uout, VAL INT getwait, wait)
-- This is a first attempt at the "leaf" PROC pseudocode of the
-- orchard sensors. It is like MIDhack except that it is missing the
-- communication with slaves.
PROC leaf(CHAN OF EVENT uin, CHAN OF PACKET uout, VAL INT getwait, wait)
  TIMER clock :
  PORT OF EVENTS get : -- this represents triggering the sensors
  PORT OF PACKET back : -- this represents reading the sensors
  BOOL trigger :
  PACKET dta :
  INT time, timeget :
  SEQ
    WHILE TRUE
      SEQ
        -- waits here until parent wakes up with a trigger event
        uin ? trigger -- rising edge signal wakes up
        clock ? time -- register current time
        get ! TRUE -- tell the sensors to register
        timeget := time PLUS getwait -- define a sleep for sensors
        -- waits here until defined gettime after incoming trigger
        clock ? AFTER timeget
        back ? dta -- get the local data from sensors
        time := time PLUS wait -- define a sleep for output
        -- waits here until defined time after incoming trigger
        clock ? AFTER time
        uout ! dta
:
}}}
```

Table 4.8: Leaf hack

perfectly in all the parameter specifications.

4.3.3 Startup, failure, and reconnect

In a perfect world, this first hack would be almost enough. It lacks one essential component: the "over the air" addressing that Bluetooth will require. If the links were wires connected to different pins, the arrays of channels would suffice to describe them. But they use a shared resource and distinguish signals with a hidden frequency-hopping mechanism that requires the master to address the slave.

Another, tougher problem comes from the finite lifetime of the parts. A serious design, especially one that is expandable in principle, needs a means of dealing with the fact that the sensors will burn out unpredictably, like light bulbs. This failure may happen conveniently by a node going silent between

```
{{{  PROC MC([3]CHAN OF EVENT out, [3]CHAN OF PACKET in, VAL INT inlen, wait)
-- This is a first attempt at the "mission control" PROC pseudocode of
-- the orchard sensors. It loops through three level-2 mid-sensors and
-- their slaves, and then calls hourly.output on the data.
PROC MC([3]CHAN OF EVENT out, [3]CHAN OF PACKET in, VAL INT inlen, wait)
  TIMER clock :
  PORT OF EVENTS get : -- this represents triggering the sensors
  PORT OF PACKET back : -- this represents reading the sensors
  BOOL trigger :
  [21]PACKET dta :
  INT time :
  SEQ
    out[0] ! FALSE -- set up for events transmitted to children
    out[1] ! FALSE
    out[2] ! FALSE
    clock ? time -- register current time
    WHILE TRUE
      SEQ
        -- this part is the gathering of data
        SEQ k FROM 0 FOR 3
          SEQ
            clock ? AFTER time -- wake at specified time
            out[k] ! TRUE -- trigger k-th child immediately
            -- a rather long wait may happen before first input
            SEQ i FROM (k*inlen) FOR inlen -- get data from k-th child
              in[k] ? dta[i]
            out[k] ! FALSE -- reset the k-th trigger
            time := time PLUS wait -- define next wakeup time
        -- this part is the using of the data
        -- which is assumed to take less time than "wait" (20 min)
        hourly.output(dta) -- do requirements implied by dta
  :
}}}
```

Table 4.9: Naive Mission Control

```
{{{  main program with local resources
[3][2][2]CHAN OF EVENT to0 :
[3][2]CHAN OF EVENT to1 :
[3]CHAN OF EVENT to2 :
[3][2][2]CHAN OF PACKET from0 :
[3][2]CHAN OF PACKET from1 :
[3]CHAN OF PACKET from2 :
PAR
  MC(to2, from2, 7, 1200)
  PAR k FROM 0 FOR 3
    PAR
      mid(to2[k], to1[k], from2[k], from1[k], 3, 390)
      PAR j FROM 0 FOR 2
        PAR
          mid(to1[k][j], to0[k][j], from1[k][j], from0[k][j], 1, 105)
          PAR i FROM 0 FOR 2
            leaf(to0[k][j][i], from0[k][j][i], 30, 45)
}}}
```

Table 4.10: Orchard scatternet via nested PAR

transmissions. Unfortunately, it may also happen by a node going silent in the middle of a transmission. In the latter case, it has an inconvenient tendency to "hang" its communication partner.

4.3.3.1 MAC addresses and scatternet setup

Each Bluetooth entity has a world-unique MAC address burned into its hardware, and a master uses the slave's MAC address when establishing a conversation link with a slave. The slave does not need to know the master's MAC address. Each low-energy Bluetooth has three connector link ends, each of which may communicate either with a master or with a slave. A mid-sensor will communicate with one master and two slaves; a leaf sensor will communicate with one master and no slaves; and the mission control will communicate with three slaves.

Using the information already described, it is therefore easy to see that all the information needed for a static array is contained in Table 4.11.

There are 22 indices (IND) in the table, 0 for mission control and 1 through 21 for the nodes. The next three numbers (FAD) are "FORTRAN addresses" describing the branches. I use the term "FORTRAN address" because real branches are numbered starting from 1 as in the classic FORTRAN language. Thus, 3 2 1 refers to the third connection coming from root (i.e., mission control), the second connection coming from level 2 mid-sensor, and the first

```
IND /-FAD-\ NC IC MAC DFI
  0  0  0  0  3  1   -   -
  1  1  0  0  2  4   a   6
  2  2  0  0  2  6   b  13
  3  3  0  0  2  8   c  20
  4  1  1  0  2 10   d   2
  5  1  2  0  2 12   e   5
  6  2  1  0  2 14   f   9
  7  2  2  0  2 16   g  12
  8  3  1  0  2 18   h  16
  9  3  2  0  2 20   i  19
 10  1  1  1  0   -   j   0
 11  1  1  2  0   -   k   1
 12  1  2  1  0   -   l   3
 13  1  2  2  0   -   m   4
 14  2  1  1  0   -   n   7
 15  2  1  2  0   -   o   8
 16  2  2  1  0   -   p  10
 17  2  2  2  0   -   q  11
 18  3  1  1  0   -   r  14
 19  3  1  2  0   -   s  15
 20  3  2  1  0   -   t  17
 21  3  2  2  0   -   u  18
```

Table 4.11: Width-first node information table

connection coming from level 1 mid-sensor, thus corresponding to the connel whose channels are from0[2][1][0] and to0[2][1][0], and the level-0 node at the far end of it. But 1 0 0 refers to the first connection coming from root, and goes no farther, thus corresponding to the connel whose channels are from2[0] and to2[0], and the level-2 node at the far end of it. So the FAD amounts to a routing table from mission control to the node.

The value NC is the number of children of this node, and the value IC is the index of the first child in this table. The letter under MAC represents a full MAC address for the Bluetooth connector link end that is pointing toward its node's master, if its node has a master. This may be considered to be the MAC address of the link between this node and its master. Finally, DFI is the depth-first index of the same node, used by the array dta in the code.

In the orchard, the signals from all the Bluetooth devices overlap, at least in principle, and require addressing of slave MACs to assemble the scatternet.

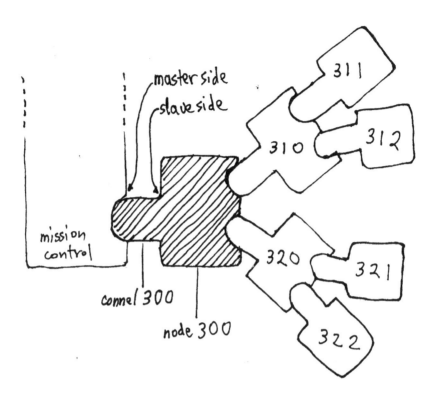

Figure 4.6: Part of orchard nodes and connels

Figure 4.6 displays some of the nodes and connels that are implied by Table 4.11. Each connel is shown connected to the node on its slave end, because its MAC is that of the slave, and the master must address that MAC.

Table 4.12 shows the connels in use by each MAC. In case IND = 0, all the MACs are slave MACs owned by nodes directly connected to mission control. For the others, the first MAC is the one owned by the current node, and the others, if any, are slave MACs that it communicates with. The last row of Table 4.12 is a special broadcast row, needed in startup.

If a node fails, the information in its row in Table 4.12 will suffice to set up communication using a replacement node. Its first MAC, new and belonging to the replacement node, is transmitted to the replacement node's master or parent, and the other MACs, if any, are transmitted to the replacement node itself, informing it of the addresses of its children. A compound failure can also be handled this way, as long as reconstruction information goes to the parent first.

At the beginning, when all nodes are powered but they do not have the

```
IND /-FAD-\   /-MACs\
  0   0  0  0   a  b  c
  1   1  0  0   a  d  e
  2   2  0  0   b  f  g
  3   3  0  0   c  h  i
  4   1  1  0   d  j  k
  5   1  2  0   e  l  m
  6   2  1  0   f  n  o
  7   2  2  0   g  p  q
  8   3  1  0   h  r  s
  9   3  2  0   i  t  u
 10   1  1  1   j
 11   1  1  2   k
 12   1  2  1   l
 13   1  2  2   m
 14   2  1  1   n
 15   2  1  2   o
 16   2  2  1   p
 17   2  2  2   q
 18   3  1  1   r
 19   3  1  2   s
 20   3  2  1   t
 21   3  2  2   u
 22  -1 -1 -1   -
```

Table 4.12: Node and slave MACs for each node

information they need about their children's addresses, a sequence of Table 4.12 rows can be transmitted. This starts with row 0, which informs the mission control about the MACs of its three children, so that communication can begin. Each of the other rows is passed along according to its routing information to its proper target sensor, except for the last row, which is broadcast (each node copies it to all its children). The broadcast row causes a state change (from setup to loop) after which the regular code takes over.

It is worth noticing that this approach can transmit any information to newly connected nodes, not just their slave addresses. In Transputer networks, an extremely small network boot capability made it possible even to transmit *all its coding* to each newly awakened part. This made the loading of Transputer networks a very simple process, and eliminated the need for each chip to have its code burned separately.

4.3.3.2 Failure-based replacement

If all parts were eternal, this would finish the job. Since it's not so, we have to design for failure detection and replacement insertion. We will start with the latter, which is not so hard a job.

Assuming we know that a failure has happened, and where, *and that all the other sensors can be assumed still to be working, including any descendants of the failed sensor,* the replacement can take place in a three-step process. (A) Place and power up the replacement sensor. (B) Add the replacement sensor's MAC address to Table 4.12 in the correct two places (its row and its parent's row). (C) Transmit the replacement sensor's row to its parent and, if it is not a leaf, to itself.

Notice that (C) is a single operation because the route of the sensor's row always includes its parent. When the parent (which is alive) receives the new row, it gleans the replacement's MAC address and is able to initiate communication with it. If the replacement is not a leaf, the parent transmits its row to it and the replacement receives its children's MAC addresses and initiates communication with them. This process can obviously be extended to multiple replacements, parent first.

Since the Table 4.12 packets are small, they can be squeezed in right after the trigger and its immediately following (non-blocking) instructions, before `in[0] ? dta[0]` in Table 4.6 and before `clock ? AFTER timeget` in Table 4.8. There are at least 45 seconds available here, which should be plenty. It is done in both cases by a loop spinning on a PRI ALT until Table 4.12 packets (if any) stop coming. Of course, `uin` (and `out[k]`) must change type so that it can carry these packets as well as the trigger event. Normally it is done by making each a `CHAN OF ANY` and then retyping it at need to the informative spec, but the state machine must be checked to make sure this setup can never get out of whack. Or an occam variant PROTOCOL can be set up.

The really important thing is the state machine. The way we are doing it, all replacement packets must be sent immediately after the trigger to any child needing them, so that the child's PRI ALT can never allow its own child to communicate until the replacement packets are done. That probably means that the possibly time-consuming process of reviving a connection with a child should wait until after the `uout ! dta` communication, which in turn means there should be no more than one replacement packet sent by mission control per trigger. This makes the 45-second timing race easy, and should not be a problem, since weeks or months should elapse between sensor failures on average.

4.3.3.3 Detection and orderly response to failure

We finally come to the part of the design that is most often ignored or underestimated. This is the response of the system to an unexpected failure. It must include detection of the failure while avoiding systemic seize-up due to transmitted state.

The design of Tables 6 through 9 is deliberately friendly to this task. Each level is activated by a trigger, and then transmits this triggering to its descendants. So if an ancestor cuts out, they should in principle just wait patiently. If a sensor cuts out, its immediate parent should in principle be able to detect this at the point where the child is supposed to be returning data. That parent in turn should stay on time with its parent, if any, but return a special packet in place of the normal one expected from the failed child.

The deep-seated state machine problems happen when the failure takes place in the middle of a communication. If the partner is a PORT (or is sending an EVENT) this does not matter; it just goes on. But if the partner is executing a true, handshaken channel communication, it may (in standard occam) seize up and never continue. As discussed in [5], not even an ALT can prevent this, because it has already committed to the communication.

In [5], the Transputer solution is explained: special communications that forcibly time out and return a failure BOOL if the time limit is exceeded. They reset their communication channel in so doing, and prevent a "hang." This can be done both for input and for output, and so all communication partners of the failing node are insulated from a "hang." The input is

```
PROC InputOrFail.t(CHAN OF ANY c, []BYTE message,
                   TIMER clock, VAL INT thetime,
                   BOOL aborted)
```

I will wrap this in a more convenient form, by inverting the Boolean:

```
PROC InputOrNot.t(CHAN OF ANY c, []BYTE message,
                  TIMER clock, VAL INT thetime,
                  BOOL success)
  BOOL aborted :
  SEQ
    InputOrFail.t(c, message, clock, thetime, aborted)
    success := NOT aborted
:
```

Here it must be remembered that all occam arrays have a length (which would be another formal parameter in C or other languages). Also, occam

PROCs, unlike C void functions, are call-by-reference (unless VAL precedes the formal type), so that BOOL aborted or BOOL success is actually the value returned by the PROC. Finally, in the Transputer definition, thetime is an expiration time, not a delay.

The output is PROC OutputOrFail.t with the same calling sequence, to which I similarly define a variant PROC OutputOrNot.t.

Finally, it is desirable that an ALT be bulletproofed. Since the enable, wait, and disable assembly instruction set for a Transputer ALT, like a C select but unlike the occam ALT expression, does not execute its winning communication but branches to code that will execute it, it is possible to use the same techniques as in [6] in this case. For details see [2] section 10.4.2, and [7]. For simplicity I will add a FAILURE branch to an ALT, e.g.

```
PRI ALT
  bool1 & c1 ? mess1
    -- code
  -- more channel guards if needed
  clock ? AFTER timeout
    -- code, e.g. timedout := TRUE
  FAILURE
    -- code, e.g. notdone := FALSE
```

If a channel guard, e.g. c1, is selected and hangs, then the equivalent of

InputOrFail.t(c1, mess1, clock, timeout, aborted)

returns aborted with value TRUE, and the FAILURE branch is taken. If none of the channel guards are selected, then the standard timeout fires. Thus, under no conditions does this ALT hang.

This horrible hack will probably get the CSP purists after me with knout and knobkerrie, but it does work. The reason it works is that once an inputting link channel guard is selected, and before its communication is done, its process's address remains in its channel word and can be recovered as in [6]. If the first, "unsolicited byte" (see [7]) has not been sent, or has not finished coming, the channel's branch of the ALT is not ready, and the timer branch wins. If it has arrived in time, the channel's branch is ready and wins the ALT, and a standard unconditional input necessarily follows, which will use the InputOrFail.t mechanism and branch to FAILURE if it does not finish in time. Under all conditions, the ALT terminates and the process continues, and it terminates within time timeout, which is also used as the deadline for the implied InputOrFail.t.

Why care what Transputers did to solve this problem? Because the design is very simple (see [6]) and we can check that whatever mechanism our connel offers is consistent with its behavior. Basically, it must kill the stuck transmission, reset its communication device, and continue its process on the side of the unfailed node.

Examination of the code from Tables 4.6 through 4.9 reveals that the only potential "hang" points are in the CHAN OF PACKET communications involving in[k] and uout. No PORT can hang, nor can a CHAN OF EVENT, with its simple, ACK-free way of firing. Because of this, we will change each CHAN OF PACKET to a CHAN OF ANY when necessary for the above devices to be made to work.

Finally, as long as I am cutting a swath with my horrible hacks, I will make one more extension of occam syntax. The purpose of this extension is mainly to deal with the tested blocks that arise in situations where C and similar languages do an early error exit from a loop. To get the same result in occam you need to check a BOOL like notdone or stillAlive that, when searched on, reveals all early error places in the code.

I will extend the "boolean &" expression to more general use than just an ALT guard. (This works because an ALT guard is currently the only place where an ampersand is used.) Namely, I define

```
boolean & codeblock
```

to be shorthand for the voluminous and common

```
IF
  boolean
    codeblock
  TRUE
    SKIP
```

Here codeblock is any process in occam's sense: a block of code consisting of one line (e.g. SEQ, PAR, IF, ALT, statement), possibly preceded by declarations and definitions (things ending in :), at the current indentation, and then zero or more dependent lines at greater indentations. Example:

```
IF
  levelind < 2
    [3][6]MAC RETYPES [MACbytes FROM 3 FOR 18] :
    SEQ k = 0 FOR 2
      initialize.connel(MAC[k+1], out[k], in[k])
  TRUE
    SKIP
```

134

will be represented by

```
(levelind < 2) & [3][6]MAC RETYPES [MACbytes FROM 3 FOR 18] :
SEQ k = 0 FOR 2
  initialize.connel(MAC[k+1], out[k], in[k])
```

And I will also permit line breaks after &.

4.3.4   The orchard.occ pseudocode

Table 4.13 below is the pseudocode produced according to the above considerations. It is still rough-edged, but shows all the key parts of the necessary code, both on the mission control and on each sensor station. It is complex enough to point up the need for a pseudocode compiler to check correctness, but this does not exist yet.

Two more cross-hardware efforts are now added to the single effort, that of sensor data handling, seen in the naive pseudocode. Now, before any sensor data handling, there is setup, which takes place once in the history of the entire network. In parallel to sensor data handling, there is sensor node failure and replacement handling, which shares the connels but mostly uses different data and timing. Each of these uses a careful state machine design which spreads through all the PROCs.

In Table 4.14, as in all the PROCs, [21]BYTE setupdta is used for setup and for failure and replacement handling, while PACKET dta[i] is used for sensor data handling. The direction of data flow for setupdta is out the fan, from mission control to leaf, because it informs each parent of its and its children's MAC addresses. The direction of data flow for dta is inward, toward mission control, carrying the sensor data. The single exception is that when a mid node detects a child's failure, it modifies dta[i] for that child so that information about the failure flows back to mission control.

```
-- This is a revised 21-sensor orchard system described in the Crawl
-- Space book. It uses extraordinary link transmissions including ALT
-- FAILURE, and uses conditional process shorthand (boolean &).
...  PROC mid(CHAN OF ANY uin, [2]CHAN OF ANY out, CHAN OF ANY uout,
...  PROC leaf(CHAN OF ANY uin, CHAN OF ANY uout, VAL INT getwait,
...  PROC MC([3]CHAN OF ANY out, [3]CHAN OF ANY in, VAL INT inlen,
...  main program with local resources
}}}
```

Table 4.13: Toplevel view of orchard.occ in origami (top comments removed)

135

```
{{{  PROC mid(CHAN OF ANY uin, [2]CHAN OF ANY out, CHAN OF ANY uout,
PROC mid(CHAN OF ANY uin, [2]CHAN OF ANY out, CHAN OF ANY uout,
  [2]CHAN OF ANY in, VAL INT levelind, inlen, chwait, totwait, shortwait)
  -- uin, out[k] is [21]BYTE until broadcast (setup)
  --            but in loop is EVENT; (0 or more times [21]BYTE)
  --            where the [21]BYTE setupdta's are immediate and
  --            continue until a in[0] child trigger comes
  -- uout is [2*inlen+1]PACKET
  -- in[k] is [inlen]PACKET
  -- NOTE: levelind is always < 2 in mid, always = 2 in leaf.
  TIMER clock :
  PORT OF EVENTS get : -- this represents triggering the sensors
  PORT OF PACKET back : -- this represents reading the sensors
  [2]BOOL upch : -- is child connel currently working?
  [7]PACKET dta :
  INT time, t1, t4 :
  -- The following variables are dedicated to failures and restarts
  [21]BYTE setupdta : -- BYTE is equivalent to unsigned char
  [3][6]BYTE MAC :
  PACKET errordta IS ERRORDTA : -- some special error values for dta
  INT t2 :
  SEQ
    ... setup
    WHILE TRUE
      INT indexdown : -- in case a replacement is moving below
      [21]BYTE wassetupdta :
      BOOL notdone : -- pseudocode test of hardware failure
      [2]BOOL wasupch :
      SEQ
        -- When you come BACK to here, this sensor has failed and a
        -- new one was installed. Notice that the code can never
        -- detect this (no place in the code sets notdone to FALSE).
        -- The "notdone := FALSE" is implicitly done by hardware.
        -- The replacement sensor must not look for a full setup (with
        -- broadcast at end), but must start here.
        (PORT out[0]) ! FALSE -- set up for events transmitted to children
        (PORT out[1]) ! FALSE
        notdone := TRUE
        indexdown := -1
        wasupch := upch
        WHILE notdone
          INT wasindexdown : -- in case a replacement came last time
          BOOL trigger, upparent :
          ... loop on each trigger from parent
  :
}}}
```

Table 4.14: Pseudocoding for mid sensor PROC

```
{{{  setup
uin ? setupdta
WHILE setupdta[0] <> (BYTE 255)
  SEQ
    IF
      setupdta[levelind+1] = 0(BYTE)
        -- setupdta has reached its destination
        SEQ
          [18]BYTE MACbytes RETYPES MAC :
          MACbytes := [setupdta FROM 3 FOR 18] -- record MAC addrs
          SEQ k = 0 FOR 2
            SEQ
              initialize.connel(MAC[k+1], out[k], in[k])
              upch[k] := TRUE -- communicating with children
      TRUE
        -- pass the setupdta along its route
        out[(INT setupdta[levelind+1]) - 1] ! setupdta -- handshaken data
    uin ? setupdta
-- final setupdta packet is broadcast
SEQ k = 0 FOR 2
  out[k] ! setupdta
}}}
```

Table 4.15: Mid sensor setup

setupdta and dta use different node ordering schemes, one width-first and the other depth-first.

Because out[i] is now a CHAN OF ANY with a dual function of outputting EVENT and setupdta, the notation (PORT out[i]) is used when a non-blocking Boolean PORT output is used to cause the EVENT. Booleans upparent and upch[i] (meaning "upchild") are used to show whether the connection to parent or child respectively is still alive. Since the parent is the timing master, upparent is local to a single loop on the trigger. After failure, code will restart at the top of the WHILE TRUE (without a new setup) and proceed to the uin ? trigger input EVENT, at which time both this node and its connector link to its parent will be functional.

Each child Boolean upch[i] is by contrast a global. A dead child connection does not cause this mid sensor to stop looping, but does cause failure notification to ride back toward mission control. Each child has an independent Boolean, allowing for partially functioning network subtrees.

Table 4.15 shows the standard setup procedure, which is in the width-first order implied by Tables 4.11 and 4.12. This permits each mid node to come alive with its children's MAC address information before waking up the

```
{{{  loop on each trigger from parent
SEQ
  -- waits here until parent wakes up with a trigger event
  upparent := TRUE -- communicating with parent
  uin ? trigger -- rising edge signal wakes up
  clock ? time -- register current time
  t1 := time PLUS shortwait
  t2 := time PLUS (chwait MINUS shortwait)
  t4 := time PLUS (totwait MINUS shortwait)
  (PORT out[0]) ! TRUE -- trigger first child immediately
  get ! TRUE -- tell the sensors to register
  -- At most one setupdta is sent per full cycle. Usually
  -- none is sent, but one may arrive at any time, dealing
  -- with replacements in this node's dependent tree.
  ...  setupdta (t1), then input first child (t2)
  (PORT out[0]) ! FALSE -- reset the event line
  ...  if still running, input 2nd child (t2) || sensor data
  ...  if still running, output to parent
  ...  if child just replaced, connect to new MAC
}}}
```

Table 4.16: Mid sensor loop pseudocode

connel to each child via `initialize.connel`. At the end, a special `setupdta` is broadcast to all nodes, carrying the information that setup is done and the other two efforts are to begin.

The loop code of Table 4.16 is the most complex, since it is interleaved of two simultaneously running state machines: the sensor data handling effort and the sensor failure and replacement effort. The latter, though essential, is rarely operational, but bulks up to more than half of the pseudocode.

This loop code spends most of its time asleep, awaiting an EVENT from its parent at `uin ? trigger`. It spends on the order of a microsecond doing time read and timeout calculation, then passes the EVENT onto its first child. The timeout calculations cause sensor data return to fit Figure 2.3 of Chapter 2, but replacement `setupdta` packets are also slipped in there if necessary, at most one to a loop.

The failure and replacement effort runs almost independently of the data handling effort. With a lot of extra local channels, a design effort beyond the scope of this book might have created a pseudocode PAR for these two efforts. This is most appropriate for chip and board design where independent areas of silicon are to be used. In our case here, the flows are kept separate by careful state machine design. As is typical of state machine pseudocode, the Booleans used in it will probably actually appear in the final C code.

```
{{{ setupdta (t1), then input first child (t2)
IF
  indexdown = 0
    upch[0] & OutputOrNot.t(out[0], setupdta, clock,
      t1, upch[0])
  indexdown > 0
    wassetupdta := setupdta
  TRUE
    SKIP
wasindexdown := indexdown
indexdown := -1
PRI ALT
  uin ? setupdta -- communicating with parent at this point
    SEQ
      indexdown := (INT setupdta[levelind+1]) - 1
      -- Has this arrived? Then store local data and speak to children
      (indexdown < 0) & SEQ
        deal.with.local.restart(levelind, setupdta, MAC, in, out)
        (PORT out[0]) ! TRUE
  clock ? AFTER t1 -- usual case
    SKIP
  FAILURE
    upparent := FALSE
-- 1st child data: possibly wait quite a while for this
upch[0] & InputOrNot.t(in[0], [dta FROM 0 FOR inlen], clock,
      t2, upch[0])
}}}
```

Table 4.17

In Table 4.17, all but the last (upch[0] &) code line is replacement code. This replacement code takes place as soon as possible after trigger. It deals with an overlap of the replacement state machine. First, if the LAST loop brought in a replacement for child 0 or below, it transmits that. Then it remembers that last replacement setupdta as wassetupdta in case it's needed for child 1, and brings in a CURRENT loop setupdta if available. Each communication is hang-tested.

It could be that the incoming setupdta is destined for this node and is not to be passed on, in which case deal.with.local.restart is called. Its block re-imposes (PORT out[0]) ! TRUE after what is assumed to be a quick re-connect with the already live slave.

The usual case for all that code is to do nothing, and after a comparatively

```
{{{  if still running, input 2nd child (t2) || sensor data
SEQ
  time := time PLUS chwait -- define a sleep
  t1 := t1 PLUS chwait -- same function as before
  t2 := t2 PLUS chwait -- same function as before
  -- waits here until chwait after incoming trigger
  clock ? AFTER time
  (PORT out[1]) ! TRUE -- trigger second child after chwait
  ((wasindexdown = 1) AND upch[1]) & OutputOrNot.t(out[1],
    wassetupdta, clock, t1, upch[1])
  -- second child data and local data
  PAR
    upch[1] & InputOrNot.t(in[1],
      [dta FROM inlen FOR inlen], clock, t2, upch[1])
    back ? dta[2*inlen] -- get the local data from sensors
  (PORT out[1]) ! FALSE -- reset the event line
}}}
```

Table 4.18

long wait, a data handling packet to come up from child 0. It will contain data from that child's whole subtree.

The code of Table 4.18 does much the same as the last, but for child 1. It uses the wrapped-over wassetupdta if necessary to send replacement data to that subtree. Its main job is, after a wait, to bring up a data handling packet from child 1's subtree. It does this in parallel to grabbing its own local sensor data. (Since C does not have a PAR, the coder will have to hand-code this behavior. The main thing is not to spend any extra time bringing in the local sensor data, but to fit it in the waits imposed by the child transmission.)

Table 4.19 starts by detecting child error, and marking the dta[i] belonging to that child with errordta. Then it sleeps till the proper time, and if the parent connel is working, it sends all of its tree's sensor data to its parent.

Finally, special code (Table 4.20) can happen once the timed data transmission to the parent is over with. This operates on replacement activation being parent-first. That means that if a child is down and a replacement comes, it must have the correct MAC address for the replacement for that child, and thus initialize.connel is called to reconnect to the child. That setupdta will later be copied on the new connection on the next loop, as the failure and replacement effort wraps around. This arrangement is because

```
{{{  if still running, output to parent
SEQ
  (wasupch[0] AND (NOT upch[0])) & dta[inlen-1] = errordta
  (wasupch[1] AND (NOT upch[1])) & dta[(2*inlen)-1] = errordta
  wasupch := upch
  time := time PLUS chwait -- define a sleep
  -- waits here until 2 * chwait after incoming trigger
  clock ? AFTER time
  upparent & OutputOrNot.t(uout,
    [dta FROM 0 FOR (2*inlen+1)], clock, t4, upparent)
}}}
```

Table 4.19

```
{{{  if child just replaced, connect to new MAC
((indexdown >= 0) AND (NOT upch[indexdown])) & SEQ
  MAC[indexdown+1] := [setupdta FROM 3 FOR 6]
  initialize.connel(MAC[indexdown+1], out[indexdown],
    in[indexdown])
  upch[indexdown] := TRUE
}}}
```

Table 4.20

initialize.connel may take awhile in Bluetooth.

It is true that the failure could have been more recent than the one that triggered a replacement and its setupdta. In that rare case, this node will fail again, and the parent will send yet another notification to mission control.

Table 4.21 is the leaf pseudocode. It is a lot like the mid code, except it does not have to worry about children.

The setup (Table 4.22) is much simpler than that in the mid code. We could have gotten by with no setup at all, since the leaf is a Bluetooth slave only, but I'm passing some information in here in case an inquiry function is later instituted. The broadcast packet, too, terminates here.

The main job of the loop (Table 4.23) is to get data from its local sensors. But a replacement packet could be sent here, for the inquiry reason I just mentioned.

Table 4.24 waits till exactly timeget in all cases. Rarely, it may get a replacement packet, but mostly it does nothing.

```
{{{  PROC leaf(CHAN OF ANY uin, CHAN OF ANY uout, VAL INT getwait,
PROC leaf(CHAN OF ANY uin, CHAN OF ANY uout, VAL INT getwait,
  outwait, totwait, shortwait)
  -- uin is [21]BYTE until broadcast (setup)
  --        but in loop is EVENT; (0 or more times [21]BYTE)
  --        where the [21]BYTE setupdta's are immediate and
  --        continue until wait is done
  -- uout is EVENT; PACKET
  TIMER clock :
  PORT OF EVENTS get : -- this represents triggering the sensors
  PORT OF PACKET back : -- this represents reading the sensors
  BOOL notdone :
  PACKET dta :
  INT time, t4 :
  -- The following variables are dedicated to failures and restarts
  -- and sensor waits
  [21]BYTE setupdta : -- BYTE is equivalent to unsigned char
  [3][6]BYTE MAC :
  INT timeget :
  SEQ
    ... setup
    WHILE TRUE
      BOOL notdone : -- pseudocode test of hardware failure
      SEQ
        -- When you come BACK to here, this sensor has failed and a
        -- new one was installed. Notice that the code can never
        -- detect this (no place in the code sets notdone to FALSE).
        -- The "notdone := FALSE" is implicitly done by hardware.
        -- The replacement sensor must not look for a full setup (with
        -- broadcast at end), but must start here.
        notdone := TRUE
        WHILE notdone
          BOOL trigger, upparent :
          ... loop on each trigger from parent
  :
}}}
```

Table 4.21: Pseudocoding for leaf sensor PROC

```
{{{  setup
uin ? setupdta
WHILE setupdta[0] <> (BYTE 255)
  SEQ
    [18]BYTE MACbytes RETYPES MAC :
    MACbytes := [setupdta FROM 3 FOR 18] -- record MAC addrs
    uin ? setupdta
-- final setupdta packet is broadcast
}}}
```

Table 4.22: Leaf sensor setup

```
{{{  loop on each trigger from parent
SEQ
  upparent := TRUE
  -- waits here until parent wakes up with a trigger event
  uin ? trigger -- rising edge signal wakes up
  clock ? time -- register current time
  t4 := time PLUS (totwait MINUS shortwait)
  get ! TRUE -- tell the sensors to register
  timeget := time PLUS getwait -- define a sleep for sensors
  ...  deal with at most one setupdta before timeget
  ...  if still running, get sensor data and output it (t4)
}}}
```

Table 4.23: Leaf sensor loop pseudocode

```
{{{  deal with at most one setupdta before timeget
PRI ALT
  uin ? setupdta
    SEQ
      deal.with.leaf.restart(setupdta, MAC)
      clock ? AFTER timeget
  clock ? AFTER timeget
    SKIP
  FAILURE
    upparent := FALSE
}}}
```

Table 4.24

143

```
{{{  if still running, get sensor data and output it (t4)
SEQ
  back ? dta -- get the local data from sensors
  time := time PLUS outwait -- define a sleep for output
  -- waits here until defined time after incoming trigger
  clock ? AFTER time
  upparent & OutputOrNot.t(uout, dta, clock, t4, upparent)
}}}
```

Table 4.25

In Table 4.25 we grab the local sensor data and, at the proper time, send it to the parent.

Table 4.26 is mission control. Of course, I have left out much of the complexity on the output side, which is probably more typical UI code on an OS-based system.

Table 4.27 reads the setup data in (see Table 4.12) and, after bringing up the near connels for the first time, is passed out into the sensor fan. Then a broadcast is sent out along each branch. A Boolean `failed[i]` is set up to maintain information about the state of every node.

Triggering by this master (Table 4.28) is based on a timer. Sometimes, a replacement packet needs to be sent out too. Normally, a long set of `dta[i]` packets is received from a direct child after a rather long wait. Failure results in this child (one directly connected to mission control) being marked as failed.

We have reserved `updwait` time for the full output and failure handling for this Table 4.29 loop. `update.failures` checks whether any descendants farther out the fan have been reported failed. `hourly.output` does normal output. `one.replacement` is NOT caused to fire by a failure, but by (unspecified) user input, telling it that a sensor has been replaced, and what its new MAC address is. If that replaced sensor is a direct child, `initialize.connel` happens here.

In general, most of the effort needed to manage the output can be offloaded to a process running in parallel to mission control. That makes it realistic that the output and failure handling can be done within so little time. In this case, further design can be done via pseudocode if necessary.

Table 4.30 is the program, not the PROC. Each member represents a different piece of hardware. Notice there is no SEQ, even though we consider the possibility a sensor may be replaced. The replacement sensors are activated by returning to the WHILE TRUE (not the setup) in their PROCs and awaiting the first EVENT.

```
{{{   PROC MC([3]CHAN OF ANY out, [3]CHAN OF ANY in, VAL INT inlen,
-- This is a second attempt at the "mission control" PROC pseudocode of
-- the orchard sensors. It loops through three level-2 mid-sensors and
-- their slaves, and then calls hourly.output on the data.
PROC MC([3]CHAN OF ANY out, [3]CHAN OF ANY in, VAL INT inlen,
   chwait, updwait, shortwait)
   -- out[k] is [21]BYTE until broadcast (setup)
   --        but in loop is EVENT; (0 or more times [21]BYTE)
   --        where the [21]BYTE setupdta's are immediate and
   --        continue until a in[0] child trigger comes
   -- in[k] is [inlen]PACKET
   TIMER clock :
   [21]PACKET dta :
   [3]BOOL upch : -- is child connel currently working?
   INT time, t2 :
   -- The following variables are dedicated to failures and restarts
   [23][21]BYTE setupdta :
   [22]BOOL failed :
   INT replace.index, replace.k :
   INT t1 :
   SEQ
     ... setup and get everything to talk
     SEQ k FROM 0 FOR 3
       (PORT out[k]) ! FALSE -- set up for events transmitted to children
     WHILE TRUE
       SEQ
         -- this part is the gathering of data
         SEQ k FROM 0 FOR 3
           ... trigger child and deal with child's response
         ... output and analyze results from whole orchard
   :
}}}
```

Table 4.26: Pseudocoding for mission control PROC

```
{{{  setup and get everything to talk
fill.in.setupdta(setupdta) -- as in Ch 4 Table 12: real MAC addresses
SEQ k FROM 0 FOR 3
  initialize.connel([setupdta[k+1] FROM 3 FOR 6], out[k], in[k])
SEQ i FROM 1 FOR 21
  VAL INT k IS (INT setupdta[i][0]) - 1 :
  out[k] ! setupdta[i]
SEQ k FROM 0 FOR 3
  SEQ
    out[k] ! setupdta[22] -- the broadcast end signal
    upch[k] := TRUE
replace.index := 0 -- no replacement right after setup
replace.k := -1
SEQ i FROM 0 FOR 22
  failed[i] := FALSE
clock ? time -- register current time
}}}
```

Table 4.27: Mission control setup

The times are given in seconds, not in millionths of a minute as in the first hack (an error for millionths of a second).

All the pseudocode except for mission control is expected to be coded on small embedded processors. The principle to follow is that every part of the pseudocode defines behavior that is mimicked by the real code. Any trick necessary to do that is OK. In addition, more features may be added to the real code to aid debugging.

4.4 Data-flow pseudocoding of the satellite CDMA receiver

The satellite CDMA receiver requires a different set of capabilities from the orchard sensors. Here, the rate of data flow and calculation is great, and best design involves a lot of vector programming methods. I will also use this design to give an example of buffering, because that is a key technique needed to avoid the "hiccups" so prevalent even in polished commercial software products.

Since the purpose is didactic, the buffering may not be necessitated by the real behavior of USB. Similarly, the Raspberry Pi (RPi) and Parallella specifications may be slightly idealized in order to illustrate some points. In particular, one RPi variant will contain fast analog input ports, a 25MHz

```
{{{  trigger child and deal with child's response
SEQ
  clock ? AFTER time -- wake at specified time
  t1 := time PLUS shortwait -- for a setupdta
  t2 := time PLUS (chwait - updwait) -- enough time for dta
  time := time PLUS chwait -- define next wakeup time
  (PORT out[k]) ! TRUE -- trigger k-th child immediately
  -- act upon one replacement if necessary
  (replace.k = k) & SEQ -- upch[k] TRUE if reach here
    OutputOrNot.t(out[k], setupdta[replace.index], clock,
      t1, upch[k])
    -- note: replace.index = k+1 if reaches here
    upch[k] & failed[replace.index] = FALSE
    replace.index = 0 -- these two are unconditional
    replace.k = -1
    -- If NOT upch[k], then failed[incoming replace.index]
    -- remains TRUE at this point, because replacement then
    -- must be retried after immediate child[k] is replaced.
  -- A rather long wait may happen before first input.
  upch[k] & InputOrNot.t(in[k],
    [dta FROM (k*inlen) FOR inlen], clock, t2, upch[k])
  (NOT upch[k]) & failed[k+1] := TRUE -- immediate child[k]
  (PORT out[k]) ! FALSE -- reset the k-th trigger
}}}
```

Table 4.28: Mission control child handler

```
{{{  output and analyze results from whole orchard
-- this part is the using of the data, which is assumed
-- to take less time than "updwait" (<< 7 minutes)
update.failures(dta, failed) -- add to list of failed if needed
hourly.output(dta) -- do requirements implied by dta
-- The following call allows user input of a new MAC address;
-- otherwise returns replace.k < 0
one.replacement(setupdta, replace.index, replace.k)
-- The following fires only if the replacement is directly
-- connected to MC
((replace.k >= 0) AND (replace.index = (replace.k+1))) & SEQ
  initialize.connel([setupdta[replace.index] FROM 3 FOR 6],
    out[replace.k], in[replace.k])
  upch[replace.k] := TRUE
}}}
```

Table 4.29: Mission control output and replacement pseudocode

```
{{{  main program with local resources
[3][2][2]CHAN OF ANY to0 : -- EVENT and [21]BYTE
[3][2]CHAN OF ANY to1 :
[3]CHAN OF ANY to2 :
[3][2][2]CHAN OF ANY from0 : -- PACKETs
[3][2]CHAN OF ANY from1 :
[3]CHAN OF ANY from2 :
PAR
  MC(to2, from2, 7, 1200, 180, 15)
  PAR k FROM 0 FOR 3
    PAR
      mid(to2[k], to1[k], from2[k], from1[k], 0, 3, 390, 1200, 15)
      PAR j FROM 0 FOR 2
        PAR
          mid(to1[k][j], to0[k][j], from1[k][j], from0[k][j], 1, 1,
            105, 390, 15)
          PAR i FROM 0 FOR 2
            leaf(to0[k][j][i], from0[k][j][i], 30, 45, 105, 15)
}}}
```

Table 4.30: Pseudocoding for orchard hardware network

dual-channel ADC, and a TCM arrangement with DMA to a circular buffer. Finally, I will stick with the original Zac Manchester CDMA algorithm, 640-bit SLCE.

The interesting thing is that allowing the computer to perform its tasks as quickly as possible is often the enemy of smoothness of output. Since Deep Programming usually ignores questions of timing, it falls into this trap by default. The Wide approach, which easily avoids it as long as there is enough computing power, is closely analogous with physical flow engineering. Compare outIQdriver in scatter.occ below.

4.4.1 Copy, move, read and write

Before going into detailed pseudocode for the satellite receiver, it's necessary to face the issue of robust zero-copy data moving. This is an issue not faced by occam, but there are constructions that have the same effect, if you keep a clear idea of the distinction between a copy and a move. In order to avoid the abstraction problems of Deep programming, where one loses control of the entities and bugs creep in, it is also necessary to have a physical analogue in mind at all times.

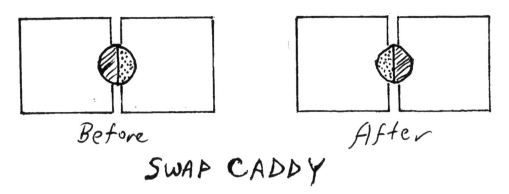

Figure 4.7: Swap caddy

Look at Figure 4.7. Here is a caddy with two memory modules, one available to each (square) piece, and it spins 180 degrees, moving each module and its contents to the other piece.

In Table 4.31 is pseudocode that does the same (repeatedly). For convenience of comparing them, the two processes are written side by side.

The critical thing about understanding the Swap Caddy is the distinction between *copy* and *move*. Taken literally as written, the inner PAR does a copy in both directions. This may take a long time if PACKET is big. After it is done, the second member's buf[ind] contains the same data as the first member's buf[1-ind] but at a different address. Similarly, the first member's buf[ind] contains the same data as the second member's buf[1-ind] but at a different address.

To show what is really intended, I invoke an obscure rule of occam: Once part of an array is abbreviated (i.e. IS or RETYPES definitions), the rest of the array is unavailable to that code block for anything except further abbreviations. Since I abbreviate only buf[ind] in each member, the innermost SEQ has no access of any kind to buf[1-ind]. The reason is that the Swap Caddy really does a move, not a copy. This means that after the communication PAR, the source of the output (buf[1-ind] in each member) is no longer there. It has lost its memory module.

If we strictly adhere to this rule of unavailability, THEN WE CAN RE-PLACE EACH DATA COMMUNICATION WITH A POINTER COMMUNI-CATION. This is a major saving that can prevent "hiccups" in rapid timed operations.

After the pointer communications, treated as moves, are done, the second member's buf[ind] has the same data **and address** as the first member's buf[1-ind] used to have, but the first member's buf[1-ind] has no data or

```
CHAN OF PACKET left, right :
PAR
   -- code for first member          -- code for second member
   [2]PACKET buf :                    [2]PACKET buf :
   INT ind :                          INT ind :
   SEQ                                SEQ
     ind := 1                           ind := 1
     WHILE TRUE                         WHILE TRUE
       SEQ                                SEQ
         ind := 1-ind                       ind := 1-ind
         PAR                                PAR
           right ! buf[1-ind]                 right ? buf[ind]
           left  ? buf[ind]                   left  ! buf[1-ind]
         PACKET a IS buf[ind] :              PACKET b IS buf[ind] :
         SEQ                                SEQ
           -- do stuff with a                 -- do stuff with b
```

Table 4.31: Two processes with swap caddy

address. Similarly, the first member's buf[ind] has the same data and address as the second member's buf[1-ind] used to have, but the second member's buf[1-ind] has no data or address. Developing the computer linguistic implications of this is a big part of the language development some of my colleagues and I have proposed.

In the meantime, implementing this in C will involve arrays of pointers, but the correspondence to real packets must be strictly controlled. For instance, it is a good idea to place an invalid pointer, perhaps a NULL, in the source slot after every move. This strictly corresponds to the memory module that isn't there.

A slight variant on this approach can be used for drivers. The same design (Figure 4.8) works for read, for write/modify, and for write with no modification allowed. I call it a *flip driver* because its driver member, which is identical with the second member of Table 4.31, flips the role of its two PACKETs after operating and before the next communication PAR.

Its circular buffer member (Table 4.32) outputs the leading buf[ind] and inputs the trailing buf[wasind]. If pointer moves are used, it is easily seen that (except for the one invalid buf[ind]) the actual pointers stay the same at the same place in the circular array. Thus it amounts to "loaning" a pointer to the driver and getting it back.

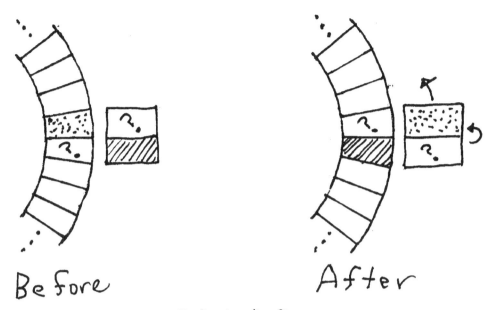

Before   After

FLIP DRIVER

Figure 4.8: Flip driver

```
-- code for first member
[N]PACKET buf :
INT ind :
SEQ
  ind := 0
  WHILE TRUE
    INT wasind :
    SEQ
      -- do stuff with buf except buf[ind]
      wasind := ind -- move 1 notch forward around circular buffer
      ind := ind + 1
      (ind >= N) & ind := 0
      -- if write or write/modify, valid data is in buf[ind]
      -- if read, there is space in buf[wasind]
      PAR
        right ! buf[ind]
        left  ? buf[wasind]
      -- if read or write/modify, new data is in buf[wasind]
      -- do stuff with buf except buf[ind]
```

Table 4.32: Flip driver circular buffer process

151

4.4.2 Provisional computational cores

In the orchard sensor case we did two "subwaves": the naive design, followed by the design including start and replacement. It similarly makes sense to do a couple of approaching steps in this high-powered electromagnetic filtering problem.

Because the flow structure is so simple (almost unidirectional) but the computing task is challenging, it is advisable to start with provisional pieces that do the computing. These pieces will have channel formals from which data flow in and out can be determined, and delays calculated and controlled. "Glue" can then be designed to fit these needs.

4.4.2.1 CDMA test integral node

At the center, repeated on each of many nodes, each node a Parallella core, is pseudocode of the form of Table 4.33. Two of these nodes will serve each of the 182 templates (PRN0 and PRN1 for each of the 91 twist values, spaced by 72 degrees, and spanning the expected +-2ppm variation in the carrier frequency caused by crystals at various temperatures). In one of the two, I0 will be a twisted I template and Q0 a twisted Q template, while in the second (quadrature) node, I0 will be a twisted -Q template and Q0 a twisted I template.

Examination of the code shows it does, as expected, "stamp" the template on the incoming (I,Q) for 1920 steps starting from an arbitrary step. Since $1919 - k$ equals $1920 - (k+1)$, the first stamp after `acfirst[1919-k]` is set to zero is the `aclast[0]` stamp involving I0[0] and Q0[0]. The index of I0 and Q0 increases by 1 for each succeeding stamp until `acfirst` is finally output after 1920 steps. This is the delay: $1920/(192\text{kHz}) = 10$ milliseconds.

Several of the blocks, especially the replicated SEQ blocks, are equivalent to and intended to represent efficient core-level vector operations.

The PAR in the setup is a standard swap caddy operation, used because the process that supplies this twisted test template has to serve up to 62 different nodes. Also, the way memory is structured on the Parallella is friendly to this approach. The communication is then notification of ownership.

Another point of interest is the use of 0.0 in I and in the output to mean reset. If by chance a real 0.0 appears, it is replaced with a very small positive number that will make no difference in the calculations.

The innermost two replicated SEQs in the WHILE notdone loop are each a long vector operation on average, a scalar-multiply-accumulate (MAC) pair. Given vector-friendly indexing, the first, after setup, should consume 4j cycles and the second 7680-4j cycles, thus totalling 7680 cycles. The overhead of the

```
PROC CDMAtest(CHAN OF REAL32; REAL32 inIQ, CHAN OF REAL32 outmatch,
  CHAN OF [1920]REAL32; [1920]REAL32 inIQ0, outIQ0)
  [2][1920]REAL32 I0b, Q0b : -- may be -Q0, I0 for quadrature test
  [1920]REAL32 ac : -- accumulator
  REAL32 I, Q :
  SEQ
    WHILE TRUE
      BOOL notdone :
      SEQ
        -- setup (the PARs denote caddy swaps)
        PAR
          inIQ0  ? I0b[1]; Q0b[1]
          outIQ0 ! I0b[0]; Q0b[0] -- lend IQ0 to crystal.occ
        PAR
          inIQ0  ? I0b[0]; Q0b[0] -- return IQ0 from crystal.occ
          outIQ0 ! I0b[1]; Q0b[1]
        SEQ i FROM 0 FOR 1920
          ac[i] := 0.0(REAL32)
        notdone := TRUE
        -- loop
        VAL [1920]REAL32 I0 IS I0b[0] : -- write unchangeable
        VAL [1920]REAL32 Q0 IS Q0b[0] :
        WHILE notdone
          SEQ j FROM 0 FOR 1920
            []REAL32 acfirst IS [ac FROM 0 FOR (1920-j)] :
            []REAL32 aclast IS [ac FROM (1920-j) FOR j] :
            VAL []REAL32 I0first IS [I0 FROM 0 FOR j] :
            VAL []REAL32 I0last IS [I0 FROM j FOR (1920-j)] :
            VAL []REAL32 Q0first IS [Q0 FROM 0 FOR j] :
            VAL []REAL32 Q0last IS [Q0 FROM j FOR (1920-j)] :
            notdone & SEQ
              inIQ ? I; Q
              (I = 0.0(REAL32)) & notdone := FALSE
              SEQ i FROM 0 FOR j
                aclast[i] := (aclast[i] + I*I0first[i]) + Q*Q0first[i]
              SEQ i FROM 0 FOR (1920-j)
                acfirst[i] := (acfirst[i] + I*I0last[i]) + Q*Q0last[i]
              notdone & REAL32 theoutput IS acfirst[1919-j] :
              SEQ
                (theoutput = 0.0) & theoutput := 1.1755E-38(REAL32)
                outmatch ! theoutput -- never outputs 0.0 here
              acfirst[1919-j] := 0.0
          outmatch ! 0.0(REAL32) -- end signal
  :
```

Table 4.33: Provisional CDMA test integral node

loop should be around 20 more cycles, not counting waits for communication, totalling under 1.479 billion cycles per second, within a Parallella node's capability. Assuming readiness to transmit and receive, the communications, which are independent, can be moved around the loop so they have at least 8 cycles to complete before their space or data is needed. If that is not adequate, some NOPs can be added; over 100 cycles per step are available within the 1.5GHz limit.

You may ask why the two innermost replicated SEQs in the loop are not placed in a PAR, thus saving around 25% clock time. Such a PAR would actually be quite legal since none of the written-to abbreviations overlap.

The answer is that this is unrealistic given the target processor, which is a single core of the 64-core Parallella. It has a limited capacity to do MACs (one per two cycles), and not in parallel. Pseudocoding should be adapted to the target processor, identified in the First Wave, but should have structure simple enough so that it can be enhanced if a differently optimized processor comes along. To attempt to optimize for all processors at once is a kind of abstraction and should usually be avoided. (The replicated SEQs themselves are adapted for a vector processor, and could be expressed differently for a core with high internal parallelism.)

4.4.2.2 IF demodulator and filter

Another major computational node is the Intermediate Frequency demodulator and filter. It was described in some detail in the First Wave, and will be fleshed out here.

The IF data is analog and produced by an analog demodulator. Because of the wide range of possible effective carrier frequencies, due to Doppler even more than to the temperature inaccuracy of the crystal, we need to be flexible about the waveforms getting the IF to baseband. Since we are operating at 25MHz, a cycle of 5000 data points will repeat every 200 microseconds, and by choosing the IF-to-baseband demodulator frequency to be a multiple of 5kHz, we can get baseband carrier rotation to between -5kHz and +5kHz. Given knowledge of the expected Doppler, that can be added to the twist frequencies presented to the CDMA nodes, and absolute twist remain under 6kHz, which should be tractable at the slow sampling of 192kHz.

The feedback channel `kill` can at any time interrupt the filter's operations, and cause it to send out an end signal (in which I is 0.0) to propagate reset to downstream processes.

The first, one-time setup (Table 4.35) relates to Figure 2.6 of Chapter 2. There are 24 possibilities (we repeat the one at the end for convenience) for

```
PROC filter(CHAN OF INT16; INT16 inIQIF, CHAN OF REAL32; REAL32 outIQ,
  CHAN OF [5000]REAL32; [5000]REAL32 inIQ0, outIQ1, CHAN OF EVENT kill)
  [2][5000]REAL32 I0b, Q0b : -- to demod the IF to baseband
  [25]REAL32 a, b : -- starters for the filter
  REAL32 Iac, Qac, Iacback, Qacback : -- accumulators
  INT16 I16, Q16 -- incoming IF data
  REAL32 I, Q : -- incoming IF data
  REAL32 IBraw, QBraw : -- after raw demod
  INT abind : -- stepping 5 of 24
  INT nsteps : -- either 129 or 130
  INT inddemod, ind :
  SEQ
    ... setup
    -- loop
    WHILE TRUE
      BOOL notdone, down :
      SEQ
        ... setup new demod
        VAL [5000]REAL32 I0 IS I0b[ind] : -- write unchangeable swap caddy
        VAL [5000]REAL32 Q0 IS Q0b[ind] :
        WHILE notdone
          REAL32 aj, ajm1, ajm2, bj, cj :
          SEQ
            ... input, demod, and handle inddemod
            ... hat node accumulate excluding end signal
            ... prepare for next hat node
            SEQ i FROM 0 FOR nsteps
              notdone & SEQ
                ... input, demod, and handle inddemod
                ... standard accumulate
        outIQ ! 0.0(REAL32); 0.0(REAL32) -- end signal
:
```

Table 4.34: Low pass filter, 25MHz to 192kHz

```
{{{ setup
-- hat spacing of 3125/24, slope 24/3125 = 0.00768
SEQ i FROM 0 FOR 25
  SEQ
    a[i] := (REAL32 i*i)/150000.0
    b[i] := 0.00384 + 0.00032*(REAL32 i)
ind := 1 -- swap caddy index
}}}
```

Table 4.35: Setup for hat functions

```
{{{  setup new demod
-- demod to within +-2.5kHz of expected Doppler
ind := 1 - ind -- swap caddy index
-- This PAR denotes a double-buffer swap
[5000]REAL32 I0 IS I0b[ind] :
[5000]REAL32 Q0 IS Q0b[ind] :
[5000]REAL32 I1 IS I0b[1-ind] :
[5000]REAL32 Q1 IS Q0b[1-ind] :
PAR
  inIQ0 ? I0; Q0
  outIQ1 ! I1; Q1
-- PAR-legal multiple assignments are legal in occam
Iac, Iacback, Qac, Qacback := 0.0, 0.0, 0.0, 0.0
abind := 24 -- start value for step-by-5
inddemod := 0 -- start value for demod cycle
notdone := TRUE
}}}
```

Table 4.36: Setup for Doppler target within +-2.5kHz

the location of the hat nodes relative to the 25MHz input nodes. The ratio 24/3125 comes out exact in decimal as 0.00768.

The Doppler setup (Table 4.36) can change the demod tables after every reset. This will happen because a downstream process has detected a pause in message bits. As with Table 4.33, a double-buffer swap is indicated for I0 and Q0 to allow a parallel process to recalculate the demod tables during reset time. If this is done by pointers, this Doppler setup is very fast.

In Table 4.37, the latest IF data is pulled from the TCM FIFO and subjected to raw demodulation, which leaves in the double frequency term. From now on, everything is **REAL32** instead of **INT16**. This exact same code is found in two places, because it is the same whether we are at a hat node or not. This code is never executed if **notdone** is already FALSE.

The **kill** channel is expected to interrupt here to take down **notdone** when it is time for a reset. This can be accomplished without **select** or similar tools, if the programmer can access interrupt code. No more data are pulled from the TCM FIFO in this pseudocode once the kill comes in, until reset is accomplished via the double buffer on I0 and Q0.

Table 4.38 does the three-accumulator work at the center of Chapter 2, Figure 2.6. After **acback** is output, it is assigned to the next hat (previously

```
{{{ input, demod, and handle inddemod
PRI ALT
  kill ? down
    notdone := FALSE
  inIQIF ? I16; Q16 -- pulled out of the TCM FIFO
    SKIP
I := (REAL32 I16)
Q := (REAL32 Q16)
IBraw := I*I0[inddemod] + Q*Q0[inddemod]
QBraw := Q*I0[inddemod] - I*Q0[inddemod]
inddemod := inddemod + 1
(inddemod > 4999) & inddemod := 0
}}}
```

Table 4.37: Input digital IF and demod: appears twice in code

```
{{{ hat node accumulate excluding end signal
aj := a[abind]
ajm2 := a[24-abind]
bj := b[abind]
ajm1 := (1.0 - aj) - ajm2
Iacback := 0.00768*(Iacback + ajm2*IBraw)
Qacback := 0.00768*(Qacback + ajm2*QBraw)
notdone & SEQ
  (Iacback = 0.0) & Iacback := 1.1755E-38(REAL32) -- smallest float
  outIQ ! Iacback; Qacback -- no end signal
Iacback := Iac + ajm1*IBraw
Qacback := Qac + ajm1*QBraw
Iac := aj*IBraw
Qac := aj*QBraw
}}}
```

Table 4.38: Hat node accumulate and output

```
{{{  prepare for next hat node
abind := abind - 5 -- value to be used on next loop
IF
  abind > 0
    nsteps := 129
  TRUE
    SEQ
      nsteps := 130
      abind := abind + 24
}}}
```

Table 4.39: Prepare for next hat node in tables

```
{{{  standard accumulate
Iac := Iac + bj*IBraw
Qac := Qac + bj*QBraw
cj := 1.0 - bj
Iacback := Iacback + cj*IBraw
Qacback := Qacback + cj*QBraw
bj := bj + 0.00768
}}}
```

Table 4.40: Standard accumulate, away from hat node

ac) and a new hat is started. For simplicity, I do not check for the special case of the first two outputs, which are invalid because of inadequate data. The third output pins down the delay, which is two output steps, or $2/(192\text{kHz}) = 10.4167$ microseconds.

Notice that this code never outputs an end signal.

The block of Table 4.39 deals with the fact that $3125/24 = 130\frac{5}{24}$. Sometimes there are 129 standard steps between hat node steps, and sometimes 130.

The block of Table 4.40 accumulates for a standard step, away from any hat node. Notice that a full unit weight of Braw is partitioned between acback and ac. That is why the end result has to be multiplied by 0.00768 before output.

It's worth noting that a different strategy is used here than in Chapter 2 Section 2.6.2. Because there are more multiply-accumulates, Table 4.40 saves one cycle compared with the temp-based approach in Chapter 2. We lose (probably) two cycles due to the branched increment in Table 4.37, and at one cycle per 16-bit input from the TCM FIFO, that is probably 24 cycles per inner loop, not counting loop overhead (which can probably be minimized). At 25MHz that uses up 600 million cycles per second, well under the RPi limit of 700MHz. This approach would also work for the 28.8MHz case, just barely, even without taking advantage of the simpler filter description (integer ratio).

This code is set up in such a way that `kill` (or reset) propagates down from the filter through the CDMAtest nodes. This is because the Doppler is changing, but dozens of message bits can be picked up before it moves the frequency out of range. The gatherer and detector, to be discussed next, will take advantage of the fact that Zac Manchester's protocol gives pauses between bytes during which no message waveforms are transmitted, and adjustments can be made.

4.4.2.3 Concessions to C in pseudocode

The occam purist will notice that I am allowing a few C-like conventions to creep into pseudocode. In occam there is no arithmetic operator precedence, in fact every order is supposed to be defined by parentheses except repeated AND and repeated OR expressions (which are evaluated by the usual "early exit" technique that allows expressions like `(x > 0) AND ((y/x) < 100)` to avoid runtime failure). In pseudocode, this cumbersome requirement is relaxed by allowing C-like precedence, although when ordering matters, as it does here (due to the favored status of MAC evaluations), putting the parentheses in is recommended.

Another concession I've made is on explicit typing, which occam requires for `REALnn` constants, any `nn`. Still, occam is a strict typing language and that should be respected at least in the comments of pseudocode. The concrete nature of Wide programming always leans toward knowing what are the storage and computational demands of variables and expressions, and keeping a finger on roundoff errors and overflow possibilities. It would actually be best if the occam family of types were expanded by adding ones like `UNSIGNED INT` for time variables, but I don't do that here.

4.4.3 Gatherer and detector

The structure of the above pseudocode is part of a system with two main states: detection and bit continuation. It remains in detection state, searching at a fixed Doppler and a range of +-900Hz in twist, until it finds either a PRN0 or PRN1 message bit. Then it expects more message bits at 100 Hz, either PRN0 or PRN1. This is bit continuation state. When it fails to detect a bit at the expected time, it sends a reset on `kill` and re-enters detection state, awaiting new demod and CDMA arrays before listening again. This is made possible by Zac Manchester's silent times between bytes, which are variable and at least 0.5 second long, plenty of time for calculating demod and CDMA arrays.

4.4.3.1 Signal behavior

If the orbital speed is 7.8km/s and the Sprite passes overhead at 160km, then the rate of change of the frequency is $\frac{v^2 f}{Hc} = 555$ Hz/s. However, it drops off as about the inverse cube of the distance, so at 30 degrees above the horizon it is only about 70 Hz/s. This means that an appropriate target PRN0 or PRN1 with constant twist would work (worst error in twist position $0.5(555\text{cycles/s}^2)(10\text{ms})^2 = 10$ degrees, which would hardly affect the detection integral).

Rob Fryer points out that the total change in frequency due to Doppler is from about +10kHz to -10kHz, which could actually work in favor of detection, since it is much more than the expected error due to the crystal, and by pointing toward an approaching satellite with a Doppler-corrected frequency with an antenna that spans more Doppler than the error range, it would hit it right on at some point. This might not work if the satellite is not passing overhead.

Another complication is that Doppler expands and compresses all time values, not just frequency. Thus a message bit is not exactly 10ms or 1920 filter output steps. Though the error is less than 0.05 filter output step per message bit, and is thus insignificant for a single detection integral, it can accumulate over dozens of message bits. The same holds for the twist rate change of up to 20 degrees per message bit, which can soon cause a twist index move, given that the twist step is 72 degrees. Thus after a bit is detected, the next bit is expected at a filter output advance between 1919 and 1921, and at a twist index change of -1, 0, or +1. Since both PRN0 and PRN1 are tested in both in-phase and quadrature, this will survey 36 CDMAtest outputs. The trend over several message bits will give information on Doppler and on crystal error.

According to the Link Budget [8], which is not substantially changed, the signal-to-noise ratio (Eb/N0) for the full message bit is 20. This is despite the carrier being much weaker than the noise (ratio 0.04), because the integration with the target template tends to cancel the noise. Because of SLCE, other Sprites' signals act as noise in this respect. A signal, rotated by any amount, is detected by a linear combination of the integrals of the in-phase and quadrature products:

$$P_I = I * I_0 + Q * Q_0$$
$$P_Q = Q * I_0 - I * Q_0 \tag{4.1}$$

Perfect detection is if $I + iQ = (I_0 + iQ_0)\gamma$ where $i = \sqrt{(-1)}$, γ is a nonzero complex number, and the MSK templates are as shown in Chapter 2 Figure 2.6. Then the sum of the squares of the two integrals is $|\gamma|^2 L^2$ where L is the length of the interval. This is multiplied by an *effectiveness number* η when I and Q are twisted by a small linearly varying angle, or shifted by a small offset.

Because for MSK we have $I_0^2 + Q_0^2 \equiv 1$, a constant, it is easily seen that for total twist α the effectiveness number is

$$\eta_\alpha = \left(\frac{\sin(\alpha/2)}{\alpha/2}\right)^2 \tag{4.2}$$

Not quite so obvious is the effectiveness number for a shift β, where β is the ratio between the shift and a symbol bit. It turns out the worst case is a sequence of identical symbol bits, which yields a sine wave of period 4 symbol bits, and hence

$$\eta_\beta \geq \left(\cos(\frac{\pi}{2}\beta)\right)^2 \tag{4.3}$$

In the case described in Chapter 2, where α is 72 degrees and β is 1/3, we get

$$\eta_\alpha = 0.87514$$
$$\eta_\beta \geq 0.75000 \tag{4.4}$$

The product of these *energy* ratios is 0.65636, so even applying both together, the signal-to-noise ratio is still 13.

4.4.3.2 Gatherer

This means that a clear, extended peak should appear, and that a minimax check over 2 by 2 neighbor arrays of sums of form

$$\left(\int P_I(t)dt\right)^2 + \left(\int P_Q(t)dt\right)^2$$

should do the trick, where neighbors are in filter output steps (at 192kHz) and in twist steps (separated by 72 degrees). Three winners for each Parallella should suffice, where 2 x 1 winners are permitted at the twist edges, since a hit may straddle the twist assignments of two Parallellas. I am assuming that

161

each Parallella is dedicated either to PRN0 or to PRN1, so it can show all test outputs for 30 or 31 twists.

There is an instance of **gather** (Table 4.41) on one node of each of the six Parallellas, and it collects from 30 or 31 IQ pairs, and thus from 30 or 31 twists. The outer WHILE loop cycles at the beginning and at each reset, and thus corresponds to a fixed filter Doppler +-900Hz. After that, for every filter output step (192,000 times a second) it performs the inner WHILE loop. At 1.5GHz, it has 7800 cycles to do this.

The 60 or 62 CDMAtest nodes feed their accumulator output to this node, as indicated by the PAR. Each CDMAtest node responds independently to a reset, which is propagated by the filter to them all, so the reset signal should come almost at the same time, but not necessarily exactly. The **active[i]** device keeps **acs[i]** at 0.0 after its reset, so following steps, if any, flatline these nodes and ignore them, till all the **active[i]** values go FALSE, which is indicated by **nactive = 0**.

The actual math is glossed over in this pseudocode. The main math is in **winnotes.update** which updates a scratchpad **winnotes** and, if the minimum of one or more 2×2 or twist-edge 2×1 is discovered to beat **criterion**, adds the best three to **windata**, sets **valid** to TRUE, and outputs **windata**. Otherwise it sets **valid** to FALSE. Thus there is at most one PACKET output per step. After reset is complete, a final, distinctive signal end is output, thus passing reset back to the detector, which initiated it using its **kill** channel.

Notice the **BOOL::[]PACKET** channel protocol. This is an occam counted protocol where the BOOL counts 0 if FALSE and 1 if TRUE. This permits the **outwin** channel communication to be merely one BOOL if, as almost always happens, a significant accumulator array is not detected.

You may ask why not omit the **outwin** communication completely if there is no detection. It could have been programmed that way, but then there will have to be a complex construction of ALTs on the input side, together with the passing of a step count, because the receiver gets no step tick in most cases. This way, the connels are more busy, but we get a clear tick.

How busy? Usually it's six bytes per step, but the theoretical maximum would be six packets per step. Each packet needs to transmit up to 12 Is and Qs, but it should suffice for them to be normalized to the largest. Since two decimal places should be plenty of resolution, this would be 24 data bytes and one exponent byte, plus information about twist index (3 bytes) and minimums (3 data bytes and one exponent byte), totalling 32. If all six were screaming at once, that, plus six more bytes for the BOOLs, would total 198*192000 bytes per second, or 38MB/s, well within the capability of USB 2, even if unbuffered.

Finally, **count.of.TRUE** is used because decrementing **nactive** within each

```
PROC gather([62]CHAN OF REAL32 inmatch, CHAN OF BOOL::[]PACKET outwin,
  VAL REAL32 criterion, VAL INT ntwist)
  INT nconnect :
  WHILE TRUE -- loop on restarting of message bit streams
    [62]BOOL active :
    [62]REAL32 acs :
    INT nactive :
    INT32 nhats :
    PACKET windata :
    NOTES winnotes :
    SEQ
      -- setup
      nconnect := ntwist * 2 -- really should do this only once
      SEQ i FROM 0 FOR nconnect
        active[i] := TRUE
      winnotes.initialize(winnotes) -- for coherence between ticks
      nactive := nconnect -- this one will decrease
      nhats := 0 -- this long int will count the filter output steps
      WHILE (nactive > 0) -- loop on filter output steps
        SEQ
          -- All the still-active CDMAtest nodes feed in here
          PAR i FROM 0 FOR nconnect
            active[i] & SEQ
              inmatch[i] ? acs[i]
              (acs[i] = 0.0) & SEQ -- this is the reset flow
                active[i] := FALSE -- acs[i] now stuck at 0.0
          nactive := count.of.TRUE(active, nconnect) -- or spinlock?
          (nactive > 0) & BOOL valid :
          SEQ
            nhats := nhats + 1
            winnotes.update(winnotes, acs, nhats, criterion, ntwist,
              windata, valid)
            outwin ! valid
            valid & outwin ! windata
      signal.end(windata)
      outwin ! TRUE
      outwin ! windata -- end signal
:
```

Table 4.41: The gatherer node in a Parallella

reset flow detection is illegal within members of a PAR. A spinlock could be used, and if so, would be represented by an extra member of the PAR to handle `nactive`, and a local channel array.

4.4.3.3 Detector

The detector code appears in Table 4.42. `BOOL::[]PACKET` channels result in 6 bytes per tick, or a "hum" of 1.2MB/s even when no incoming accumulator passes the criterion. This permits the reception to be done with a simple PAR.

If the BOOL were not transmitted, the "hum" would disappear, but at the cost of an ALT arrangement to catch the data when there is some. A looping fair ALT can be done, as interrupt programmers know, but I will not cover that just now. The current setup makes it easy to keep track of ticks, too.

The key is `check.all.win`, which is called every tick (192,000 times per second), but most of the time does nothing. Thanks to `initialize.params`, `initialize.notes`, and `determine.params`, it knows when the node is just coming out of a reset, which puts it in detecting state. It keeps going until it detects a bit, either 0 or 1, and then `validbit` comes true, a bit is output, and it goes into continuing state. After that it listens only 1919, 1920, and 1921 ticks after the last bit, and to the last bit's twist and its two neighbors. As long as it keeps finding bits (either 0 or 1) in that narrow window, it keeps transmitting them, but when it fails, it sets `killing` to TRUE and forces a reset. The reset takes one or two ticks to percolate back to here, and then `nactive` goes to 0 and the detector returns to the setup and to detecting state.

Movement of the twist value, which can be determined to a fraction of a radian using the 2×2 accumulator packet data, determines the rate of change of frequency, due to a combination of Doppler and crystal inaccuracy. This permits `determine.params` to place the Doppler prediction arrays in the right place for the next bit sequence, assuming that is placed according to the Zac Manchester byte approach (22 bits followed by a quasi-random silence between 0.5 and 1.5 seconds).

Since we can maintain a tick count, we can detect the case where the Sprite has passed below the horizon; a wait of more than 2 seconds will do. In this case, `killing` can be set TRUE and `determine.params` can reset the parameters to correspond to a later capture of an approaching satellite on the next orbit.

```
PROC detect([6]CHAN OF BOOL::[]PACKET inwin, CHAN OF PARAMS outparams,
  CHAN OF BOOL messagebits, CHAN OF EVENT kill)
  [6]PACKET windata :
  NOTES bitnotes :
  PARAMS fornextsetup :
  SEQ
    initialize.params(fornextsetup)
    outparams ! fornextsetup
    (PORT kill) ! FALSE
    WHILE TRUE -- loop on restarting of message bit streams
      INT nactive :
      [6]BOOL active, valid :
      BOOL outbit, killing :
      SEQ
        -- setup
        active := [TRUE, TRUE, TRUE, TRUE, TRUE, TRUE]
        nactive := 6
        killing := FALSE
        initialize.notes(bitnotes)
        WHILE (nactive > 0) -- loop on filter output steps
          SEQ
            -- All the still-active CDMAtest node data feeds in here
            SEQ i FROM 0 FOR 6
              active[i] & SEQ
                inwin[i] ? valid[i]
                valid[i] & inwin[i] ? windata[i]
                is.end(windata[i]) & SEQ -- this is the reset flow
                  active[i] := FALSE -- windata[i] stuck at END
                  nactive := nactive - 1
            (nactive > 0) & BOOL validbit, killing :
            SEQ
              check.all.win(windata, bitnotes, valid, outbit,
                validbit, killing)
              IF
                validbit
                  messagebits ! outbit
                killing
                  SEQ
                    determine.params(bitnotes, fornextsetup)
                    (PORT kill) ! TRUE -- start reset process
                    outparams ! fornextsetup
                TRUE
                  SKIP
        (PORT kill) ! FALSE -- after end of reset process
:
```

Table 4.42: The detector node in a Raspberry Pi

165

4.4.4 Glue and buffering

USB 2 is pretty fast and does its own buffering, but I am going to proceed on the assumption that the data flow staggers at times, perhaps due to operating system problems. In fact, according to [9], the bulk transfer works 8000 times a second, at which time it can send a "microframe" of up to 13 packets of 536 bytes each, payload 512 bytes and framing 24 bytes. This implies a maximum throughput of 53.248 MB/s.

Also of interest is that the standard defines a maximum response time of 192 bits (400 nanoseconds). This does not change the packet count limit, but does imply that interrupt response and raw communication overhead must be at least this good. The fact that one of 64 sets of 6 bits must be subjected to "bit stuffing" and increase to 7 bits results in average packets being 537.38 and does not change the count of 13. However, worst case bit stuffing would result in packets of length 624 and only 11 packets in a microframe. This would imply a worst-case throughput of 45.056 MB/s. However, shortening the packets by one byte (payload 511, length 623) would allow 12 packets and a worst-case throughput of 49.056 MB/s.

Though the Parallella has a USB slave port, and the RPi defaults to master mode, it turns out that a USB slave cannot have two masters. Therefore the LAN capability shared by the RPi and the Parallella will have to work on one side. The RPi supports only 100 Megabit Ethernet, but that is enough to deal with the *average* throughput on the downstream side, between the gatherers and the detector. The fan of upstream IQ data coming from the filter is 9.3MB/s, using the pair of REAL32s shown in the code. However, the RPi can broadcast and thus use only 1.6MB/s on its side of the LAN switch.

4.4.4.1 LAN transmission buffer pieces

According to [10] and [11], the best latency that can be expected from a LAN communication is about 600 microseconds. Using regular packets, with TCP timestamps, without 802.1q, gives a 90-byte overhead and maximum net packet payload 1462 bytes for regular packets, according to [12]. 90 bytes at 100Mb/s, at 8 bits per byte, is 7.2 microseconds, which is too much burden at 192kHz, so multiple IQ communications must be packaged per packet. If we expect latency of 625 microseconds, and spend 375 microseconds (72 steps) gathering IQ sets, then that gives maximum latency of 1 millisecond, and about 375 microseconds between arrival of packets.

But packet arrival is expected to be choppy, so it makes sense to enforce a uniform delay of much more than 1 millisecond. Average arrival times can be used to smoothly correct the firing of IQ to CDMAtest nodes within each Parallella, if there is any possibility of cumulative error due to disagreement of the clocks.

All of this can be accomplished if a circular buffer is used, with output about 180 degrees delayed from input, thus allowing the maximum variability so that jitter can be smoothed out by a numerical "shock absorber." Buffer swap needs to be nearly instantaneous if the output is to tick along smoothly at about 192kHz, so the best swap is an exchange of pointers, represented as in `filter` by a PAR of exchanges.

The structure of the LAN transmission pieces is fourfold. On the RPi side, `package` gathers IQ and broadcasts it in groups of 72, or every 375 microseconds. On each Parallella, a passive `IQbuffer` with a circular buffer array supports a pair of swap caddy drivers. One, `inIQdriver`, receives a whole group of 72 in one shot, and the other, `outIQdriver`, broadcasts 192,000 IQ data pairs per second, at constant or nearly constant time intervals, each to 60 or 62 CDMAtest nodes.

The last three together comprise a double (read/write) flip driver occupying a *scatterer* node on a Parallella, and there are six Parallellas. Their broadcast times must be carefully calibrated so as to minimize any timing drift, as all the streams must be regathered at the output. The timing of the LAN receptions make this calibration possible.

The packager, in Table 4.43, is a simple progressive double buffer arrangement. The PAR shows that at the same time as a new set of 72 IQ pairs is coming in from the filter at the 192kHz rate, the last set, completed, is being broadcast all at once through the LAN. The delay of one set (up to 375 microseconds) is managed by the Boolean `notstarting` and the index `indswap`.

Of course, the packager must be implemented in code native to the Raspberry Pi. This requires true parallelism, which can be managed with soft interrupts that deposit `I[i]` and `Q[i]` at the correct location in a TCP/IP buffer each time the filter outputs, and TCP/IP output of the other half-buffer using DMA and a completion interrupt.

Tables 4.44 through 4.46 show the scatterer's structure and its two drivers. `inIQdriver` reads a batch from `fromLANbroadcast`, and `outIQdriver` broadcasts timed outputs to the CDMAtest nodes via `IQbroadcast[j]`. In `update.outIQdriver.notes` and `next.outIQdriver.time`, coding is assumed to exist that smoothly spaces the outputs and, using `arrivaltime` and `time`, keeps the write from wandering too far from 180 degrees (5/2 batches) from the read. The use of 5 as the count of buffers is probably low, but it expresses the principle. Actual buffering will depend on experiments having to do with

167

```
PROC package(CHAN OF REAL32; REAL32 inIQ,
  [6]CHAN OF [72]REAL32; [72]REAL32 toLANbroadcast)
  [2][72]REAL32 Iswap, Qswap : -- doublebuffer
  -- loop
  WHILE TRUE
    BOOL notdone, notstarting :
    INT indswap :
    SEQ
      notdone := TRUE
      notstarting := FALSE
      indswap := 0
      WHILE notdone
        SEQ
          [72]REAL32 I IS Iswap[indswap] :
          [72]REAL32 Q IS Qswap[indswap] :
          VAL [72]REAL32 Iout IS Iswap[1-indswap] :
          VAL [72]REAL32 Qout IS Qswap[1-indswap] :
          PAR
            SEQ i FROM 0 FOR 72
              IF
                notdone
                  SEQ
                    inIQ ? I[i]; Q[i]
                    (I[i] = 0.0) & notdone := FALSE
                TRUE -- stop receiving after a reset detected
                  I[i], Q[i] := 0.0, 0.0
            notstarting & PAR j FROM 0 FOR 6 -- implemented by LAN switch
              toLANbroadcast[j] ! Iout; Qout
          indswap := 1 - indswap
          notstarting := TRUE
      VAL [72]REAL32 Iout IS Iswap[1-indswap] :
      VAL [72]REAL32 Qout IS Qswap[1-indswap] :
      PAR j FROM 0 FOR 6 -- implemented by LAN switch
        toLANbroadcast[j] ! Iout; Qout
:
```

Table 4.43: The packager node in a Raspberry Pi

```
PROC scatter(CHAN OF [72]REAL32; [72]REAL32 fromLANbroadcast,
  [62]CHAN OF REAL32; REAL32 IQbroadcast, VAL INT ntotal)
  TIMER clock : -- shared by buffer and both drivers
  CHAN OF [72]REAL32; [72]REAL32 in, inback, out, outback :
  CHAN OF BOOL intrigger, outtrigger :
  CHAN OF INT64 intime, outtime :
  PAR
    ...  inIQdriver
    ...  outIQdriver
    ...  IQbuffer
:
```

Table 4.44: Scatterer on a Parallella

latency irregularities.

Notice, in Table 4.44, the large number of channels internal to PROC scatter. Their action will probably have to be modeled by interrupt code or asynchronous driver code in C. The behavior implied by the pseudocode must be emulated by the C code, sometimes not a trivial task.

Table 4.47 shows the circular buffer process, which is not smart in any way, but merely offers the mechanics to implement both flip drivers at once without causing hiccups in the output. All the channels used by IQbuffer are internal. The swap caddy PARs are assumed to work by passing pointers, not data. The normal order of things should be wasjin = 0, wasjin = 1, wasjin = 2, jout = 0, wasjin = 3, jout = 1 ... so no collisions should ever take place.

This setup assumes latency irregularities are small, say 200 microseconds (one half batch time) at most. Long-term errors such as clock skew among the boards must be detected and handled by the programming of outIQdriver.

4.4.4.2 USB transmission buffer pieces

Now we proceed to the use of USB at the downstream end. The detector RPi will be the master, and the six Parallellas the slaves. It will not do for each filter output step on each Parallella to be associated with a USB communication, even though most of them are only one byte long, because there is a 36-byte overhead which would nearly fill the whole practical capacity of USB. Therefore, the procedure is to send packed INT::[]BYTE bursts of 160 steps each. That is about the maximum that can go in one microframe. Detection of a reset causes a short burst to be sent at the end. This is the packer1 code found in Table 4.48.

```
{{{  inIQdriver
BOOL notdone :
INT64 thetime :
[2][72]REAL32 Ib, Qb :
INT ind : -- swap caddy index
SEQ
  notdone := TRUE
  ind := 1 -- swap caddy index
  WHILE notdone
    SEQ
      ind := 1 - ind -- swap caddy index
      [72]REAL32 I IS Ib[ind] :
      [72]REAL32 Ix IS Ib[1-ind] :
      [72]REAL32 Q IS Qb[ind] :
      [72]REAL32 Qx IS Qb[1-ind] :
      SEQ
        fromLANbroadcast ? I; Q
        clock ? thetime
        notdone := (I[71] <> 0.0)
        intrigger ! notdone
        intime ! thetime
        -- This PAR denotes a flip driver read
        PAR
          in ! I; Q
          inback ? Ix; Qx
}}}
```

Table 4.45: Scatterer flip driver (read)

Because the end comes rather quickly (22 bits of 10 ms each, according to Zac Manchester's setup) we expect little skew to develop between the six Parallellas. Therefore only a two-deep burst buffer is implied by the RPi side of the transmission. (Each burst is about 833 microseconds, and the expected skew much less than that.) The code for doing this is stacker1 in Table 4.49. Although it lives on the RPi, it is for only one of the Parallellas, and therefore there will be six instances of stacker1.

Basically, packer1 and stacker1 are inverses of one another, so the output of stacker1 looks as if it was straight from gather. However, it comes in bursts. If this were undesirable (as for instance in a music application) we

```
{{{ outIQdriver
BOOL notdone :
INT64 arrivaltime, time, wastime :
NOTES outIQdriver.notes :
[2][72]REAL32 Ib, Qb :
INT ind :
SEQ
  notdone := TRUE
  ind := 1 -- swap caddy index
  initialize.outIQdriver.notes(outIQdriver.notes, ntotal)
  WHILE notdone
    SEQ
      outtrigger ! TRUE -- master signal
      outtime ? arrivaltime
      -- This PAR denotes a flip driver write
      ind := 1 - ind -- swap caddy index
      PAR
        out ? Ib[ind]; Qb[ind]
        outback ! Ib[1-ind]; Qb[1-ind]
      clock ? time
      update.outIQdriver.notes(outIQdriver.notes, arrivaltime, time)
      [72]REAL32 I IS Ib[ind] :
      [72]REAL32 Q IS Qb[ind] :
      SEQ i FROM 0 FOR 72
        notdone & SEQ
          wastime := time
          time := next.outIQdriver.time(outIQdriver.notes, wastime)
          clock ? AFTER time
          -- this is broadcast to CDMAtest nodes
          PAR j FROM 0 FOR ntotal
            IQbroadcast[j] ! I[i]; Q[i]
          notdone := (I[i] <> 0.0)
  outtrigger ! FALSE
}}}
```

Table 4.46: Scatterer flip driver (broadcast write)

```
{{{   IQbuffer
BOOL notdone, notoutdone :
INT64 thetime[5] :
INT wasjin, jin, wasjout, jout :
[5][72]REAL32 I, Q : -- circular buffers for flip drivers
SEQ
  notdone := TRUE
  notoutdone := TRUE
  wasjin := 0
  SEQ j FROM 1 FOR 3
    notdone & SEQ
      intrigger ? notdone
      intime ? thetime[wasjin]
      -- This PAR denotes a flip driver read
      PAR
        in ? I[wasjin]; Q[wasjin] -- read block
        inback ! I[j]; Q[j]
      wasjin := j
  jin := wasjin + 1 -- normally 4
  jout := 0
  wasjout := 4
  WHILE notoutdone -- notoutdone lasts longer than notdone
    ALT
      outtrigger ? notoutdone
        notoutdone & SEQ
          outtime ! thetime[jout]
          -- This PAR denotes a flip driver write
          PAR
            out ! Ib[jout]; Qb[jout] -- write block
            outback ? Ib[wasjout]; Qb[wasjout]
          wasjout := jout
          jout := jout + 1
          (jout > 4) & jout := 0
      notdone & intrigger ? notdone
        SEQ -- happens even if notdone turned FALSE
          intime ? thetime[wasjin]
          -- This PAR denotes a flip driver read
          PAR
            in ? I[wasjin]; Q[wasjin] -- read block
            inback ! I[jin]; Q[jin]
          wasjin := jin
          jin := jin + 1
          (jin > 4) & jin := 0    .
}}}
```

Table 4.47: Scatterer flip driver circular buffer

would insert a timed FIFO as with `outIQdriver` in `scatter`. As it is, timing is dictated by the `SEQ i FROM 0 FOR 6` in `detect`, which forces all six instances of `stacker1` to align timewise. The requirement that communications, other than `CHAN OF EVENT`, be acknowledged, transmits this back to the first location of a significant FIFO.

Because communications are internal and therefore very fast, we expect the output side of `stacker1` to take much less than 833 microseconds, thus permitting some skew buffering action. Of course, the six parallel instances will have to be hand-coded in equivalent C code, probably with some polling approach that is essentially sequential. It does not matter much, because the data flow here is very slow. The six parallel stackers are a convenience of data flow description, not a rigid coding guide.

4.4.4.3 Doppler and crystal twist

The `doppler` and `crystal` pieces are active only upon reset. They receive the `params` that are calculated by the detector, and recalculate the tables that are used to demod and test the incoming data at various twists. Since half a second, at least, is spent quiet between bytes under Zac Manchester's system, they have lots of time to do all their calculations and prepare for the next message bit.

Two caddy swaps can be noted at reset in `CDMAtest`. This is to allow `crystal` to write its work directly to arrays local to each of the CDMA nodes. This is an approach favored by the Parallella. For efficiency, of course, the caddy swaps should be implemented by pointer moves in some form.

4.4.4.4 Possible variations on this theme

It would be possible to place `doppler` in the setup after each reset of `filter`, and to place `crystal` in the `inIQdriver` setup of `scatter` after each reset. As I have it, the channels between filterRPi and the scatter node of each Parallella have to be overlaid by some device, not shown. They are really transmissions through the same LAN switch, all in the same direction (except for `back` which is really just an acknowledge).

The "guts" of the big PAR in `crystal` is ill-suited to a single Parallella node, and could be moved to the 62 target CDMA nodes, where it would only be a short interlude on the setup of each one. See Table 4.52, and note that all the arrays (`IPRNbase`, `QPRNbase`, `ct1`, and `st1`) are constant. In theory, therefore, shared read-only memory is OK, and the address of the four arrays could be shared by the upstream node with all 62 CDMA nodes.

```
PROC packer1(CHAN OF BOOL::[]PACKET inwin, CHAN OF INT::[]BYTE packed)
  [2][5280]BYTE packb :
  [2]INT indpackb :
  WHILE TRUE -- loop on restarting of message bit streams
    BOOL notdone, notstarting :
    INT indswap :
    SEQ
      notdone := TRUE
      notstarting := FALSE
      indswap := 0
      WHILE notdone
        SEQ
          INT indpack IS indpackb[indswap] :
          VAL INT indpackout IS indpackb[1-indswap] :
          [5280]BYTE pack IS packb[indswap] :
          VAL [5280]BYTE packout IS packb[1-indswap] :
          PAR
            BOOL valid :
            PACKET windata :
            SEQ
              indpack := 0
              SEQ i FROM 0 FOR 160
                notdone & SEQ
                  inwin ? valid
                  pack[indpack] := (BYTE valid)
                  indpack := indpack + 1
                  valid & SEQ
                    inwin ? windata
                    []BYTE winbytes RETYPES windata :
                    [pack FROM indpack FOR 32] :=
                      [winbytes FROM 0 FOR 32]
                    indpack := indpack + 32
                    notdone := NOT is.end(windata)
            notstarting &
              packed ! indpackout::[packout FROM 0 FOR indpackout]
          indswap := 1 - indswap
          notstarting := TRUE
      VAL INT indpackout IS indpackb[1-indswap] :
      VAL [5280]BYTE packout IS packb[1-indswap] :
      packed ! indpackout::[packout FROM 0 FOR indpackout]
:
```

Table 4.48: The packer piece in a Parallella

```
PROC stacker1(CHAN OF INT::[]BYTE packed, CHAN OF BOOL::[]PACKET outwin)
  [2][160]BOOL validsb :
  [2][160]PACKET windatasb :
  [2]INT indmaxb :
  WHILE TRUE -- ignore restarting of message streams
    BOOL notdone, notstarting, inputting :
    INT indswap :
    SEQ
      notdone := TRUE
      notstarting := FALSE
      inputting := TRUE
      indswap := 0
      WHILE notdone
        BOOL wasinputting :
        SEQ
          wasinputting := inputting -- goes FALSE when read done
          VAL INT indmax IS indmaxb[indswap] :
          INT indmaxin IS indmaxb[1-indswap] :
          [160]PACKET windatas IS windatasb[indswap] :
          [160]PACKET windatasin IS windatasb[1-indswap] :
          [160]BOOL valids IS validsb[indswap] :
          [160]BOOL validsin IS validsb[1-indswap] :
          [5280]BYTE pack :
          PAR
            inputting & INT indpack :
            SEQ
              packed ? indpack::[pack FROM 0 FOR indpack]
              indpack := 0
              SEQ i FROM 0 FOR 160 -- need to detect reset here
                inputting & SEQ
                  indmaxin := i
                  validsin[i] := (BOOL pack[indpack])
                  indpack := indpack + 1
                  validsin[i] & SEQ
                    []BYTE winbytes RETYPES windatasin[i] :
                    [winbytes FROM 0 FOR 32] :=
                      [pack FROM indpack FOR 32]
                    indpack := indpack + 32
                    inputting := NOT is.end(windatasin[i])
            notstarting & SEQ i FROM 0 FOR (indmax+1)
              SEQ
                outwin ! valids[i]
                valids[i] & outwin ! windatas[i]
          indswap := 1 - indswap
          notstarting := TRUE
          notdone := wasinputting
  :
```

Table 4.49: The stacker piece in a Raspberry Pi

```
PROC doppler(CHAN OF PARAMS inparams, [6]CHAN OF PARAMS outparams,
  [6]CHAN OF BOOL back, CHAN OF [5000]REAL32; [5000]REAL32 outIQ0, inIQ1)
  [5000]REAL32 I1, Q1 : -- dummies for write unchangeable swap
  [5][5000]IOb, QOb : -- -2 -1 0 1 2 times 5000 Hz Doppler center
  PARAMS theparams :
  VAL REAL32 pi IS 3.1415926536 :
  SEQ
    -- setup (this can be done more efficiently)
    SEQ j FROM 0 FOR 5
      VAL INT jm2 IS j - 2 :
      SEQ i FROM 0 FOR 5000
        REAL32 x IS (REAL32 i*jm2)*pi/2500.0 :
        IOb[j][i], QOb[j][i] := cos(x), -sin(x)
    -- loop
    WHILE TRUE
      INT inddoppler :
      SEQ
        -- demod to within +-2.5kHz of expected Doppler
        inparams ? theparams
        PAR j FROM 0 FOR 6
          BOOL gotcha :
          SEQ
            outparams[j] ! theparams -- to one of the Parallellas
            back[j] ? gotcha -- signal that this Parallella is ready
        -- current.doppler is nearest integer to doppler/(5000 Hz)
        -- and is always between -2 and +2
        inddoppler := current.doppler(theparams) + 2
        -- This PAR denotes a double-buffer swap
        VAL [5000]REAL32 I0 IS IOb[inddoppler] :
        VAL [5000]REAL32 Q0 IS QOb[inddoppler] :
        PAR
          outIQ0 ! I0; Q0 -- This can really share the data (VAL)
          inIQ1  ? I1; Q1 -- This is actually not needed
        -- This PAR passes stuff on to the six Parallellas
:
```

Table 4.50: The doppler piece on a Raspberry Pi

```
PROC crystal([62]CHAN OF [1920]REAL32; [1920]REAL32 outIQ0, inIQ1,
  CHAN OF PARAMS inparams, CHAN OF BOOL back,
  VAL BOOL isPRN1, VAL INT ntwiststart, ntwistcount)
  VAL INT ntotal IS ntwistcount*2 :
  VAL REAL32 pi IS 3.1415926536 :
  PARAMS theparams :
  [1920]REAL32 IPRN, QPRN, IPRNbase, QPRNbase :
  [9600]REAL32 ct1, st1 :
  SEQ
    -- setup (this can be done more efficiently)
    enter.untwisted.PRN(isPRN1, IPRN, QPRN) -- FALSE is PRN0, TRUE is PRN1
    SEQ i FROM 0 FOR 9600
      REAL32 x IS (REAL32 i)*pi/4800.0 : -- 72 degree twist over 1920
      ct1[i], st1[i] := cos(x), sin(x)
    -- loop
    WHILE TRUE
      REAL32 twist :
      SEQ
        inparams ? theparams
        twist := get.basetwist(theparams) -- total twist, message bit
        SEQ i FROM 0 FOR 1920
          REAL32 c IS cos((REAL32 i)*twist/1920.0) :
          REAL32 s IS sin((REAL32 i)*twist/1920.0) :
          SEQ
            IPRNbase[i] := IPRN[i]*c + QPRN[i]*s
            QPRNbase[i] := QPRN[i]*c - IPRN[i]*s
        PAR k FROM ntwiststart FOR ntwistcount
          PAR j FROM 0 FOR 2 -- I,Q or -Q,I
            ...   calculation for a CDMAtest node
        back ! TRUE -- signal doppler that this Parallella is done
:
```

Table 4.51: The crystal piece on a Parallella

In practice, it is not clear that such heavy simultaneous memory access would work well. In fact, the issue is unimportant, because a huge amount of time intervenes between the moment when a reset is signaled (which is when this calculation of trigonometry tables begins) and the moment when the next message byte will begin.

Finally, the use of swap caddies everywhere is overkill. See Figure 4.9 below for a simpler device, the slider slot, which however has two modes of action. This is the simplest client/server, using a pair of single moves in opposite directions, and with care could be substituted for most of our swap caddies. Even simpler variations on it are possible in the read-only case: an address can be broadcast, and after use an acknowledge received from each target.

```
{{{  calculation for a CDMAtest node
INT i IS (k-ntwiststart)*2 + j :
[1920]REAL32 I0, Q0, I1, Q1 :
INT m :
SEQ
  PAR
    outIQ0[i] ? I0; Q0 -- This can really share the data (VAL)
    inIQ1[i]  ! I1; Q1 -- This is actually not needed
  m := 0
  SEQ n FROM 0 FOR 1920
    SEQ
      IF
        j = 0
          SEQ -- twisted template in-phase
            I0[n] := IPRNbase[n]*ct1[m] + QPRNbase[n]*st1[m]
            Q0[n] := QPRNbase[n]*ct1[m] - IPRNbase[n]*st1[m]
        TRUE -- j = 1
          SEQ -- twisted template in quadrature
            I0[n] := IPRNbase[n]*st1[m] - QPRNbase[n]*ct1[m]
            Q0[n] := IPRNbase[n]*ct1[m] + QPRNbase[n]*st1[m]
      m := m + k
      (m < 0) & m := m + 9600
      (m >= 9600) & m := m - 9600
  PAR
    outIQ0[i] ! I0; Q0 -- This can really share the data
    inIQ1[i]  ? I1; Q1 -- This is actually not needed
}}}
```

Table 4.52: The crystal calculation

```
CHAN OF INT16; INT16 inIQIF : -- TRUE INPUT (from the ADC at 25 MHz)
CHAN OF BOOL messagebits : -- TRUE OUTPUT (100 bits/second or less)
CHAN OF PARAMS nextparams : -- detectRPi feeds back to filterRPi
[6]CHAN OF PARAMS params.broadcast : -- filterRPI feeds to Parallellas
[6]CHAN OF BOOL back.signal : -- Parallellas feed back to filterRPi
[6]CHAN OF [72]REAL32; [72]REAL32 LAN.broadcast : -- I,Q package
[6]CHAN OF INT::[]BYTE packed : -- 160-step packages to detectRPi
VAL [3]INT ntwists IS [30, 31, 30] : -- breakup of twist steps from
VAL [3]INT mintwists IS [-45, -15, 16] : -- -45 to +45 inclusive
VAL REAL32 criterion IS get.criterion("linkBudget") : -- external info
PAR
  -- This is the filter node, an enhanced RPi
  CHAN OF [5000]REAL32; [5000]REAL32 IQ0, IQ1:
  CHAN OF REAL32; REAL32 IQ :
  PAR
    filter(inIQIF, IQ, IQ0, IQ1, kill)
    package(IQ, LAN.broadcast)
    doppler(nextparams, params.broadcast, back.signal, IQ0, IQ1)
  -- This is the set of six Parallellas
  PAR k FROM 0 FOR 3
    PAR j FROM 0 FOR 2
      -- Within each Parallella, there are 1 + 62 + 1 nodes
      [62]CHAN OF REAL32; REAL32 IQbroadcast :
      [62]CHAN OF [1920]REAL32; [1920]REAL32 localIQ0, localIQ1 :
      [62]CHAN OF REAL32 match :
      VAL INT i IS 2*k+j : -- index of a Parallella
      PAR
        -- This is the upstream node
        PAR
          scatter(LAN.broadcast[i], IQbroadcast, 2*ntwists[k])
          crystal(localIQ0, localIQ1, params.broadcast[i],
            back.signal[i], BOOL j, mintwists[k], ntwists[k])
        -- Here are up to 62 CDMA test nodes
        PAR n FROM 0 FOR 2*ntwists[k]
          CDMAtest(IQbroadcast[n], match[n], localIQ0[n], localIQ1[n])
        -- This is the downstream node
        CHAN OF BOOL::[]PACKET win :
        PAR
          gather(match, win, criterion, ntwists[k])
          packer1(win, packed[i])
  -- This is the output RPi
  [6]CHAN OF BOOL::[]PACKET win : -- FIFO for each Parallella
  PAR
    PAR i FROM 0 FOR 6
      stacker1(packed[i], win[i])
    detect(win, nextparams, messagebits, kill)
```

Table 4.53: The complete satellite CDMA receiver software

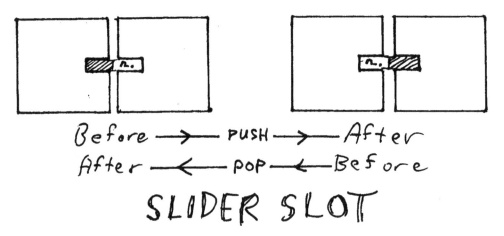

Figure 4.9: Slider slot

4.4.5 Overview

Table 4.53 shows all the code of the satellite CDMA receiver.

There are multiple nestings of PARs, and both internal and external channels. This is openly mapped onto the hardware, and all communications are through channels that live on the *outermost levels* of this code description. There are, in fact, more channels than there are hardware connections, even if you consider a full duplex connection to be two connections. This is because it is a purpose of pseudocode to elucidate DATA FLOWS, and in normal design there can be more than one data flow sharing a connection.

Mapping a pseudocode description like this back into C code and hardware will often involve simplification. For instance, `params.broadcast` and `LAN.broadcast` will be different usage times of the same LAN switch in broadcast mode. Some of the pieces will disappear, or be distributed into sequential code found in other pieces.

However, the pseudocode design retains its value through all that, as a *criterion of judgement* that can be applied to any code changes to see if they are faithful to the design. This value can extend over decades and many changes of personnel, and be relied upon by external users.

4.5 References

[1] Dickson, Lawrence: "Transparent Analogy as a Foundation for Language," 6 April 2006. http://www.tjoccam.com/tacliwhp.pdf

[2] Inmos Limited: *Transputer Instruction Set, a compiler writer's guide* (Document Number 72 TRN 119 05). Prentice Hall, 1988. PDF found at `http://www.transputer.net/iset/iset.asp`

[3] Inmos Limited: *occam 2 Reference Manual* (Document Number 72 occ 45 01 or 72 occ 45 02). Prentice Hall, 1988. PDF found at `http://www.transputer.net/obooks/obooks.asp`

[4] Inmos Limited: *Transputer Architecture Reference Manual* (Document Number 72-TRN-048-03). INMOS, July 1987. `http://www.transputer.net/fbooks/tarch/tarch.html`

[5] Inmos Limited: *Extraordinary use of transputer links* (Document Number 72-TCH-001). `http://www.transputer.net/tn/01/tn01.html`

[6] Rabagliati, Andy: "Sources of extraordinary link handling libraries". `https://groups.google.com/forum/#!topic/comp.sys.transputer/BT28d5o5lEc`

[7] Harriman, Guy: Transputer Instruction Set Appendix. November 29, 1988. `http://www.transputer.net/iset/appendix/appendix.html`

[8] Manchester, Zac: Sprite Spacecraft Link Budget. `https://github.com/zacinaction/kicksat-groundstation/blob/master/Link%20Budgets.xlsx`

[9] Electrical Engineering Stack Exchange: "Why are USB devices slower than 480 MBit/s." `http://electronics.stackexchange.com/questions/24700/why-are-usb-devices-slower-than-480-mbit-s`

[10] arstechnica: "LAN latency (cisco)". `http://arstechnica.com/civis/viewtopic.php?f=10&t=68851`
Best expected (2006) about 0.6ms, and 0.13ms was derided as unrealistic.

[11] Coulouris, Dollimore and Kindberg: *Distributed Systems: Concepts and Design,* Edn. 3 Instructor's Guide. Pearson Education, 2001. `http://www.cdk3.net/ig/slides/Chapter3Slides.pdf`
Figure 3.1 Network types
LAN 10-100 Mbps Latency 1-10ms

[12] P. Dykstra: "Protocol Overhead." March 2001 - August 2013. `http://sd.wareonearth.com/~phil/net/overhead`
Yes TCP timestamps, IPV4, no 802.1q: (1500-52)/(1500+38) 38 is Ethernet

[13] Niiler, Eric: "Have New Cars Gone Haywire?" *Discovery News,* April 3, 2014, 5:00 PM ET. `http://news.discovery.com/autos/drive/have-new-cars-gone-haywire-140403.htm`

Programming Using Connel   5

Abstract

This chapter continues, in the light of the science of Chapter 4, the Connel introduction started in Chapter 3. Using pseudocode and Connel tools, some simple communicating C programs are developed, running in both Linux and Windows. These are programs actually found in the Connel source distribution. Some use serial communications, and others use SOCKLOCAL (Linux socket or Windows named pipe) communications. The techniques of their construction can be extended to general communicating programs, including masters of heterogeneous, embedded, or graphics pieces.

5.1   How to use Connel tools

The best place to start is the spirit of Chapter 4, Section 4.1. There, a distinction was made between "regular" and "critical" programming, where in this context "critical" programming is that which depends significantly on outside behavior. Compare [2].

Here by "outside behavior" I mean outside *your* code, if you are the software creator. This would create an insuperable mountain of critical code in standard Deep programming, since it would have to include all the hidden driver and method code supplied from outside, with its many-layered unpredictable features. Almost all reused code becomes critical because there are no limits on its behavior. Even something as apparently straightforward as data structures ("objects") is critical because they are laden with callbacks and communication addresses of unfathomable complexity.

That's why Deep programming has to proceed side by side with a battery of tests that are run at every step. You, the software creator, are basically along for the ride, and only by experimentation can you find out where your wild horses are going to take you. It's an inductive, not a deductive, process. And as for all the things you did not test—oh well, the customers will test them, sooner or later. We just saw that happen in October 2013 with the "Obamacare" rollout.

Wide programming, *consistently applied,* avoids all this. All the whiplash delivered by the outside world is on the outside of your program structure, as in Chapter 4. (By the way, one point needs to be made clear. Not just communications and events are "outside world," but also timeouts, timer waits, and so-called exceptions of every kind, like sensor failure in the Orchard and loss of satellite communication in the Receiver.) As the software creator, you are able to reuse code, *both regular and critical*, without adding any uncertainty to the behavior of your program. You can even change reused code (or hardware) in midstream, because you are confident it does the same thing—like a new alternator in a classic car.

The Connel contribution is to make it easy to separate pieces that are typically tangled in a centralized "program build." This is based on real distinctions between major functions whose programming (and reused code) is significantly different. Using Connel, they can be separated into independent programs, *separately testable,* and their timing and communications moved to the top of the designs. Another motivator for independent programs is the nature of their IO, or the hardware with which they naturally communicate. The bigger the project, the more different kinds of "specialty" are imposed by this diversity, and if their nearest programming can be kept separate, the rewards are great downstream.

Each Connel-based piece is a different program. Timing is communicated using connels as described above, and small packets may as well be sent this way too. Large blocks of data may be passed using robust shared memory techniques, which are also controlled by connels passing ownership signals. In some cases large blocks are transmitted across especially fast channels, which are different from the standard connels. This kind of thing is easily designed, in a way similar to FTP, and I will not go into further detail about it here.

Timing usually uses the system clock, and we give examples of that in this chapter. However, each system clock has a granularity, and this is often too coarse. Special hardware can be added if needed, supporting a fine-grained timer queue by communicating on a low-latency channel. That is really embedded code and won't be covered in this chapter.

The main thing in writing practical Connel-based code is, like any other low-level communications library, to patch together blocks from known good examples and modify them to work in the new code. The examples given here will be a good start for that. As a rule, Connel-based code is bulky, and I mitigate that with a folding editor. Other techniques may be used, such as macros, but I do not explore them here.

Once the communicating backbone of a piece has been written, "ballast" can be introduced in the form of loops that use about the same CPU and time as the ultimate calculations. Then they can be made to communicate with other pieces or with dummies. The data or controls that fly between them can be made to pass through spies, one of which is detailed in this chapter.

5.2 Rundown of pseudocode for sercomio

One program has already been exhibited in full. I will here show its pseudocode, which can be related to the actual code in Chapter 3. This is in reverse of the normal procedure, but should be instructive.

The first thing you will notice is that the pseudocode is very short compared to the actual C code expanded in Chapter 3, Section 3.6. This is not because of large amounts of regular code. All that `sercomio` does is send bytes across a serial connection and display them (although, to be sure, some blocks of the display and command-line argument code are summarized in single lines in the pseudocode). It is mostly because the occam-like primitives expand into several Connel entities each.

The first thing to do is to enumerate the external conditions of the piece. They are to be consistent with either a call in a script or a keyed-in command-line call taking over a whole screen.

`CHAN OF BYTE kbd, scr` are different from `CHAN OF BYTE serial` in this respect. `kbd` and `scr` are, in the current Connel, the standard terminal IO—not always equivalent to `stdin` and `stdout`, although redirection works for the latter. Terminals can be manipulated using the `expect` interactive programming tool (see [3]). They are specifically targeted by connel type CONNEL_STD.

By contrast, `serial` is of connel type CONNEL_SERIAL. Where `kbd` and `scr` are unique (they are placed external only because what connects to them is external), `serial` can be one of many. If it were real occam, the channels (full duplex) would be determined by whatever called PROC sercomio. In an OS, we need an extra formal, `name`, and will have to open the connel to get two channels, `serialin` and `serialout`.

Thus, the existence of connels requires `connel_list_init`, `connel_begin`, and `connel_open`, while the use of machines (ALT) requires `connel_set_init`, `connel_machine_begin`, and `connel_machine_add`. These are summarized by `open.*` calls in the pseudocode. Similarly, the `close.*` calls in the pseudocode stand for `connel_close`.

Added complications arise with the ALT, which as described in Chapter 3 follows a more general approach, intended to use `connel_listen` and `connel_deafen` to deal with a TRUE or FALSE `boolean &`, and to allow the WaitForMultipleObjects (asynchronous IO) model. Therefore each machine must involve `connel_listen` and each incoming communication involves `connel_read_start` and CONNEL_FINISH as well as `connel_select`.

That involves only the reads (`kbd` and input `serial`). The output on `serial` is synchronous (`connel_write`) and `scr` is actually not used at all. Instead,

```
-- This is pseudocode for sercomio.c.
PROC sercomio(CHAN OF BYTE kbd, scr, serial, CHAN OF EVENT interrupt,
  VAL []BYTE name, VAL PACKET args, BYTE exit, BOOL notInterrupted)
  CHAN OF BYTE serialin, serialout :
  BOOL noexitchar, isbinary, notQuiet, yesdrop :
  BYTE exitchar :
  INT ret :
  SEQ
    notInterrupted := TRUE -- updated later by interrupt
    getargs(args, noexitchar, isbinary, notQuiet, yesdrop, exit)
    (exit = 0(BYTE)) & SEQ
      open.kbd(kbd, ret)
      open.scr(scr, ret)
      open.serial(name, serial, serialin, serialout, ret)
      BYTE thechar, thechar2 :
      BOOL notdone :
      SEQ
        notdone := (ret > 0) AND notInterrupted
        WHILE notdone
          PRI ALT
            interrupt ? ANY -- represents a Ctrl-C interrupt
              notInterrupted := FALSE
            kbd ? thechar
              SEQ
                comment.kbd(isbinary, notQuiet, thechar)
                serialout ! thechar
                notdone := (noexitchar OR (thechar <> exitchar)) AND
                  notInterrupted
            serialin ? thechar2
              SEQ
                comment.serial(isbinary, notQuiet, thechar2)
                notdone := (noexitchar OR (thechar2 <> exitchar)) AND
                  notInterrupted
      close.scr(scr, ret)
      yesdrop & close.serial(serial, serialin, serialout, ret)
      close.kbd(kbd, ret)
:
}}}
```

Table 5.1: View of sercomio.occ in origami (top comments removed)

`CONNEL_DINFO` and `CONNEL_DWARN` are used to make output show up on the screen.

This is the main theme of communication for `sercomio`, but a good deal of other detail is found in the pseudocode call. It relates to the top and bottom of Chapter 4, Figure 4.5. `CHAN OF EVENT interrupt` and `BOOL notInterrupt` refer to the Ctrl-C that is capable of causing `sercomio` to halt. `VAL []BYTE name` and `VAL PACKET args` refer to the arguments input in the call, as handled in Chapter 3 Table 5.6: `name` is the leftover, unspecific argument (`remargv`), and `args` plus `getargs` refer to the specific arguments `--q` etcetera in the `for` loop. Finally, `BYTE exit` is output by `PROC sercomio` and thus corresponds to the one-byte exit value of a process, where 0 means success.

The main action, both in the pseudocode and in the C code, is in the `WHILE notdone` loop. It is assumed that both `kbd` and `serialin` are pumping input into the loop, so each of them continually gets a `connel_read_start` right after its last input is finished. In the Windows case, that commits to the next input that will affect WaitForMultipleObjects, while in the Linux case (which does not use asynchronous IO) it does nothing but set some bits. Then the key (ALT) step is `connel_select` which responds to the winner(s) of the race. `CONNEL_FINISH` winds up the asynchronous read in the case of Windows, and does the read in the case of Linux. So all of them taken together amount to an ALT win.

Between the `if (finish)` and the `connel_read_start` in each response branch to the `connel_select` is the "guts" of the ALT branch in the pseudocode. In more complex Connel code, done in proprietary work, this can get quite extensive and have dependencies that involve the data flowing in from both (or all) machines. In addition, the decision which `connel_read_start` to trigger, if any, can become complex, and `connel_deafen` is the usual alternative if a `connel_read_start` is not appropriate.

Thus, the communication-handling code, whose bulk completely dominates this example, is not necessarily dominant in "real" cases. But its structure remains basically the same. The most nonintuitive part of handling the C code is the `connel_read_start`, which has to be called if the **next** ALT in the loop is to have this communication as a live option. And if it's not a live option, a `connel_deafen` is probably appropriate.

5.3 tapper: a client/server system

This code refers to a server and up to two clients at any time. Here, as mentioned before, Connel does not offer "spawning" and unlimited client spinoffs in the manner of standard sockets (as in [4], Chapter 13). Instead, the `tapper.occ` server sets up a fixed number of named SOCKLOCAL channels, and clients pick them up and set them down at will. This is actually more like what real httpd daemons do in OS systems like Linux, and it avoids the "infinite = finite" metaphor described in [2].

The history of this code is interesting. What was written first was a set of single-OS programs like `servecho.c` for Linux and `[server|client]-win32-[console|echoer].c` for Windows. These were used to develop the SOCKLOCAL (CONNEL_TYPE = CONNEL_NAMED_PIPE or CONNEL_SOCKET) code in Connel. Then the pseudocode for an OS-independent version was written, and the catch/tap code followed the pseudocode in C.

5.3.1 tapper.occ pseudocode as a secure firmware OS

The pseudocode program embraces all the OS entities that are needed to run this simple client/server system.

People tend to think of an OS as a practically infinite bag of tricks, all of which are needed for any programs to run. This is untrue, as is known by classic programmers who are familiar with DOS. The important thing to remember about DOS is that it is *a self-sufficient embedded operating system*—something that has become essentially unknown since its day. That means: (a) it is capable of doing everything that an OS needs to do, and (b) all of its code is on the surface, and can be dumped as assembly that is both understandable and deals with all the hardware. Since the 1990s you only have Deep OSs (with millions of lines of code including hidden Ring 0 drivers) to satisfy (a), and embedded cross-compilers like Arduino to satisfy (b). Most people do not even remember that the original DOS PC ran an *embedded* CPU, the 8088 or 8086. And all of its hardware interfaces were fully described in a small booklet ([1]).

The importance of this observation is that the design implied by `tapper.occ` is perfectly capable of running in an embedded system, or even implying the design of a stub OS that will permit design of an embedded system that can be used to support flexible and changeable programming of this sort.

The lost art of a fully capable embedded OS is one of the most important Wide Programming agenda items.

In the pseudocode of Table 5.2, two nonstandard types are used: TYPE and COMMANDSTRING. This is an immediate clue that significant structural information about the programming and response are carried in the "out-of-band" parts of these types and their users. TYPE is essentially BYTE (from 0 through 255) with two out-of-band values, `connecting` and `disconnecting`.

```
-- Version 2 supporting catch.c and tap.c using connel tools, which
-- require type[i] be used in place of type, as ALT target cannot
-- overlap with connel. Also check for 'x' before quit.
VAL TYPE connecting IS -1 :
VAL TYPE disconnecting IS -2 :
VAL COMMANDSTRING exit IS "exit" :
-- The occam PROCs correspond to programs in an OS
...   PROC catch(CHAN OF ANY kbd, scr, [2]CHAN OF ANY pipe)
...   PROC tap(CHAN OF ANY kbd, scr, pipe)
-- The occam kbd and scr declarations correspond to command windows
[3]CHAN OF ANY kbd, scr : -- 3 windows must be open
-- The occam pipe declarations correspond to starting the catch early
-- and running setup code
[2]CHAN OF ANY pipe : -- 2 pipes or a pipe with 2 INSTANCEs
-- The occam PAR corresponds to running the programs
...   main program
}}}
```

Table 5.2: View of tapper.occ in origami (top comments removed)

The **CHAN OF ANY** in the case of **pipe[i]** is a bit lazy: it could have been **CHAN OF TYPE**. But **kbd[i]** and **scr[i]** alternate between TYPE, BYTE, and COMMANDSTRING.

The number of pipes active in the server **catch** (Table 5.3) can be 0, 1, or 2. The ampersand expression in the ALT means that it listens to its keyboard only when the count of active pipes is 0. That means this program is written so that a shutdown requires all clients be disconnected.

The two out-of-band values of TYPE allow the server to keep track of how many clients are connected, and to which pipes they are connected. The server also displays the incoming (in-band) data. It's not clear from the above pseudocode that a client can't talk unless it is connected, but that is implied by the client code in Table 5.4.

The client **tap** is simpler than the server. The code in Table 5.4 implies that each client session starts by sending **connecting** along the pipe, then zero or more data bytes, and finally **disconnecting**. (The fact that it won't send another **connecting** is not obvious, but follows from the fact that **kbd** never inputs a **connecting** value, although it is capable of inputting **disconnecting**— a signal that is implementation-dependent.)

The main program (Table 5.5) illustrates two possible commands: **exit**, and everything else as an alias for **tap**. The **exit** command is not to be confused with the action of **disconnect** within a command. In fact, **disconnect** causes

```
{{{  PROC catch(CHAN OF ANY kbd, scr, [2]CHAN OF ANY pipe)
PROC catch(CHAN OF ANY kbd, scr, [2]CHAN OF ANY pipe)
  INT npipes :
  BOOL notdone :
  BYTE char :
  [2]TYPE type : -- pseudocode
  SEQ
    npipes := 0
    notdone := TRUE
    WHILE notdone
      -- The pipes take higher priority than the keyboard
      -- Also, keyboard input is ignored unless both clients are
      -- disconnected
      ALT
        ALT i FROM 0 FOR 2
          pipe[i] ? type[i]
            CASE type[i]
              connecting
                npipes := npipes + 1
              disconnecting
                npipes := npipes - 1
              ELSE
                scr ! type[i]
            --END CASE
        npipes = 0 & kbd ? char -- does not listen unless npipes = 0
          IF
            char = 'x'
              notdone := FALSE -- forces termination
            TRUE
              scr ! char
          --END IF got an 'x' to signal termination
      --END ALT
    --END WHILE notdone
}}}
```

Table 5.3: The server program (corresponds to catch.c)

```
{{{  PROC tap(CHAN OF ANY kbd, scr, pipe)
PROC tap(CHAN OF ANY kbd, scr, pipe)
  BOOL notdone :
  BYTE char :
  TYPE type :
  SEQ
    notdone := TRUE
    pipe ! connecting
    WHILE notdone
      SEQ
        kbd ? type
        pipe ! type -- disconnecting is the Linux signal, not 'x'
        notdone = ( type <> disconnecting ) -- <> is occam !=
        IF
          notdone
            scr ! type
          TRUE
            SKIP
    --END WHILE notdone
}}}
```

Table 5.4: The client program (corresponds to tap.c)

a "program run" (i.e. **tap**) to shut down, and moves to the stable state, **kbd[i]** ? **command**. There, the main program (not to be confused with the server) waits patiently for the user to enter the next command. While it is in this state, its pipe is disconnected from the server.

Thus, normal termination is to disconnect any running instances of **tap**, to enter **exit** as the next command for each such instance, and to kill the instance of **catch** by using the keyboard which has become available there since no pipes are connected.

This DOS-like but limited-program-list OS model is very good for computer security. It is applicable on any level of programming, including firmware, drivers, and Ring 0. More flexible than a monolithic firmware burn, it still allows only a finite list of code sequences to be executed.

5.3.2 tap.c—a client

This is the C code for the tapper client, using a SOCKLOCAL. It starts and opens up communication using a pre-existing connel (a named pipe in Windows,

```
{{{   main program
PAR
  -- Because connecting is the first communication from an
  -- instance of tap, and disconnecting is the last, catch has a
  -- running count of currently open taps, and will not shut
  -- down unless both taps are shut down. To make it absolutely
  -- robust, the "exit" command for a tap should be required to
  -- send a special signal before catch shuts down (not done
  -- here). Either that, or exit should cause something to stay
  -- open until it receives a signal from catch that says it is
  -- shutting down (requires extra channels). Neither is done
  -- here, which would allow a tap to come on line and hang
  -- because the catch got signaled to go away.
  catch(kbd[2], scr[2], pipe)
  -- The subsidiary PAR corresponds to running and closing
  -- programs at will. This is possible with an OS.
  PAR i FROM 0 FOR 2
    -- At this point is one of the client windows
    COMMANDSTRING command : -- pseudocode
    SEQ
      kbd[i] ? command
      WHILE command <> exit
        SEQ
          tap(kbd[i], scr[i], pipe[i])
          kbd[i] ? command
      --END WHILE command <> exit
  --END PAR i FROM 0 FOR 2
--END PAR
}}}
```

Table 5.5: Main program for tapper (server/client system)

192

or a socket in Linux).

I am dealing with the client first, because it is simpler than the server, and closer to **sercomio**, the Connel program detailed in Chapter 2. Like **sercomio** it is dominated by **harness** code, the Wide "piping" superstructure that handles data flow and timing. In fact, the similarity is so strong that the best approach is to proceed through the code, block by block, in parallel with that of **sercomio**, and compare them.

The `tap.c` toplevel in Table 5.6 is actually shorter than the **sercomio** toplevel in Chapter 3 Table 3.4. It eliminates two global functions, `ctrlc` and `legalize`, a lot of standard arguments, and the **remarg** argument filter, while adding the standard OS-dependent `#define SOCKLOCAL` and a **namein** prefix `"tapper"`. These are all important program features, which tend to blow by due to the huge volume of hardly-varying Connel calls.

You will note that the five major fold titles are substantially unchanged from those of **sercomio**. This is a crude way of hinting that I do a lot of cutting and pasting!

In the connel declarations (Table 5.7), the only change is to exchange **serial** for **pipe** in connel names and pointers, and **mserinp** for **mpipe** in machine name and pointer. This implies, fairly enough, that the SOCKLOCAL pipe will take the place of the serial connection. That can work in detail, because according to the pseudocode, there is *only one* connect and *only one* disconnect per client session, and they are at the beginning and end, respectively.

The handling (Table 5.8) of the input arguments is much simpler for **tap**. There is merely a digit, `0` or `1`, which when appended to the prefix **tapper** gives the correct filename of an already existing SOCKLOCAL. Of course, a real application can be more extensive (a count of around 10 simultaneous clients is typical of Linux **httpd** daemon usage).

Table 5.9 is nearly identical with REAL CODE BEGINS (Connel setup code) in **sercomio**, except that the place of **scr** with respect to the non-STD connel is reversed.

Tables 5.10, 5.11, and 5.12 are identical with Chapter 3 Tables 3.8, 3.9, and 3.11 respectively. Table 5.13 compares to Chapter 3 Table 3.10 for the non-STD connel. The big difference is that **sercomio** added a machine for **serial**, while **tap** omits the machine, even though its space was reserved (an oversight). This is because the client in **tapper** only outputs, never inputs. A more general server/client implementation would be bidirectional, like **sercomio**.

An invisible difference is that the **connel_open** call for a SOCKLOCAL carries out a C **connect**. This corresponds to transmitting the TYPE value **connecting** in the pseudocode, and blocks until the server does a C **accept**.

```
/*
 * This one functions as a client sending to SOCKLOCAL pname[i]
 * and receiving from the keyboard. Start it AFTER catch.c.
 */
#ifndef CONNEL_LINUX
#define CONNEL_WINDOWS
#else
#undef CONNEL_WINDOWS
#endif
#ifdef CONNEL_WINDOWS
#include "..\LAZM\connel.h"
#define SOCKLOCAL CONNEL_NAMED_PIPE
#else
#include "../LAZM/connel.h"
#define SOCKLOCAL CONNEL_SOCKET
#endif
#define LNAMEOUT 200
int main(int argc, char *argv[])
{
   char namein[20] = "tapper";
   char nameout[LNAMEOUT];
   char *pname;
   int ret;
   ...  declare connel structs and their pointers
   ...  introduce test program self
   ...  REAL CODE BEGINS
   ...  DO THE ACTION
   ...  END
   return 0;
}
}}}
```

Table 5.6: View of tap.c in origami (top comments removed)

194

```
{{{  declare connel structs and their pointers
connel_list_t scl;
connel_list_t *cl = &scl;
connel_set_t scs;
connel_set_t *cs = &scs;
connel_t sckbd, scscr, scpipe;
connel_t *ckbd = &sckbd;
connel_t *cscr = &scscr;
connel_t *cpipe = &scpipe;
connel_machine_t scmkbd, scmpipe;
connel_machine_t *cmkbd = &scmkbd;
connel_machine_t *cmpipe = &scmpipe;
}}}
```

Table 5.7

```
{{{  introduce test program self
#ifdef CONNEL_LINUX
printf("Linux test case\n");
#else
printf("Windows test case\n");
#endif
CONNEL_DINFO("sizeof(connel_t) is %d.\n", sizeof(connel_t));
CONNEL_DINFO("sizeof(connel_list_t) is %d.\n", sizeof(connel_list_t));
CONNEL_DINFO("sizeof(connel_machine_t) is %d.\n", sizeof(connel_machine_t));
CONNEL_DINFO("sizeof(connel_set_t) is %d.\n", sizeof(connel_set_t));
CONNEL_DINFO("sizeof(connel_timeout_t) is %d.\n", sizeof(connel_timeout_t));
if ((argc>1)&&(strlen(argv[1])==1)) {
  strcat(namein, argv[1]);
} else {
  CONNEL_DINFO("Syntax: tap <single digit number>\n");
  exit(1);
}
CONNEL_MAKENAME(SOCKLOCAL, LNAMEOUT, namein, nameout, pname);
if (pname) CONNEL_DINFO("Concocted name: %s\n", pname);
}}}
```

Table 5.8

```
{{{ REAL CODE BEGINS
/* REAL CODE BEGINS */
... init list and set
... kbd begin, open, machine begin, add
... scr begin and open
... pipe begin and open
}}}
```

Table 5.9

```
{{{ init list and set
ret = connel_list_init(cl);
CONNEL_DINFO("connel_list_init returned %d\n", ret);
ret = connel_set_init(cs);
CONNEL_DINFO("connel_set_init returned %d\n", ret);
}}}
```

Table 5.10

```
{{{ kbd begin, open, machine begin, add
ret = connel_begin(cl, ckbd);
CONNEL_DINFO("connel_begin(cl, ckbd) returned %d\n", ret);
ret = connel_open(CONNEL_STD, NULL, CONNEL_READ_BIT, ckbd);
CONNEL_DINFO("connel_open(%d, NULL, %d, ckbd) returned %d\n",
  CONNEL_STD, CONNEL_READ_BIT, ret);
ret = connel_machine_begin(ckbd, cmkbd, 0);
CONNEL_DINFO("connel_machine_begin(ckbd, cmkbd, 0) returned %d\n", ret);
ret = connel_machine_add(cs, cmkbd);
CONNEL_DINFO("connel_machine_add(cs, cmkbd) returned %d\n", ret);
}}}
```

Table 5.11

```
{{{ scr begin and open
ret = connel_begin(cl, cscr);
CONNEL_DINFO("connel_begin(cl, cscr) returned %d\n", ret);
ret = connel_open(CONNEL_STD, NULL, CONNEL_WRITE_BIT, cscr);
CONNEL_DINFO("connel_open(%d, NULL, %d, cscr) returned %d\n",
  CONNEL_STD, CONNEL_WRITE_BIT, ret);
}}}
```

Table 5.12

```
{{{ pipe begin and open
ret = connel_begin(cl, cpipe);
CONNEL_DINFO("connel_begin(cl, cpipe) returned %d\n", ret);
ret = connel_open(SOCKLOCAL, pname, CONNEL_READ_BIT, cpipe);
CONNEL_DINFO("connel_open(%d, %s, %d, cpipe) returned %d\n",
  SOCKLOCAL, pname, CONNEL_READ_BIT, ret);
}}}
```

Table 5.13

```
{{{ DO THE ACTION
/* DO THE ACTION */
{
  char thechar = '#';
  int notdone;
  ... listen kbd
  if (notdone) {
    ... first read_start and notdone if success
  }
  while (notdone) {
    unsigned long newready = 0;
    ret = connel_select(cs, NULL, &newready);
    CONNEL_DINFO(
      "connel_select(cs, NULL, &newready) output %ld, returned %d\n",
      newready, ret);
    ... keyboard response, pipe out and read_start or notdone:=FALSE
  }
  ... deafen kbd
}
}}}
```

Table 5.14

After that, the client is released to continue communication just as if a serial connection or Transputer link were set up.

The active part (Table 5.14) of the program, corresponding to the part of pseudocode after **pipe ! connecting**, is structured like that in **sercomio**. First, **connel_listen** is called for relevant machines (the ones with TRUE or implied Booleans in the ALT), and **connel_read_start** is called for each of these. (It is enclosed in a **notdone** branch because the listen can fail.) After that, the WHILE loop is the same as in the pseudocode.

The listen and the read_start (Tables 5.15 and 5.16) are similar to those in **sercomio**, except for only one machine instead of two. If the client had been bidirectional, the SOCKLOCAL machine would have been serviced too.

```
{{{  listen kbd
ret = connel_machine_listen(cmkbd, 0);
CONNEL_DINFO("connel_machine_listen(cmkbd, 0) returned %d\n", ret);
if (ret<1) {
  ret = connel_machine_listen(cmkbd, 1);
  CONNEL_DINFO("connel_machine_listen(cmkbd, 1) returned %d\n", ret);
}
notdone = (ret > 0);
}}}
```

Table 5.15

```
{{{  first read_start and notdone if success
ret = connel_read_start(cmkbd, &thechar, 1, 1);
CONNEL_DINFO(
  "connel_read_start(cmkbd, &thechar, 1, 1) returned %d\n", ret);
notdone = (ret > 0);
CONNEL_DINFO("nbytes %d ndone %d\n",
  cmkbd->cm_nbytes, cmkbd->cm_ndone);
}}}
```

Table 5.16

In Table 5.17, the keyboard response is simpler than that in **sercomio** because of the lack of options. However, the minimal tests with **newready** and CONNEL_FINISH are still there.

Actually, this code is more complex than it needs to be. With only one input and no timeouts, it could all be done with synchronous reads in place of the select.

In Table 5.18, as usual, the **connel_deafen** call is made to happen when the **connel_read_start** did not happen. Thus, in every case, you get a **connel_listen**, followed by a number (perhaps zero) of **connel_read_start**—**connel_select** win—CONNEL_FINISH sequences, followed by a **connel_deafen**.

The END, in Table 5.19, consists as usual of **connel_close** calls that are symmetrical with the **connel_open** calls. These are nested outside the listen/deafen pairs, if applicable, which in turn are nested outside the read_start/select win/FINISH triplets.

```
{{{  keyboard response, pipe out and read_start or notdone:=FALSE
if ((ret > 0)&&(newready&1)) {
  unsigned long finish = 0;
  notdone = 0;
  CONNEL_FINISH(cs, 0, finish);
  CONNEL_DINFO(
    "CONNEL_FINISH(cs, 0, finish) returned finish = 0x%lX\n",
    finish);
  if (finish) {
    CONNEL_DINFO("============= KEY byte: 0x%02X %c\n",
      (int)thechar, thechar);
    notdone = (thechar != 'x');
    if (notdone) {
      connel_write(cpipe, &thechar, 1);
      CONNEL_DINFO("  PIPE output KEY byte.\n");
      ret = connel_read_start(cmkbd, &thechar, 1, 1);
      CONNEL_DINFO(
        "connel_read_start(cmkbd, &thechar, 1, 1) returned %d\n", ret);
    }
  }
}
}}}
```

Table 5.17

```
{{{  deafen kbd
ret = connel_machine_deafen(cmkbd, 0);
CONNEL_DINFO("connel_machine_deafen(cmkbd, 0) returned %d\n", ret);
if (ret<1) {
  ret = connel_machine_deafen(cmkbd, 1);
  CONNEL_DINFO("connel_machine_deafen(cmkbd, 1) returned %d\n", ret);
}
}}}
```

Table 5.18

```
{{{ END
/* END */
ret = connel_close(cpipe);
CONNEL_DINFO("connel_close(cpipe) returned %d\n", ret);
ret = connel_close(cscr);
CONNEL_DINFO("connel_close(cscr) returned %d\n", ret);
ret = connel_close(ckbd);
CONNEL_DINFO("connel_close(ckbd) returned %d\n", ret);
}}}
```

Table 5.19

5.3.3   catch.c—a server

This is the C code for a server using SOCKLOCALs. It starts and creates two connels (named pipes in Windows, or sockets in Linux). Clients can pick these up and use them—at most two at a time.

This code is examined with both sercomio.c and tap.c in mind. It is more complex than these, for several reasons. First, it includes part of the outdented declaration code of the pseudocode, just as seen in Chapter 3 Table 3.1. This is implemented by connel_create calls. Second, it deals in full with the response to the out-of-band TYPEs, connecting and disconnecting. Thus its Connel structure is more complex. Finally, it deals with an *array* of SOCKLOCALs which can be operational in arbitrary order.

In another way, catch.c is more like sercomio.c: it has more than one machine in its ALT. In fact, here we deal with a replicated ALT array.

Compared with the top view of tap.c, one significant feature is found in Table 5.20: a state machine (actually an array of two state machines, one for each SOCKLOCAL) with the values DISCONNECTED, CONNECT-ING, and READING. In addition, both link names (tapper0 and tapper1) are explicitly listed. This corresponds to part of the implementation of [2]CHAN OF ANY pipe : in the outer declarations of the pseudocode.

In the declarations in Table 5.21, as would be expected, the key difference is an array of two connels and two corresponding input machines.

No program call arguments are expected in Table 5.22, because the server "knows" all the possible names of its connels.

Nothing unexpected happens in Tables 5.23 through 5.27, although Table 5.26 shows a new feature: an array loop for the array of two connels, and a connel_create call for each of them, instead of the connel_open

```
/*
 * This one functions as a server receiving from SOCKLOCAL
 * pname[i] as well as from the keyboard. Start it BEFORE tap.c.
 */
#ifndef CONNEL_LINUX
#define CONNEL_WINDOWS
#else
#undef CONNEL_WINDOWS
#endif
#ifdef CONNEL_WINDOWS
#include "..\LAZM\connel.h"
#define SOCKLOCAL CONNEL_NAMED_PIPE
#else
#include "../LAZM/connel.h"
#define SOCKLOCAL CONNEL_SOCKET
#endif
#define LNAMEOUT 200
#define DISCONNECTED 0
#define CONNECTING 1
#define READING 2
int main(int argc, char *argv[])
{
   char namein[2][8] = {"tapper0","tapper1"};
   char nameout[2][LNAMEOUT];
   char *pname[2];
   int pstate[2] = {DISCONNECTED, DISCONNECTED};
   int i, ret;
   ...  declare connel structs and their pointers
   ...  introduce test program self
   ...  REAL CODE BEGINS
   ...  DO THE ACTION
   ...  END
   return 0;
}
}}}
```

Table 5.20: View of catch.c in origami (top comments removed)

```
{{{  declare connel structs and their pointers
connel_list_t scl;
connel_list_t *cl = &scl;
connel_set_t scs;
connel_set_t *cs = &scs;
connel_t sckbd, scscr, scpipe[2];
connel_t *ckbd = &sckbd;
connel_t *cscr = &scscr;
connel_t *cpipe[2] = {scpipe, scpipe+1};
connel_machine_t scmkbd, scmpipe[2];
connel_machine_t *cmkbd = &scmkbd;
connel_machine_t *cmpipe[2] = {scmpipe, scmpipe+1};
}}}
```

Table 5.21

```
{{{  introduce test program self
#ifdef CONNEL_LINUX
printf("Linux test case\n");
#else
printf("Windows test case\n");
#endif
CONNEL_DINFO("sizeof(connel_t) is %d.\n", sizeof(connel_t));
CONNEL_DINFO("sizeof(connel_list_t) is %d.\n", sizeof(connel_list_t));
CONNEL_DINFO("sizeof(connel_machine_t) is %d.\n", sizeof(connel_machine_t));
CONNEL_DINFO("sizeof(connel_set_t) is %d.\n", sizeof(connel_set_t));
CONNEL_DINFO("sizeof(connel_timeout_t) is %d.\n", sizeof(connel_timeout_t));
for (i=0; i<2; i++) {
  CONNEL_MAKENAME(SOCKLOCAL, LNAMEOUT, namein[i], nameout[i], pname[i]);
  if (pname) CONNEL_DINFO("Concocted name: %s\n", pname[i]);
}
}}}
```

Table 5.22

```
{{{  REAL CODE BEGINS
/* REAL CODE BEGINS */
...  init list and set
...  kbd begin, open, machine begin, add
...  pipes begin, create, machine begin, add
...  scr begin and open
}}}
```

Table 5.23

```
{{{  init list and set
ret = connel_list_init(cl);
CONNEL_DINFO("connel_list_init returned %d\n", ret);
ret = connel_set_init(cs);
CONNEL_DINFO("connel_set_init returned %d\n", ret);
}}}
```

Table 5.24

```
{{{  kbd begin, open, machine begin, add
ret = connel_begin(cl, ckbd);
CONNEL_DINFO("connel_begin(cl, ckbd) returned %d\n", ret);
ret = connel_open(CONNEL_STD, NULL, CONNEL_READ_BIT, ckbd);
CONNEL_DINFO("connel_open(%d, NULL, %d, ckbd) returned %d\n",
  CONNEL_STD, CONNEL_READ_BIT, ret);
ret = connel_machine_begin(ckbd, cmkbd, 0);
CONNEL_DINFO("connel_machine_begin(ckbd, cmkbd, 0) returned %d\n", ret);
ret = connel_machine_add(cs, cmkbd);
CONNEL_DINFO("connel_machine_add(cs, cmkbd) returned %d\n", ret);
}}}
```

Table 5.25

```
{{{  pipes begin, create, machine begin, add
for (i=0; i<2; i++) {
  ret = connel_begin(cl, cpipe[i]);
  CONNEL_DINFO("connel_begin(cl, cpipe[%d]) returned %d\n", i, ret);
  ret = connel_create(SOCKLOCAL, pname[i], CONNEL_READ_BIT, cpipe[i]);
  CONNEL_DINFO("connel_create(%d, %s, %d, cpipe[%d]) returned %d\n",
    SOCKLOCAL, pname[i], CONNEL_READ_BIT, i, ret);
  ret = connel_machine_begin(cpipe[i], cmpipe[i], 0);
  CONNEL_DINFO(
    "connel_machine_begin(cpipe[%d], cmpipe[%d], 0) returned %d\n",
    i, i, ret);
  ret = connel_machine_add(cs, cmpipe[i]);
  CONNEL_DINFO(
    "connel_machine_add(cs, cmpipe[%d]) returned %d\n", i, ret);
}
}}}
```

Table 5.26

203

```
{{{  scr begin and open
ret = connel_begin(cl, cscr);
CONNEL_DINFO("connel_begin(cl, cscr) returned %d\n", ret);
ret = connel_open(CONNEL_STD, NULL, CONNEL_WRITE_BIT, cscr);
CONNEL_DINFO("connel_open(%d, NULL, %d, cscr) returned %d\n",
  CONNEL_STD, CONNEL_WRITE_BIT, ret);
}}}
```

Table 5.27

met with in `tap.c` and `sercomio.c`. This finishes the implementation of [2]`CHAN OF ANY pipe :` in the outer declarations of the pseudocode. The analogy to a declared channel in the pseudocode is a created SOCKLOCAL in the OS's file system: a named pipe if Windows, and a socket if Linux.

The `connel_create` also does the equivalent of a `connel_open`, placing the server-side SOCKLOCAL in a listening state. It's worth noting here that there is nothing intrinsic about **tapper**'s restriction to client writing and server reading. I could have allowed both, with a somewhat more complicated state machine, but the read-only server is enough to demonstrate the key feature of a SOCKLOCAL: its ability to connect and disconnect.

The toplevel ACTION code in Table 5.28 shows a new kind of communication, one that is found on SOCKLOCALs but not on serial or STD connels. This is the **connect** input, which is different from a **read** in C, but is expressed by an out-of-band input in pseudocode. There is also a **disconnect** input, handled differently from either **read** or **connect** in C, and not yet visible in this fold. The reason it is not visible is that, once the pipe has entered the `connel_listen` state (which is to be distinguished from the C `listen` state), it does not leave it, even when its clients disconnect. All it does is to change what it is listening for: a C connect, or a read.

The `connel_connect_start` calls found in Table 5.30 are to be called when a server SOCKLOCAL is in state DISCONNECTED. They actually correspond to the C **accept** call. Once the connect has started, the server SOCKLOCAL is in the state CONNECTING, which will last until it wins the ALT and receives either a connection or a disconnection. That will put it in state READING or DISCONNECTED respectively.

This contrasts with `kbd` in Table 5.31, which as a STD only has a `connel_read_start` call. This is legitimate according to the pseudocode, since `npipes = 0`.

Table 5.31 is a standard keyboard response. Notice that the bit in **newready** that corresponds to the keyboard depends on the order in which machines are

```
{{{  DO THE ACTION
/* DO THE ACTION */
{
  int npipes = 0;
  char keychar = '#';
  char pipechar[2] = "&&";
  int notdone;
  ...  listen kbd, pipes, set notdone if successful
  ...  start read on kbd and connect on both pipes
  while (notdone) {
    int wasnpipes = npipes; /* whether kbd deaf coming in */
    unsigned long newready = 0;
    ret = connel_select(cs, NULL, &newready);
    CONNEL_DINFO(
      "connel_select(cs, NULL, &newready) output %ld, returned %d\n",
      newready, ret);
    newready |= cs->cs_ready;
    if (ret > 0) {
      ...  kbd response
      for (i=0; i<2; i++) {
        int ind = i + 1;
        ...  pipe[i] response
      }
      ...  change state of deaf or listening as appropriate
    }
  }
  ...  deafen pipes, and if necessary, kbd
}
}}}
```

Table 5.28

added. The response code does not test for whether the ALT kbd line is deaf, since connel_select itself will not be responsive under those conditions, and newready will never show kbd ready.

Table 5.32 below is a pipe[i] response (in a replicated ALT) which has new features. Unlike the pseudocode, the C code must be explicitly clear about state. Any ALT win must be checked for disconnection, as this can happen either when a read was expected or when a connect was expected. CONNEL_STATE_SERVER_DISCONNECTED_BIT is the sign, and always forces the pipe into state DISCONNECTED, while if it is absent, then the pipe goes into (or stays in) state READING. A disconnection happens when the client closes its end of the pipe.

In either case, the pipe remains ready to hear. However, in all cases (kbd

```
{{{  listen kbd, pipes, set notdone if successful
ret = connel_machine_listen(cmkbd, 0);
CONNEL_DINFO("connel_machine_listen(cmkbd, 0) returned %d\n", ret);
if (ret<1) {
  ret = connel_machine_listen(cmkbd, 1);
  CONNEL_DINFO("connel_machine_listen(cmkbd, 1) returned %d\n", ret);
}
for (i=0; i<2; i++) {
  if (ret > 0) {
    ret = connel_machine_listen(cmpipe[i], 0);
    CONNEL_DINFO(
      "connel_machine_listen(cmpipe[%d], 0) returned %d\n", i, ret);
    if (ret<1) {
      ret = connel_machine_listen(cmpipe[i], 1);
      CONNEL_DINFO(
        "connel_machine_listen(cmpipe[%d], 1) returned %d\n", i, ret);
    }
  }
}
notdone = (ret > 0);
}}}
```

Table 5.29

```
{{{  start read on kbd and connect on both pipes
if (notdone) {
  int rets[2];
  ret = connel_read_start(cmkbd, &keychar, 1, 1);
  CONNEL_DINFO(
    "connel_read_start(cmkbd, &keychar, 1, 1) returned %d\n", ret);
  CONNEL_DINFO("nbytes %d ndone %d\n",
    cmkbd->cm_nbytes, cmkbd->cm_ndone);
  for (i=0; i<2; i++) {
    rets[i] = connel_connect_start(cmpipe[i], 1);
    CONNEL_DINFO(
      "connel_connect_start(cmpipe[%d], 1) returned %d\n",
      i, rets[i]);
    if (rets[i] > 0) pstate[i] = CONNECTING;
  }
  notdone = (ret > 0)||(rets[0] > 0)||(rets[1] > 0);
}
}}}
```

Table 5.30

```
{{{  kbd response
if (newready&1) {
  unsigned long finish = 0;
  CONNEL_FINISH(cs, 0, finish);
  CONNEL_DINFO(
    "CONNEL_FINISH(cs, 0, finish) returned finish = 0x%lX\n",
    finish);
  if (finish) {
    int knotdone;
    CONNEL_DINFO("   KBD INPUT WAS <%c>\n", keychar);
    knotdone = (keychar != 'x');
    if (knotdone) {
      ret = connel_read_start(cmkbd, &keychar, 1, 1);
      CONNEL_DINFO(
        "connel_read_start(cmkbd, &keychar, 1, 1) returned %d\n", ret);
      knotdone = (ret >= 0);
    }
    notdone = (notdone && knotdone);
  }
}
}}}
```

Table 5.31

or `pipe[i]`), reception of the kill character causes everything to shut down, gracefully or not.

Tables 5.33–5.35 use `connel_listen` and `connel_deafen` to respond according to the pseudocode to the current count of live pipe connections. These implement the Boolean part of the ALT guard. Notice that only `kbd` is deafened.

Table 5.36 is executed only when `catch` is committed to terminating.

Table 5.37 is the usual close procedure, mirroring the create/open sequence.

5.4   sockspy: a channel spy program

The next example is a very useful tool: `sockspy`. It works, one byte at a time, as a channel spy. The structure is very simple (see Figure 5.1), and is based on the SOCKLOCAL character of a server and a single client at any point of time. In the SOCKLOCAL design, both the server process and the bidirectional connel must pre-exist any run of a client. This means an "extension cord" such as `sockspy` can always be placed between the server and its connel, on the one hand, and its client on the other.

```
{{{ pipe[i] response
if (newready&(((unsigned long)1)<<ind)) {
  unsigned long finish = 0;
  CONNEL_FINISH(cs, ind, finish);
  CONNEL_DINFO(
    "CONNEL_FINISH(cs, %d, finish) returned finish = 0x%lX\n",
    ind, finish);
  if (finish) {
    int pnotdone;
    if ((cpipe[i]->c_state)&(~CONNEL_STATE_SERVER_DISCONNECTED_BIT)) {
      if (pstate[i]!=READING) npipes++;
      pstate[i] = READING;
    } else {
      if (pstate[i]==READING) npipes--;
      pstate[i] = DISCONNECTED;
    }
    if (pstate[i]==READING) {
      if (cpipe[i]->c_laststart&CONNEL_READ_BIT)
        CONNEL_DINFO("PIPE[%d] INPUT WAS <%c>\n", i, pipechar[i]);
      pnotdone = (pipechar[i] != 'x');
      if (pnotdone) {
        ret = connel_read_start(cmpipe[i], pipechar+i, 1, 1);
        CONNEL_DINFO(
          "connel_read_start(cmpipe[%d], &pipechar[%d], 1, 1) returned %d\n",
          i, i, ret);
        pnotdone = (ret >= 0);
      }
    } else {
      ret = connel_connect_start(cmpipe[i], 1);
      CONNEL_DINFO(
        "connel_connect_start(cmpipe[%d], 1) returned %d\n",
        i, ret);
      if (ret > 0) pstate[i] = CONNECTING;
      pnotdone = (ret >= 0);
    }
    notdone = (notdone && pnotdone);
  }
}
}}}
```

Table 5.32

```
{{{ change state of deaf or listening as appropriate
if (wasnpipes != npipes) {
  CONNEL_DINFO("CHANGED NUMBER OF CONNECTIONS FROM %d TO %d\n",
    wasnpipes, npipes);
  if (wasnpipes>0) {
    if (npipes<1) {
      ... start listening to kbd
    }
  } else if (npipes>0) {
    ... stop listening to kbd
  }
}
}}}
```

Table 5.33

```
{{{ start listening to kbd
ret = connel_machine_listen(cmkbd, 0);
CONNEL_DINFO("connel_machine_listen(cmkbd, 0) returned %d\n",
  ret);
if (ret<1) {
  ret = connel_machine_listen(cmkbd, 1);
  CONNEL_DINFO("connel_machine_listen(cmkbd, 1) returned %d\n",
    ret);
}
}}}
```

Table 5.34

```
{{{ stop listening to kbd
ret = connel_machine_deafen(cmkbd, 0);
CONNEL_DINFO("connel_machine_deafen(cmkbd, 0) returned %d\n",
  ret);
if (ret<1) {
  ret = connel_machine_deafen(cmkbd, 1);
  CONNEL_DINFO("connel_machine_deafen(cmkbd, 1) returned %d\n",
    ret);
}
}}}
```

Table 5.35

209

```
{{{  deafen pipes, and if necessary, kbd
for (i=1; i>=0; i--) {
  ret = connel_machine_deafen(cmpipe[i], 0);
  CONNEL_DINFO(
    "connel_machine_deafen(cmpipe[%d], 0) returned %d\n", i, ret);
  if (ret<1) {
    ret = connel_machine_deafen(cmpipe[i], 1);
    CONNEL_DINFO(
      "connel_machine_deafen(cmpipe[%d], 1) returned %d\n", i, ret);
  }
}
if (npipes<1) {
  ret = connel_machine_deafen(cmkbd, 0);
  CONNEL_DINFO("connel_machine_deafen(cmkbd, 0) returned %d\n", ret);
  if (ret<1) {
    ret = connel_machine_deafen(cmkbd, 1);
    CONNEL_DINFO("connel_machine_deafen(cmkbd, 1) returned %d\n", ret);
  }
}
}}}
```

Table 5.36

```
{{{  END
/* END */
ret = connel_close(cscr);
CONNEL_DINFO("connel_close(cscr) returned %d\n", ret);
ret = connel_close(cpipe[1]);
CONNEL_DINFO("connel_close(cpipe[1]) returned %d\n", ret);
ret = connel_close(cpipe[0]);
CONNEL_DINFO("connel_close(cpipe[0]) returned %d\n", ret);
ret = connel_close(ckbd);
CONNEL_DINFO("connel_close(ckbd) returned %d\n", ret);
}}}
```

Table 5.37

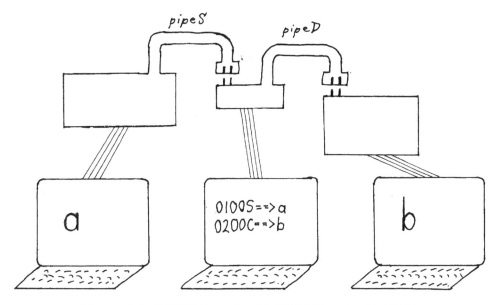

Figure 5.1: SERVER==(>SOCKSPY==(>CLIENT

```
-- sockspy
VAL INT DISCONNECTED IS 0 :
VAL INT CONNECTING IS 1 :
VAL INT READING IS 2 :
VAL INT SPY.BREAK IS 0 :
VAL INT SPY.SERVER IS 1 :
VAL INT SPY.CLIENT IS 2 :
VAL TYPE connecting IS -1 :
VAL TYPE disconnecting IS -2 :
VAL COMMANDSTRING exit IS "exit" :
...   PROC sockspy(CHAN OF ANY kbd, scr, pipeS, pipeD, VAL BOOL isnotext)
...   main program together with client(s) of pipeD
}}}
```

Table 5.38: View of sockspy.occ in origami (top comments removed)

The exhibits of code for this and following programs will focus on the pseudocode. The C code is very bulky, and follows the pseudocode in essential organization. I will touch the "high spots" and new features of the C in passing. The actual C code is available as part of the Connel source distribution, plus the special header file `LAZMcmnt.h`.

5.4.1 Coding details of sockspy

The server and its connel (`pipeS`) are started first; then `sockspy` starts, connects to `pipeS` as a client, and starts the diagnostic connel `pipeD` as a server; finally, the original client connects to `pipeD`. The `pipeD` connel "looks like" a direct `pipeS` connection to the client (or clients: for clients can terminate and new ones start in the quasi-OS behavior described above for `tapper`).

Not shown in the pseudocode is the calling sequence of `sockspy`: `sockspy <pipeSname> <pipeDname> [--notext]` where the names are of the SOCKLOCAL connels (sockets or named pipes) in the file system. `pipeS` must pre-exist and `pipeD` will be created. `--notext` resets the Boolean `doText` to FALSE.

Looking at Table 5.38, a new state machine is seen: the spy state, which can be SPY.BREAK, SPY.SERVER, or SPY.CLIENT. This refers to `sockspy`'s very simple operation, which when a client is connected merely captures data from either side, one byte at a time, and passes it to the other. The last sender of data (server or client) then determines SPY.SERVER or SPY.CLIENT. The other state, SPY.BREAK, refers to times when no client is connected.

Table 5.39 includes a non-occam pseudocode innovation which is related to the actual behavior of `connel_select`: the `ALTALL` block, which is merely a `PRI ALT` block in which *all the ready branches are executed in sequence*. This is actually natural for most implementations of `select`, since they return a bitmap showing every branch that is ready. Since `wasConnectedD` and `triggerD` refer only to the last (`pipeD`) branch, the `ALTALL` is actually substantially equivalent to an ordinary `PRI ALT`, but is slightly more efficient, and corresponds to the `sockspy.c` code as it actually exists.

Another minor violation of the occam standard is in the CHAN formals, of which `pipeS` and `pipeD` are bidirectional. I finesse this by the `connel.machine` definitions which split away an input channel, leaving the formals for use only for output. This also follows what actually happens in the C code.

The argument `--notext` is expressed as `isnotext`; there is a compile parameter DEBUG seen in the C code also. A new Connel call is introduced here: `connel_timebase`, which reads a clock value to `connel_timeout_t sctstart`, using its pointer. This is represented by `INT tstart` in the pseudocode.

```
{{{  PROC sockspy(CHAN OF ANY kbd, scr, pipeS, pipeD, VAL BOOL isnotext)
PROC sockspy(CHAN OF ANY kbd, scr, pipeS, pipeD, VAL BOOL isnotext)
  CHAN OF ANY pipeSin IS connel.machine(pipeS) :
  CHAN OF ANY pipeDin IS connel.machine(pipeD) :
  VAL BOOL doText IS (NOT isnotext) :
  TIMER clock :
  INT tstart : -- time
  INT pstateD :
  INT discobufferind :
  [1024]BYTE discobuffer : -- for when disconnected down
  INT spy.state : -- state machine tracking
  BYTE requestK, requestS : -- flow data 1 byte at a time
  TYPE requestD : -- BYTE, or out-of-band "connecting" "disconnecting"
  BOOL notQuiet, disconnectedD, notdone :
  SEQ
     ...  setup
    WHILE notdone
      BOOL wasConnectedD, triggerD :
      SEQ
        wasConnectedD := NOT disconnectedD -- recorded at top of loop!
        triggerD := FALSE -- if TRUE by pipeD loopend, start will happen
        ALTALL -- this is a PRI ALT that does all its ready branches
          kbd ? requestK
            ... kbd response
          pipeSin ? requestS
            ... pipeS response
          pipeDin ? requestD -- can be connecting or disconnecting
            ... pipeD response
    -- deafen machines and close connels
}}}
```

Table 5.39

```
{{{  setup
pstateD := DISCONNECTED
clock ? tstart
discobufferind := 0
notQuiet := DEBUG -- compile parameter
requestK, requestS, requestD := '#', '#', TYPE '#'
spy.state := SPY.BREAK -- state
disconnectedD := TRUE
-- turn on machines here; do listen and read_start (kbd and pipeS)
-- and connect_start (pipeD); can't be connected until ALT
pstateD := CONNECTING -- assume success
notdone := TRUE -- assume success (does NOT imply pipeD client ready)
}}}
```

Table 5.40

```
{{{  kbd response
SEQ
  IF
    VALID.K(kbd)
      notdone := (requestK <> 'x')
    FINISHED.K(kbd)
      notdone := FALSE -- SHOULD NEVER HAPPEN
    TRUE
      SKIP
  spy.state := SPY.BREAK
}}}
```

Table 5.41

The index `discobufferind` points into a 1024-byte array that absorbs input from the server if there is currently no client to send it to. The other state machines are obvious: `spy.state` is at `SPY.BREAK` because no client is yet attached; `disconnectedD` is TRUE for the same reason.

A comment refers to a section of C code that starts the machines running, even before any client has necessarily communicated. Then `pstateD` turns to CONNECTING and `notdone` (assuming success) is TRUE. The support of `pstateD`, which harks back to `pstate[i]` in `tapper` and `catch.c`, is actually not needed here, as current and former values of `disconnectedD` will serve the same purpose.

Harking back to Table 5.39, a WHILE `notdone` loop is found and two Booleans, `wasConnectedD` and `triggerD`, are declared for every loop instance. As mentioned above, they relate to activity of `pipeD`, which can input the two out-of-band values, `connecting` and `disconnecting`. To the C code these amount to signals, each handled in its own way. Most important at the top of the loop is that `wasConnectedD` gives the connectedness state of `pipeD` *at this time*, before the `connel_select` fires. This is FALSE if `pstateD` is CONNECTING and TRUE if it is READING. The state of DISCONNECTED is excluded by `notdone` because under normal operation either a `connel_connect_start` or a `connel_read_start` has just succeeded. (The `connel_connect_start` happens as soon as a disconnection is detected, returning immediately, requiring following selects to try patiently for a new client.)

Immediately after this comes the ALTALL block which occupies the rest of the WHILE loop. It responds to input on keyboard or from server (`pipeS`) or client (`pipeD`) connel. For keyboard or server this input is a byte, but for client if CONNECTING it is either a connection or a disconnection, and if READING it is either a byte or a disconnection.

Table 5.41 shows the response to a local keystroke. For the sake of pseudocode, FINISHED.K is introduced to refer to the successful `finish` output of `CONNEL_FINISH(cs, 0, finish)` where 0 is the bit index of `kbd`. VALID.K refers to `finish&&ckbd->c_state`, the normal result in this case. The only result of a keystroke, other than a quit signal, is to flip the spy state to SPY.BREAK, which can cause a republication of the time in the report stream if, as normally, `notQuiet` is FALSE.

Table 5.42 is the response to communication on the server connel `pipeS`. From the point of view of `pipeS`, `sockspy` is a client, so it merely gets bytes. VALID.S is always expected to be TRUE because the alternative is a server crash. Within that, the first IF block shows a normal publication, verbose if `notQuiet`, bare (normal) otherwise. The result of a TRUE `doText` (not shown) is to publish, where the byte is ASCII, the character itself after the hex expression which is always published. This enhances readability and causes a linebreak when a newline is received.

The second IF block tests the **other** connel, and if connected it repeats the received byte to the client. If not, it tries to feed the new datum into `discobuffer` for later transmittal. If that overflows, `sockspy` is terminated by `notdone := FALSE`. Not shown in the pseudocode is the normal preparation for the next ALTALL by calling `connel_read_start` for the next input byte.

The final ALT response (Tables 5.43 through 5.45) is the most complex: `pipeD`. There are three IF blocks. The first one is like that of the `pipeS` branch but omits a VALID.D test because a client crash (or quit) is normal from the point of view of `sockspy`: it amounts to an out-of-band `disconnecting` signal. The second IF block (ampersand notation) captures a transition from connected to disconnected (here CHECK.CONNECTED.D is the inverse of the important C macro `CONNEL_IS_SERVER_CONNECTED(cpipeD)`). The third (`triggerD &`) IF block makes a distinction as to whether disconnection was found, and either (in C) calls `connel_connect_start` for the next client, or `connel_read_start` for the next input byte. In the former case, SERVER.DISCONNECT refers to the important C cleanup macro `CONNEL_SERVER_DISCONNECT(cpipeD)`.

Table 5.44 refers to a `pipeD` ALTALL win. `finish` should always pass even if a client disconnects. In C, some code involving `int hereconnectD = CONNEL_IS_SERVER_CONNECTED(cpipeD);` `if (disconnectedD || !hereconnectD) {` accomplishes the same purpose as the pseudocode. At this point, `disconnectedD` refers to the previous state of `pipeD`, before the select, and `!hereconnectD` refers to the state introduced by the select. This supports the three-way branch shown in the pseudocode.

Just disconnected state is referred to by the pseudocode out-of-band re-

```
{{{  pipeS response
SEQ
  notdone := FALSE
  VALID.S(pipeS) & SEQ
    notdone := TRUE
    IF
      notQuiet
        SEQ
          TIME.COMMENT(scr, clock, tstart, "INPUT S byte\n")
          BYTE.VERBOSE.COMMENT(scr, doText, requestS)
      TRUE
        SEQ
          (spy.state <> SPY.SERVER) & SEQ
            scr ! '\n'
            TIME.COMMENT(scr, clock, tstart, "S==>")
            spy.state := SPY.SERVER
          BYTE.BARE.COMMENT(scr, doText, requestS)
    IF
      NOT disconnectedD
        SEQ
          pipeD ! requestS
          notQuiet & OUTPUT.VERBOSE.COMMENT.D(scr)
      discobufferind < 1024 -- AND disconnectedD
        SEQ
          (discobufferind = 0) & SEQ
            BUFFER.WARNING(scr)
            spy.state := SPY.BREAK
          discobuffer[discobufferind] := requestS
          discobufferind := discobufferind + 1
      TRUE -- full buffer AND disconnectedD
        SEQ
          BUFFER.FULL.WARNING(scr)
          spy.state := SPY.BREAK -- not really needed
          notdone := FALSE
}}}
```

Table 5.42

```
{{{  pipeD response
SEQ
  IF
    FINISHED.D(pipeD)
      ... normal response to a pipeD win
    TRUE
      ... unlikely ever to happen
  ((NOT CHECK.CONNECTED.D(requestD)) AND wasConnectedD) & SEQ
    SERVER.DISCONNECT(pipeD)
    disconnectedD := TRUE
    triggerD := TRUE
  -- triggerD means prepare for next ALT
  triggerD & SEQ
    (NOT disconnectedD) & SEQ
      pstateD := READING
      -- also read_start, which could turn disconnectedD to TRUE
    disconnectedD & SEQ
      SERVER.DISCONNECT(pipeD) -- OK if repeated
      pstateD := DISCONNECTED
      -- connect_start here, which if successful...
      pstateD := CONNECTING
}}}
```

Table 5.43

ception of **disconnecting**. Change from disconnected to connected state is referred to by the pseudocode out-of-band reception of **connecting**. Other receptions are in-band (state READING).

The reception of **connecting** is capable of dumping communications that were previously buffered in **discobuffer**. It then puts spy state into SPY.BREAK so as to make sure that a time stamp is published next reception. A READING reception causes a response similar to that of **pipeS**, described for Table 5.42, but in the other direction. It is always assumed that the output to **pipeS** is possible, because a server is not supposed to disconnect.

A failure of communication from the client is not supposed to happen, but if it does, **sockspy** shuts down.

Table 5.46 shows the main pseudocode program. It is an approximation to **sockspy** plus any client calls that fall in its lifetime, due to the fact that the OS in C is capable of an unlimited supply of clients. I reduce **pipeS** to a comment as an expression of the fact that it is supposed to pre-exist the **sockspy** call. As mentioned in Chapter 3 Table 3.1, **sockspy.c** includes not only the pseudocode **sockspy** member but also the preceding CHAN OF ANY pipeD : declaration, which is modeled by a **connel_create** call.

```
{{{  normal response to a pipeD win
-- hereconnectD := (requestD <> disconnecting)
IF
  requestD = disconnecting -- is now disconnected
    SEQ --DISCONNECTED
      disconnectedD := TRUE
      COMMENT.DISCONNECT.D(scr)
  disconnectedD -- was disconnected, is now connected
    SEQ -- CONNECTING
      disconnectedD := FALSE
      COMMENT.CONNECT.D(scr)
      wasConnectedD := TRUE -- revised to current value
      (discobufferind > 0) & SEQ -- need to dump buffer?
        pipeD ! [discobuffer FROM 0 FOR discobufferind]
        BUFFER.SENT.WARNING(scr)
        discobufferind := 0
      triggerD := TRUE
      spy.state := SPY.BREAK
  TRUE -- connected both before and after
    SEQ -- READING
      IF
        notQuiet
          SEQ
            TIME.COMMENT(scr, clock, tstart, "INPUT D byte\n")
            BYTE.VERBOSE.COMMENT(scr, doText, requestD)
        TRUE
          SEQ
            (spy.state <> SPY.CLIENT) & SEQ
              scr ! '\n'
              TIME.COMMENT(scr, clock, tstart, "C==>")
              spy.state := SPY.CLIENT
            BYTE.BARE.COMMENT(scr, doText, requestD)
      pipeS ! requestD
      notQuiet & OUTPUT.VERBOSE.COMMENT.S(scr)
      notdone := TRUE
      triggerD := TRUE
}}}
```

Table 5.44

```
{{{  unlikely ever to happen
SEQ
  INCONSISTENT.FINISH.WARNING(scr)
  spy.state := SPY.BREAK
  notdone := FALSE
}}}
```

Table 5.45

```
{{{  main program together with client(s) of pipeD
-- An external server and SOCKLOCAL pipeS precede sockspy run
-- CHAN OF ANY pipeS :
-- VAL BOOL DEBUG, isnotext :
-- The occam kbd and scr declarations are of two command windows
[2]CHAN OF ANY kbds, scrs :
-- the connel pipeD is LOCAL to the run of C sockspy
CHAN OF ANY pipeD : -- its creation is part of C sockspy
PAR
  -- sockspy runs on one window
  sockspy(kbds[0], scrs[0], pipeS, pipeD, isnotext)
  -- The 2nd PAR member corresponds to running programs in an OS
  -- The other window is for client(s) of pipeD
  COMMANDSTRING command : -- pseudocode
  SEQ
    kbds[1] ? command
    WHILE command <> exit
      SEQ
        command(kbds[1], scrs[1], pipeD)
        kbds[1] ? command
}}}
```

Table 5.46

5.4.2 Summary of sockspy

The function of **sockspy** is to publish data and timing flowing in both directions on a client/server SOCKLOCAL connel. Under normal conditions (**notQuiet** FALSE) it captures the time and begins a new line each time the direction of communication changes, and also after any local keystroke. Therefore some part of the transmission shown on the line can come considerably later than the time shown (but before the next time). Also published is information about connection and disconnection of the client.

The connels of **sockspy** are operated bytewise. For control transmissions and short data, as is typical in embedded robotics applications, the inefficiencies thus introduced are insignificant. Transmission speeds of server or client are probably not affected, because of system buffering, but a slight slowdown in response is possible, even on a fast OS, due to spinning through the Connel and IO calls.

The screen output of **sockspy** can be redirected, using **tee** and similar capturing tools. Standard scripting, in both Linux and Windows, is capable of quite complex operations involving **sockspy**, even including sequences of clients. It has been used for serious debugging of a proprietary UI-based robotics and control system.

5.5 Other sketches

The rest of the current applications of Connel were written as development aids for Connel itself, or for its graphics extension. They do not fit the "pseudocode first" model, though they have many useful and illustrative blocks of code that are usable in concerted application development. Therefore, in this section, I will sketch their high points with partial pseudocode, and expand the key techniques illustrated by them.

A better approach, not driven by haste and external requirements, would be to build a library of illustrative small applications, in the manner of traditional embedded processor sample code. Such a development could proceed in tandem with language or scripting work and actual embedded extensions to Connel. My hope is that we can put our heads together about such directions, but in the meantime this book will work from the current, admittedly inadequate state of things.

The main value of these sketches is in their illustration of Wide programming itself. Each one displays an "angle" that will be needed in the most general programming tasks. Unlike whole languages devised according to the Deep paradigm, the Wide approach (using Connel or other tools) is totally general in the problems it can deal with, and that means it is uniquely good for large projects and projects that will grow in unexpected directions.

5.5.1 Serial block communication—ttester and rtester

The two programs `ttester.c` and `rtester.c` are meant to communicate with one another across a real or virtual serial connection. This differs in three ways from the SOCKLOCAL connel used by `tapper` and `sockspy`:

(1) The connel must be established outside both communicating pieces, instead of being created by one of the pieces. This model is friendly to a connector that is outside the whole OS or even outside the hardware, and able to connect heterogeneous systems. But it always requires scripting or documenting an external setup procedure, which can include specifications starting with baud rate.

(2) Both sides of the communication are equivalent. There is no server/client distinction, and either side can start first. The downside is that if the sides do not shut down in tandem, behavior can be unpredictable or implementation-dependent, ranging from a kill upon next transmission to a buffering of unsent bytes (with later surprising results).

(3) There are no special, out-of-band "connecting" or "disconnecting" messages. Thus a **CHAN OF BYTE** is OK, and pass-through to or from STD connels **kbd** and **scr** is often possible. That is not an exact fit, however, and serial-to-tty issues differ slightly in every OS. Still, the serial model is very friendly to heterogeneous embedded pieces, even when the data is not actually passing through an RS232 connection.

As detailed in Chapter 3, Section 3.7, "Standard third party tools," the Linux command **stty** and the Windows command **MODE** enable you to set up the detailed specifications of a serial connection. That serial connection may be of hardware wires, or between two virtual machines (see [5]) or part of another hardware protocol.

The pseudocode of Table 5.47 is a summary, not complete, of the code in **ttester.c** and **rtester.c**. The C code permits keystroke input and uses an ALT or **connel_select** to arbitrate between **kbd** and **serial**, but this is code inherited from other programs when the lazy coder (myself) modified them for a speed test. The right way to call them never uses a keystroke during the run, but merely performs something like

./ttester 1 16384 10

in Linux and

RTESTER 2 16384 10

in Windows, to transmit 10 packets of 16384 bytes each across a serial connection that is **/dev/ttyS1** on the Linux side and **COM2** on the Windows side.

Though the **kbd** option is useless, the **connel_select** serves a purpose in demonstrating buffering. Running the **tester** pair with the verbosity of **rtester** adjusted to show each **serial** select win, using a large buffer size, it is seen (at least for a 9600 baud VMWare virtual serial connection) that there are many such wins before **finish** goes TRUE. The big read, in this case, comes across in batches of about 10 bytes. Each of them triggers the end of a **connel_select** block, but the **CONNEL_FINISH** macro returns **finish** TRUE only when all the data has arrived.

5.5.1.1 Summary of utility—large transmissions

The new feature here is the transmission of large blocks of data across a real channel. This differs from the design of the Satellite Receiver, detailed above, in that most of the large blocks in the Receiver were *virtually* transmitted using implied pointers. In real large-block transmissions, buffering and/or DMA usually play a big role, and this implies that efficiency analysis must consider two main types of cost: *fixed cost*, or the cost (especially time—latency) for

```
-- Global resources are:
-- Externally set up serial connection
-- VAL INT PKTSZ
-- VAL INT PKTCT
PROC ttester(CHAN OF ANY serial, VAL INT pktsz, pktct)
  [65536]BYTE bigbuf :
  BYTE thechar2 :
  CHAN OF BYTE in IS (CHAN OF BYTE) connel.machine(serial) :
  CHAN OF ANY out IS serial :
  ((pktsz>0) AND (pktct>0) AND (pktsz<=65536)) & SEQ
    SEQ i FROM 0 FOR pktct
      SEQ
        out ! [bigbuf FROM 0 FOR pktsz]
        in ? thechar2 -- actually uses an ALT
:
PROC rtester(CHAN OF ANY serial, VAL INT pktsz, pktct)
  [65536]BYTE bigbuf :
  VAL BYTE thechar2 IS '&' : -- never changes
  CHAN OF ANY in IS connel.machine(serial) :
  CHAN OF BYTE out IS (CHAN OF BYTE) serial :
  ((pktsz>0) AND (pktct>0) AND (pktsz<=65536)) & SEQ
    SEQ i FROM 0 FOR pktct
      SEQ
        in ? [bigbuf FROM 0 FOR pktsz] -- actually uses an ALT
        out ! thechar2
:
CHAN OF ANY serial : -- externally connected and set up
VAL INT pktsz IS PKTSZ :
VAL INT pktct IS PKTCT :
PAR
  ttester(serial, pktsz, pktct)
  rtester(serial, pktsz, pktct)
}}}
```

Table 5.47: Summary pseudocode for tester (top comments removed)

sending the first byte of the block, and *incremental cost*, or the cost (especially time—data rate) for sending each byte of the block after that.

Things can, of course, be more complicated than that (the time curve can have "elbows"), but most real channels can be summarized this way. `ttester` and `rtester` allow an experimental test to be carried out and are especially valuable when critiquing a specification, or the designer's understanding of a specification. Often latency and data rate behave oppositely: a hardware protocol that has the best data rate may have bad latency, and vice versa. Therefore fully acknowledged "point tests" of prospective channel technologies are valuable as part of the First Wave, and "keeping up" with the results thus obtained is valuable as a critique of later programming.

5.5.2 Timer waits—test8out and test8in, and timer ALT

The `connel_timeout_t` struct uses two 32-bit integers to express time in seconds and microseconds. As in occam, the Connel timers can be used in three ways:

(1) A call to `connel_timebase` yields a current time value. It is relative to other current time values in the same program run. These are clock times, not program run times. Once you get a single timebase, all other times are relative to that, so it can be used to construct timeouts.

(2) A call to `connel_sleep` blocks until as soon as possible after the specified time. This is a sleep *for* a time, not a sleep *until* a time. If something equivalent to the occam

```
clock ? AFTER time
```

is desired, its target must be constructed using `connel_timesub` to calculate the sleep from the result of `connel_timebase`. If the time is negative, it is treated as zero, which is NOT quite the same as returning immediately: the OS swaps the program out and immediately puts it in the queue to run again.

(3) A time in the second formal parameter of `connel_select` is an ALT timeout, which like (2) is defined as waiting *for* the time and not *until* the time. Again, this is unlike the occam usage. If the second formal is negative or zero, this instance of `connel_select` will return immediately, whether or not any other branches of the ALT are ready.

The occam ALT branch

```
TRUE & SKIP
```

(which always returns immediately if nothing else is ready) can be emulated by specifying a timer branch (second formal parameter) that is negative, referring to the past. Here "past" and "present/future" are based on the sign of the relative `connel_timeout_t` struct, which is always equal to the sign of its `ct_seconds` member, because the `ct_microseconds` member is always nonnegative. Thus "1 microsecond past" is denoted by `ct_seconds = -1` and `ct_microseconds = 999999`.

The pair `test8out` and `test8in` operate by sending and receiving in a different rhythm. The sender `test8out` generates INT64s, which increment by 8, and are broken up into an 8-byte code in a peculiar fashion (see the library `eightlib.c`). It pauses a certain amount of time between each burst of 8. The receiver `test8in` receives one byte at a time, pausing another amount of time (presumably less than 1/8 that of the sender) between bytes. The receiver is also capable, from time to time, of printing a summary of what it has recently received. A `connel_select` is used by both to allow a single keyboard kill signal.

Thus, the `test8` pair exhibits both (1) and (2) of the three timer uses listed above. However, it does not provide an example of the timer ALT (the select timeout). Table 5.48 shows the bare bones of a timer ALT (unrelated to `test8`) imposing a timeout on an awaited keystroke. The arrangement shows a "comb" of timeouts, with fixed spacing of `ctdel`, which as time passes will always generate timeout wins unless the keystrokes are "screaming" to such an extent that there is always a keystroke ready. The part at the end, which prevents a negative `ctsub`, is not really necessary.

5.5.2.1 Accuracy of timers

The use of Connel timers, like those of the OSs on which Connel is built, is always approximate. In standard OSs, which are not "real-time" or embedded CPUs, the timer resolution is usually rather coarse, typically between 1 to 4 milliseconds (Linux) to up to 14 milliseconds (Windows). In my experience, the tendency is for the resolution to *degrade* (become longer) with later versions of an OS. For example, around 2008, a Linux distribution my employer was working with went from 1000 ticks per second to 250 ticks per second.

A serial connection at 115200 baud is more than ten times faster than this, and other interrupt-based communication is even faster. Therefore, if high timer responsiveness is needed, it is best to "farm out the job" to heterogeneous embedded hardware which these days can be very cheap. I will give more details on this in the embedded chapter.

Very precise time *recording* can be done by using the cycle-counting capability of most chips, e.g. RDTSC in the X86. This is not yet supported by the Connel calls, but can easily be added in OS-specific code by the programmer.

```
connel_timeout_t sct, sctnext, sctdel, sctsub;
connel_timeout_t *ct = &sct;
connel_timeout_t *ctnext = &sctnext;
connel_timeout_t *ctdel = &sctdel;
connel_timeout_t *ctsub = &sctsub;
connel_set_t scs;
connel_set_t *cs = &scs;
int notdone;
/* initialize notdone, cs, ctdel, ctsub, ctnext, etc. */
while (notdone) {
  unsigned long newready = 0;
  int kbdhit = 0;
  int timedout = 0;
  int ret = connel_select(cs, ctsub, &newready);
  newready |= cs->cs_ready;
  if (ret > 0) {
    if (newready&1) {
      unsigned long finish = 0;
      CONNEL_FINISH(cs, 0, finish);
      if (finish&&ckbd->c_state) {
        kbdhit = 1; /* = kbdhit := TRUE in pseudocode */
      } else if (finish) {
        notdone = 0; /* Input keystroke failed */
      }
    }
  } else if (!ret) { /* No keystroke; it timed out */
    timedout = 1; /* = timedout := TRUE in pseudocode */
    ret = connel_timeadd(ctnext, ctdel);
  }
  ret = connel_timebase(ct);
  memcpy(ctsub, ctnext, sizeof(connel_timeout_t));
  ret = connel_timesub(ctsub, ct);
  if (ctsub->ct_seconds < 0) {
    memset(ctsub, 0, sizeof(connel_timeout_t));
  }
}
```

Table 5.48: Connel usage in code snippet for timer ALT

5.5.2.2 Summary of utility—timers

A timer is very useful in its place, but TIMERS ARE DANGEROUS IF OVERUSED. This is because a timeout makes a state machine unpredictable, and the effects of a timeout propagate through other parts of the program, causing remote effects that can be nearly impossible to diagnose. If timeouts are used, as in the Orchard Sensors, then *the entire program must be written with timeouts treated as a normal branch,* as opposed to the Deep Programming habit of sweeping them under the rug as "exceptions."

Other, less dangerous, uses are often overlooked. *Recording* is very valuable and almost cost-free, and frequently it makes sense to add time members to any packet with a significant history, because the programs that use them will never stop being developed. The recorded times will then lead straight to the diagnosis of any bottlenecks. *Smoothing* is done by a combination of timeouts and buffering: it imposes a substantially fixed latency on all data throughput, and thus eliminates "hiccups." This fixed latency is forced to be greater than the maximum latency ever imposed by program flow, and must be carefully supported by output hardware, as in video and music. *Spacing* can be imposed on a project piece that has a tendency to be "lumpy" and deal with infrequent big batches of not-very-urgent throughput. This is accomplished by inserting frequent waits within the loops working through the "lumps." This controls hiccups from the other end, and is friendly to a mix of widely different real-time response requirements.

5.5.3 Graphics—gsflip

A final sketch in this chapter deals with an early, developmental version of the graphics slave promised to some Kickstarter backers. In addition to standard Connel, this uses the `connel_g.c` library mentioned in Chapter 3 Section 3.4. Though I will not give full details here, as some of it is still under development, the shape of things is already clear enough to be instructive.

In both Windows and Linux, the graphics machinery behaves like an independent piece, notifying the program hosting it in an asynchronous fashion. But there are great differences in the details of how this is handled. Surprisingly, a Connel approach makes it possible to get the same responsive behavior despite these details, and even to use **exactly** the same 2D array format for the color frame buffer.

The Connel approach is to make graphics responsiveness a "special case" of `connel_select`, somewhat like timeout responsiveness. Thus, the Connel application with graphics (like `gsflip.c` and the coming graphics slave) has an

```
[HEIGHT][WIDTH][4]BYTE image :
PAR j FROM 0 FOR HEIGHT -- start from top and go down
  [WIDTH][4]BYTE line IS image[j] :
  PAR i FROM 0 FOR WIDTH -- start from left and go right
    [4]BYTE pixel IS line[i] :
    PAR
      pixel[0] := blue(i, j)
      pixel[1] := green(i, j)
      pixel[2] := red(i, j)
      pixel[3] := (BYTE)0 -- unused
```

Table 5.49: Graphics fill

extra response branch each time select fires. Coding adapted to each operating system does "painting" and other operations immediately upon responding to this stimulus.

In the case of Linux, upon recommendation of William Swanson, I use the XCB library for the X Windows system. This requires, in Ubuntu, that the version be at least 10.04 (Lucid). The connel_g library in this case calls xcb_get_file_descriptor which yields a special file descriptor for graphics events, to which C select can respond. However, connel_select does not expose this special descriptor as yet another machine, but instead treats it as a response that must be checked every time. The extra effort involved in this is insignificant: the test is

```
if (cs->xcbisset) DO_GRAPHICSSTUFF;
```

and if there have been no graphics events it just branches past.

In the case of Windows, no choice of graphics toolset is required; it is part of the default OS. It uses messages and callbacks, and within connel_select the Windows code calls MsgWaitForMultipleObjects instead of WaitForMultipleObjects. As with Linux, every time the select fires there is a check made for messages, calling connel_g_peekmsgs() which uses the Windows tool PeekMessage() to catch, translate, and dispatch each message. There may be no messages, but if there are, the Windows OS code carries out callbacks to messages like WM_PAINT, and this accomplishes the same thing as the xcbisset graphics branch in Linux.

The upshot of all this is that a graphics window can be opened as a slave under either Windows or Linux, and rectangular subsets of it can be updated at full speed (currently the rectangular subset is the full window). **The same array in C works to color the pixels the same way in both Windows and Linux.** The pseudocode for it is in Table 5.49.

The extreme degree of parallelism in this pseudocode is justified by the fact that a PAR that does not involve communication can always be implemented either in parallel or sequentially. The mix of PARs and SEQs will, for example, differ depending on the graphics card in a real computer. In `gsflip` where the buffer is being filled in by the C routine `fillimage()`, all the PARs are replaced by SEQs (i.e. `for` loops or expanded code), but it is possible that optimization, by the compiler or by the CPU, is operating "under the radar" to restore some of the PARs.

5.5.3.1 Some code blocks

Table 5.50 shows the commentary that describes how to compile and link graphics programs, and Table 5.51 shows the outermost structure of the simple graphics slave, gsflip.

Table 5.50's comments are quite clear, if somewhat dated. Both `WINgs2` and `XCBgs2` are now replaced by `gsflip`, which contains the code for both OSs. And `gxconnel` is a name for *object* files compiled from `connel.c` with the modifier `CONNEL_GRFX`. The Windows linking is done in such a way as to have a standard appearance, like command line linking, without using special non-standard Windows calls.

Several features of graphics coding are shown in Tables 5.51 and 5.52. The macro GODEAFIFGONE is an example of what could be done more generally to reduce the prolixity of Connel code. The global variables support `fillimage()` and (for Windows) the Window (callback) Procedure, both of which are outside `main()`. The `fillimage()` code *is completely independent of OS* and corresponds exactly to Table 5.49, except for a single global variable, `global_flip`, which changes `blue()`, `green()`, and `red()` after each external input to `gsflip`. The `connel_grfx_t` struct and its pointer, and the Booleans `notDone` and `going`, are not really restricted to Windows, it is just that they must be declared before the callback in Windows, while in Linux they are declared at the top of `main()`. However, Booleans `notInit` and `notDC` are really for Windows only.

5.5.3.2 Summary of structure

The structure of `gsflip` is rather simple, and is applicable to any graphics slave. Because of the tight involvement with OS and graphics hardware, it is not expanded into two (or more) PAR members, but is treated as a single piece with a responsive ALT to deal with the graphics. Table 5.53 is a pseudocode summary, omitting some details, which are fully supplied in the C code and the supporting operating system calls.

```
* Windows code credit:
* From winprog.org/tutorial/simple_window.html
* Substantially changed by LJD.
* Different from standard code as used thus far
* Fixed so that debug stuff appears in a debug window
* How to make the GUI code run without the non-standard main
* int WINAPI WinMain(HINSTANCE hInstance, HINSTANCE hPrevInstance,
*    LPSTR lpCmdLine, int nCmdShow)
* Compile normally but link differently:
* cl /c WINgs2.c
* cl WINgs2.obj ..\LAZM\connel_g.obj ..\LAZM\gxconnel.obj \
* /link /entry:mainCRTStartup /subsystem:windows User32.lib Gdi32.lib
* And add the lines:
*   int nCmdShow = 1;
*   HINSTANCE hInstance = GetModuleHandle(0);
*
* Linux code credit:
* XCB application drawing an updating bitmap in a window
* Inspired by the xcb black rectangle in a window example
* Copyright 2010 V. R. Sanders, released under the MIT licence
* Substantially adapted by LJD.
* compile with:
*   gcc -c XCBgs2.c
*   gcc -Wall -lxcb-icccm -lxcb -lxcb-image -o XCBgs2 \
*     XCBgs2.o ../LAZM/connel_g.o ../LAZM/gxconnel.o
* Bug fixed (i,j swapped), color scheme changed. LJD 8/24/2013
* Further development LJD 8/28/2013
*
* LJD 8/21-29/2013 Slave Flipper
* LJD 9/10/2013 uses gxconnel
*/
```

Table 5.50: Commentary on gsflip.c

The key structure is a message event (shown) which in both Linux and Windows signals content in a queue of messages that is consumed and interpreted in each OS (hidden in `HANDLE.MESSAGES()` in the pseudocode). This is a check on `pb->xcbisset` in Linux and a call to `connel_g_peekmsgs()` in Windows. In each case, zero messages is a possibility.

The differences between Windows and Linux/XCB are hinted at by the comments involving CREATE, PAINT, CLOSE, and DESTROY. These in Linux are handled in the normal way, when the message is found. In Windows, the `PeekMessages` loop in `connel_g_peekmsgs` makes OS calls which in turn make callbacks that are defined in our Windows Procedure. These are defaults except for the messages WM_CREATE, WM_PAINT, WM_CLOSE, and

```
#ifndef CONNEL_LINUX
#define CONNEL_WINDOWS
#else
#undef CONNEL_WINDOWS
#endif
#define CONNEL_GRFX
#ifdef CONNEL_WINDOWS
#include "..\LAZM\connel.h"
#include "..\LAZM\connel_g.h"
#else
#include "../LAZM/connel.h"
#include "../LAZM/connel_g.h"
#endif

#define GODEAFIFGONE do {\
if (listening&&(!going)) {\
  ret = connel_machine_deafen(cmkbd, 0);\
  CONNEL_DINFO("connel_machine_deafen(cmkbd, 0) returned %d\n", ret);\
  if (ret<1) {\
    ret = connel_machine_deafen(cmkbd, 1);\
    CONNEL_DINFO("connel_machine_deafen(cmkbd, 1) returned %d\n", ret);\
  }\
  listening = 0;\
}\
} while(0)

#define THEWIDTH 512
#define THEHEIGHT 384

...  global variables (mostly Windows)

...  fillimage(unsigned char *p, int width, int height)
...  // Step 4: the Window Procedure (Windows)
...  int main(int argc, char *argv[])
}}}
```

Table 5.51: Top fold of gsflip.c, with commentary removed

```
{{{ global variables (mostly Windows)
int global_flip = 0;
#ifdef CONNEL_WINDOWS
int notInit = 1;
int notDC = 1;
int notDone = 1;
int going = 1;
connel_grfx_t cgb;
/* HDC cgb.hDC; device context of window */
/* HDC cgb.hMemDC; compatible DIB device context */
/* HGDIOBJ cgb.hOld; storage space for old HBITMAP */
/* HBITMAP cgb.hBitmap; the one for the DIB */
/* VOID *cgb.imagebits; return place for image */
connel_grfx_t *pb = &cgb; /* GLOBAL BASE POINTER */
#endif /* CONNEL_WINDOWS */
}}}
```

Table 5.52: Globals depending on OS

WM_DESTROY which include the code we write to accomplish those tasks. (Actually WM_CLOSE just triggers a call which sets up the OS callback to WM_DESTROY.) The final result is just the same as the responsive check-and-branch of the Linux code.

It is not incredibly clear why Windows took this extremely convoluted way of doing a simple select, but it is worth noting that responsive Object Oriented systems always seem to implement this callback approach, often using nesting callbacks that reach a great depth. Its only Deep advantage seems to be that state machine details can be hidden from the main loop.

In any case, Table 5.53 is a basic design template that can easily be expanded to any graphics slave capability. One merely replaces `kbd ? signal` with as many independent inputs to the ALT as the project needs, and allows each independent input to provide what information the graphics needs to revise its picture. Then `g.mapimage` is refined to notify the display machinery to revise the picture, often restricting its rectangular BitBlt area to just what is needed. (In the C code, the WINDOWPACKET has a pointer to `image`, so from the pseudocode point of view `g.mapimage` sees `image` and the connection to the graphics hardware as globals. Failing to show this explicitly is not good pseudocode design practice, but this design is dictated by the OS, and the pseudocode is only descriptive.)

Expanding `fillimage` and `g.mapimage` to be responsive to graphics commands is a completely general approach. It can be used for vector or for raster graphics, with or without anti-aliasing and remapping of the picture to a dif-

```
-- Approximate pseudocode for gsflip
-- Global resources are:
-- CHAN OF EVENT msg
-- CHAN OF ANY kbd
-- INT HEIGHT
-- INT WIDTH
[HEIGHT][WIDTH][4]BYTE image :
WINDOWPACKET b :
BOOL notdone :
SEQ
  g.winsetup(b) -- includes CREATE
  fillimage(image)
  g.mapimage(b, FALSE)
  g.winshow(b, WIDTH, HEIGHT)
  notdone := TRUE
  WHILE notdone
    BYTE signal :
    BOOL grfx :
    SEQ
      ALT
        kbd ? signal
          SEQ
            notdone := (signal <> endsignal)
            notdone & SEQ
              fillimage(image)
              g.mapimage(b, TRUE)
        msg ? grfx
          SKIP
      HANDLE.MESSAGES(b, image) -- includes PAINT
  g.close.and.destroy(b) -- includes CLOSE and DESTROY
}}}
```

Table 5.53: Summary pseudocode for gsflip (top comments removed)

ferent pixel density. The only restriction is the usual buffering requirement, that the part of **image** that is being modified by graphics commands should be distinct from the part that is being transmitted to the picture. In this code it's single-buffered; image modification and image mapping to the display are in a SEQ. A double-buffering scheme can easily be designed if great responsiveness is needed.

5.5.3.3 Summary of utility—graphics slave

The ability to write a graphics slave with this simple structure is one of the key rewards of Wide programming. It unwinds the most hideous code tangles, the ones dictated by a Graphical User Interface which is being forced to "branch out" its options by disorganized and unexpected user needs. It does this by striking at the root of bad GUI design: the fact that a GUI entangles both command input and informational output in the same interface.

The user interface of the graphics slave is output only. Its input, whether program-controlled or user-controlled, is decoupled from this. Not only does this disentangle the code. **It also frees the entire project from the crippling requirement that everything be an "instant response" to screen stimuli,** adapted to an attention span around fifteen seconds. This brain-damaging feature of the standard GUI is quite absent from programs using a graphics slave.

The graphics slave can have a long life, because some of its ALT inputs can be managed by server connels. This means that whole programs and pieces of hardware can be disconnected and reconnected, with inputs and controls that are quite different from each other. This is very friendly to science and complex control such as robotics. Think of it as "server stuff" that, traditionally, "you've got to do with scripts," avoiding a GUI because it's under active development and frequent design change. Now you can have immediate graphics too, and it won't react back on the rest of your work, tying it in knots.

5.6 References

[1] Choisser, John P., and John O. Foster: *The XT-AT Handbook.* Annabooks, San Diego, 1989–1992. Booklet (3.5" by 6"), 94 pgs.

[2] Dickson, Lawrence: "Transparent Analogy as a Foundation for Language," 6 April 2006. http://www.tjoccam.com/tacliwhp.pdf

[3] Libes, Don: "The Expect Home Page," NIST, 2009. This contains links to other references. http://expect.sourceforge.net

[4] Matthew, Neil, and Richard Stones: *Beginning Linux Programming.* Wrox Press Ltd, Birmingham, UK, 1997.

[5] VMWare serial connections between virtual machines, Fusion http://communities.vmware.com/message/748577#748577

Wide Embedded Programming

6

Abstract

This chapter concludes the book with an introduction to the kind of computing whose capabilities are completely general. "Embedded" computing is that computing which is part of the design of things that are not computers. It therefore avoids the self-referential, eating-its-own-tail nature of abstract "computer science," and responds to the broad variety of every other kind of science. I go beyond Connel here, and show how Wide techniques flatten out the requirements of all such projects, reducing them to tractable pieces. It doesn't matter how recent, how high-speed or how big-sized the "core" is. The arcane alphabet soup that refers to responsive driver hardware is not an alien specialty, but just offers more examples of what is done everywhere in Wide programming.

6.1   Embedded essence: time flow

From your phones, your vehicles, your household appliances up and out to space probes on Mars and Titan, embedded programming is the cutting edge not only of computing but of much of science and economics. Here, I believe, Wide Programming will stand or fall. In fact, the Wide task is to pull all that back from a mystery land of confusing icons and place it before the scientific mind in a working form as clear and understandable as a street map.

The world of embedded programming may seem so various that it cannot be conquered by a single approach. But that appearance is caused by the rush to complexity in all matters of computing. Gregg Keizer calls this a "complexity tax," and observes it bringing down Microsoft (see [7]). If you focus on the *results* that must come from embedded programming (that is, programming that supports a design with a purpose beyond information passing), then a clear common ground appears. In all actions in the real world, time flow is of critical importance. All other causes and consequences that any embedded program must deal with are mounted, so to speak, on a scaffolding of time.

6.1.1 Design principles

Each embedded program, or piece thereof, is built on the basics of a state machine in the real world. The three components they all share are:

1. Input or stimulus
2. Computation over time
3. Output or actuation

I use the term *input* to refer to some state imposed by the outside world that is digital and in the computer's address space, and thus is of the same programmable nature as the computation of step 2. Similarly, *output* is a state imposed on the outside world that is digital and from the computer's address space. Each of these is a **copy** from/to the outside world to/from the computer, and therefore forms a connection between computing inside and computing outside.

By contrast, I use the term *stimulus* to refer to any other kind of state imposed by the outside world, such as timing or analog voltage. And *actuation* is state imposed on the outside world, not just timing or voltage, but any microscopic or macroscopic physical effect. These are *at the same time* subject to the laws of programming and to the laws of physics beyond the hardware of the computer. This is not copy but **cause and consequence**, and here the physics of the external world takes complete precedence over the logic of the computer. The external world doesn't care about the state of the computer, but the computer must care about the state of the external world, or it will fail of its purpose.

Thus the critical considerations, at both ends, are power and time. Usually, power is adjustable using good engineering, since the power controlled by a switch can be any multiple of the power needed to throw the switch. That leaves time. THE ESSENTIAL FEATURE OF EMBEDDED PROGRAMMING IS SUCCESSFUL HANDLING OF TIMING CONSTRAINTS.

Notice that this implies that embedded computing can be harmed by its strengths as well as by its lacks. It's quite frequent for quality to degrade because the program is too fast for the physical device to respond properly. This includes instant changes in values, which can be alien to smooth higher derivatives that are needed by the physics.

6.1.2 Time coherence

Typically, a developer on a modern system tends to be defeated before he starts by the sheer weight of accumulated technology. This causes him to "sheer off"—either toward minor projects using standard embedded toolsets, which are designed to be introductory and not to be the whole story, or toward "app" or "web" development that approaches the programming equivalent of a fill-in-the-blanks test in the academic world. Is it really true that all the good stuff has already been done, and the individual developer is like a placeholder in a decadent school of philosophy, making minor adjustments in a huge thing far beyond his control?

To show why not, I have to unwind where we're at. When you spin the little cloud of icons on your smartphone, you are doing *magic*. What does it do? Everything, and incoherently, and instantly. It acts in a hyperactive city where every place is the same, and everything is getting more itty bitty all the time. Its design is based on psychology.

However, if you lift your eyes beyond the handheld flat screen, you discover that the world is big. The project sketches in this book reflect that, even the 21-sensor orchard. (Try going to every tree even in such a small orchard.) The Kicksat cloud, even viewed from the mother ship's point of view (with delta orbital elements of a few miles per hour), gets very large. Its path is bigger. The resource of "flyover country" is unimaginably huge—you will hail your nearest neighbor across a hill—but it bears no fruit for you, unless you are farming or prospecting or fracking, or doing something fundamental like that.

But someone is doing something fundamental like that, whether robotics or resource surveys. When you make those connected pieces work together, you are doing *science*. What do the pieces do? A simple coherent thing, or list of things, over time, and sensing or moving a weight of reality over a distance. The design of the pieces is based on nature.

Boeing made a lunar rover in 1971, before there were personal computers. Like a classic car, it implied a true embedded program, even if little or no electronics was used. Its connected and nested pieces went from cause to consequence over time, responded to reality, and moved it over a distance. Only last year (2013), after forty-two years, was its successor finally deployed, and by China. I want to return to that kind of thing. After the long Moore's Law hiatus, I think its time has come.

6.1.3 Three physical constants

Response of a mechanical or electrical system over time is usually controlled by a set of three constants, whose dimensions are related as X, XT, and XT^2, where T is time (Table 6.1).

More precisely, $X = \frac{P}{Q}$, where P is a kind of "push" and Q is a kind of "quantity," always chosen so that the product PQ is energy. Thus the dimensions become, respectively, $\frac{P}{Q}$, $\frac{P}{Q/T}$, and $\frac{P}{Q/T^2}$. The denominators are respectively "quantity", "quantity per unit time", and "quantity per unit time per unit time".

The analogy is complete between the mechanical responses and the electrical responses, and they follow exactly the same equations. (There is a third set of related mechanical responses, in which torque takes the place of force and angle takes the place of distance, which also fits the same exact analogy, and is often of even greater use in mechanical design.) These responses are always calculated in any actuator design, and the success of such designs depends on getting them right. That means the output "push" (whether voltage, force, or torque) must have the right curve, including the right smoothness. Usually, jerkiness (value or derivative discontinuity) is bad, and ringing (unwanted oscillation) is also harmful.

6.1.3.1 Physical interfaces and time constants

Digital data is naturally jerky, essentially always integer snapshots at time intervals. This holds both for input (after analog-to-digital conversion, or ADC) and port output generated by a digital device. In addition to jerkiness, one must deal with the fact that single-port digital data is only 0s and 1s, while "real-world" data takes intermediate values.

On the input/stimulus side, **debounce** is often needed. This is done by a combination of *averaging* and *hysteresis*. Averaging requires a time breadth (or a frequency cutoff) and does a moving average of the bouncing values from the switch over this time breadth (see below). Hysteresis does not admit to a state change until movement of the averaged value goes well beyond the boundary in

TYPE	MECHANICAL	ELECTRICAL
P	Force	Voltage
Q	Distance	Charge
$\frac{Q}{T}$	Velocity	Current
$\frac{Q}{T^2}$	Acceleration	Rate of change of current
$X = \frac{P}{Q}$	Spring constant	1/Capacitance
$XT = \frac{P}{Q/T}$	Friction	Resistance
$XT^2 = \frac{P}{Q/T^2}$	Mass	Inductance

Table 6.1: Constant triplet, two examples

the direction being detected. That means that to change state back, it has to go well beyond the boundary in the other direction, which eliminates chatter caused by slight ringing which can persist even after averaging.

On the output/actuator side, the first step is to change 0/1 data to the intermediate values required by the real world. This **multi-valued output** can be accomplished in two ways: *digital to analog conversion* or DAC, and *pulse-width modulation* (PWM). A DAC, changing value at certain timed intervals, simply outputs voltage that is proportional (or at least functionally dependent) on an input integer. PWM alternates the voltage in binary fashion, say between 0V and 3V, but holds each value for differing lengths of time so that the time-integrated average is the desired value.

So far, we have four time constants. Input takeup, as by an ADC, must happen at timed intervals. Input averaging for hysteresis must average over a time (though it can be more subtle than that, as described below). If an output DAC is used, the integer driving the voltage must be re-evaluated at timed intervals. And if pulse-width modulation is used, the full waveform (the 1 and 0 pattern that averages to the correct value) has a certain time duration. *All of these time constants imply controlled delays.*

6.1.3.2 Averaging and smoothing filters

There is another tradeoff. A moving average extends over a certain amount of time, which is usually expressed as a *cutoff frequency*. In Figure 6.1 we see log-log plots of the frequency response of three averaging filters, and I define the cutoff frequency to be the point of intersection of their asymptotes; 1 in every case. (Another definition is the "3DB" point, which for two of the filters is less than 1.) However, the smoother filters have steeper declines in stopband sensitivity. See Figure 6.2 for the impulse responses of the three filters.

The interesting thing is that the smoother filters have longer delays. In fact, in the filters of Figure 6.2, THE DELAY IS EQUAL TO THE SMOOTHING ORDER DIVIDED BY THE (REDUCED) ASYMPTOTIC CUTOFF FREQUENCY. The delay is here defined as the expected delay value of the impulse response, treated as a probability density, and equals the limit of phase delay and group delay as (passband) frequencies approach zero. The smoothing order is the increase in smoothness caused by the filter, where -2 is the "smoothness" of an impulse, -1 is the smoothness of a function with discontinuities (like digital input and output), 0 is the smoothness of a continuous function with corners, and n greater than 0 means continuous n-th derivatives.

The filters of Figure 6.2 are *linear averaging filters*. This means their impulse response always has a total integral equal to the impulse, it is all to the right

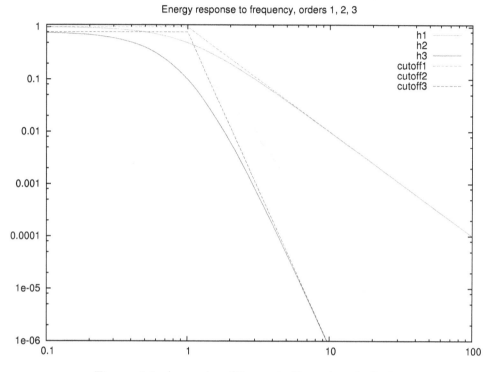

Figure 6.1: Averaging filter cutoffs, orders 1, 2, 3

of (after) the impulse, and it is everywhere nonnegative. The last condition is to avoid "ringing". The filters chosen are critically damped (have only one time constant, of multiplicity n), which means their response is as quick as possible, assuming the avoidance of ringing.

It is not necessary to pick critically damped filters; overdamped ones will also avoid ringing. But the critically damped ones are the best, if they can be achieved, and they are also simply related to one another. In Figure 6.3, a critically damped filter impulse response lies between each pair of curves, and if summed all the way to ∞ they will converge to the Heaviside "step" function (1 for $t > 0$, 0 for $t < 0$).

6.1.3.3 Real implementations using ladders

Figure 6.4 shows a general structure, called an "LC ladder", for the construction of smoothing filters. We want the **transfer function**

$$\frac{V_L}{V_0} = \frac{R_L}{R_L + R_0} \frac{1}{(\sigma + 1)^n} \qquad (6.1)$$

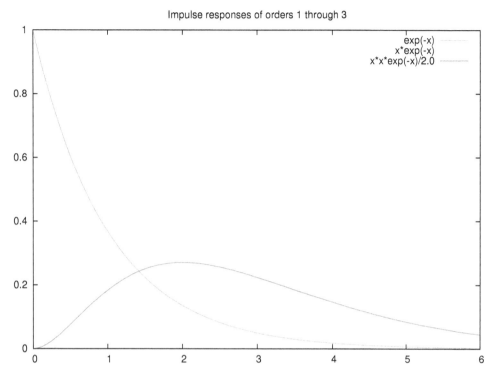

Figure 6.2: Impulse response functions, orders 1, 2, 3

where

$$\sigma \equiv \tau s \equiv \tau j \omega \tag{6.2}$$

for ω the (reduced) frequency, $j \equiv \sqrt{-1}$, and τ the (reduced) cutoff period, inverse of the cutoff frequency. Notice that the first factor of the right-hand side of (6.1) is enforced by the $\omega = 0$ behavior of each circuit, functioning as a DC voltage divider, with an inductor acting as a short circuit and a capacitor as an open circuit. Here s is a Laplace transform variable.

The most general approach to the LC ladder and similar networks is to use impedance and its inverse, admittance. Impedance extends the concept of resistance to AC by treating a sinusoid as equivalent to a complex exponential *that is rotating in the positive direction* and has the sinusoid as its real part:

$$\cos(\omega t + \phi) \sim e^{j(\omega t + \phi)}$$

It follows from the differential equations that an inductor with inductance L has impedance $j\omega L$, and a capacitor with capacitance C has admittance $j\omega C$,

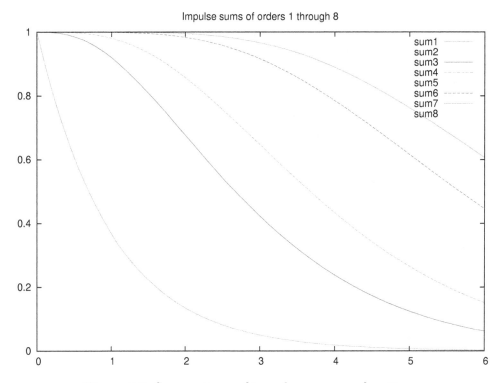

Figure 6.3: Sum pattern of impulse response functions

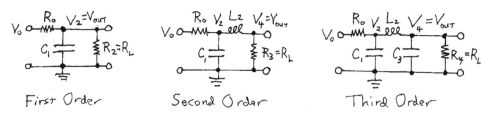

Figure 6.4: Smoothing ladder filters (electrical)

hence impedance $\frac{-j}{\omega C}$. Using this, all the circuits of Figure 6.4 can be analyzed as if they were resistive circuits.

The circuits of Figure 6.4 are analyzed by alternating impedance (voltage divider) and admittance (current divider) expressions. Giving the third order circuit as an example, and using Z for impedance and Y for admittance, we get:

$$
\begin{aligned}
Y_3 &= j\omega C_3 + \frac{1}{R_{\mathrm{L}}} \\
Z_3 &= \frac{1}{Y_3} \\
Z_2 &= j\omega L_2 + Z_3 \\
Y_2 &= \frac{1}{Z_2} \\
Y_1 &= j\omega C_1 + Y_2 \\
Z_1 &= \frac{1}{Y_1} \\
Z_0 &= R_0 + Z_1
\end{aligned}
\tag{6.3}
$$

And the transfer function is:

$$
\frac{V_{\mathrm{OUT}}}{V_0} = \frac{Z_1}{Z_0}\frac{Z_3}{Z_2}
\tag{6.4}
$$

It's actually easy to see in general that the filters of Figure 6.4, and similar higher-order filters constructed with more inductors and capacitors, are smoothing filters of the expected order. This is because equations of the type of (6.3) show inductively that for large ω each sum step is dominated by its new capacitor or inductor, and thus the magnitude of the transfer function must behave like $|\omega|^{-n}$ for large ω. Since it's easily seen to be a rational function of that order, it must have a constant numerator and an n-th degree polynomial denominator, and since it is the Laplace transform of the impulse response, that implies the expected smoothness.

However, we must still fit it to the critically damped Equation (6.1). If we make things dimensionless by defining

$$R \equiv R_{\mathrm{L}} + R_0$$

$$\epsilon \equiv \frac{R_{\mathrm{L}}}{R}$$

$$\gamma_3 \equiv \frac{R_{\mathrm{L}} C_3}{\tau}$$

$$\lambda_2 \equiv \frac{L_2}{\tau R}$$

$$\gamma_1 \equiv \frac{R_0 C_1}{\tau}$$

then it follows from (6.1) and (6.3) that

$$\lambda_2 = \frac{1}{\gamma_1 \gamma_3}$$

$$\gamma_1 = \frac{\gamma_3}{3\gamma_3 - 1}$$

and substitution in the remaining equation gives

$$(3 - 3\epsilon)\gamma_3^4 - (10 - 2\epsilon)\gamma_3^3 + 12\gamma_3^2 - 6\gamma_3 + 1 = 0. \tag{6.5}$$

The left-hand side of (6.5) is linear in ϵ. Substituting the extreme values of $\epsilon = 0$ and $\epsilon = 1$ yields, respectively, the left-hand sides $(3\gamma_3 - 1)(\gamma_3 - 1)^3$ and $-(2\gamma_3 - 1)^3$, both of which are positive for $0 \leq \gamma_3 < 1/3$ and negative for $1/2 < \gamma_3 < 1$. It follows that this is true for every ϵ between 0 and 1, so a solution exists for each such ϵ, and is between $1/3$ and $1/2$.

As long as ϵ is well away from 0 and 1 (that is, the source and load resistances are not too different in dynamic range), the solution area is well-behaved, which indicates that small deviations (like some resistance in the inductors) will not affect solvability. Similar, easier techniques prove similar results for n = 2 and n = 1. Each LC ladder implies a precisely analogous mechanical smoothing device made with springs and masses. Since three orders of smoothing will be enough for most purposes, this should be enough for good averaging and output quality.

As a side note, most discussions of ladder filters (e.g. [5]) concentrate on methods of R. M. Foster, E. Cauer, and Otto Brune that involve the driving point impedance (e.g. Z_0 in (6.3)). The derivation of driving point impedance from transfer function is alluded to but omitted in all the references I could find, and restrictions (like all poles being distinct) seem to be on the method rather than the result, as the above derivation makes clear.

6.1.4 Extra cores and fine timing

The multiple timing demands that physical responsiveness requires lead to a feature of embedded design: the desirability of multiple cores, including *cores that are independent of the operating system*. This follows from a very simple and obvious fact: **A timing signal must not be delayed.** But an OS by its very nature is in charge and can impose delays. This is true even of the simplest "real-time" OS or RTOS, the Arduino-like main program with interrupts, if there can ever be an interrupt other than the timer interrupt (or even if there is more than one timer).

Of course, sometimes a small delay is acceptable, because it is insignificant compared to what is being timed. Data uptake (or mouse movement), as long as it is combined with true, accurate timing for the data, can stand some roughness since it is just plotting points with irregularly distributed abscissas. On the other hand, manufacturing UART serial bits is quite demanding, and pulse-width modulation needs to be even more precise as to switching times, otherwise the average will suffer a lot of jitter.

Typically, a CPU or an embedded core will include "subcores" which are dedicated to some of these timing jobs. Most chips have serial input and output capability, for example. Bytes are on the "digital" side, and their bits, in a certain order (**big-endian** or **little-endian**) with some padding (start bits, stop bits), are turned into physical voltages with fixed timing. Interrupts will not usually work for this (although I got an Inmos Transputer, with its very fast high-priority [interrupt] response, to generate a 57.6 kilobaud serial waveform in 1995 for the SCS Ford automotive radar). Dedicated hardware with FIFOs is normally required. Once you understand the principles, the assembly language specs make sense, and design is easy.

6.1.4.1 Dedicated physical driver design

We start here with the absolute lowest level piece, the one closest to the physics of the outside world. A dedicated physical driver, with one purpose (though possibly capturing or driving more than one signal in a coherent fashion) is designed like my 57.6 kilobaud serial driver. It can use Field-Programmable Gate Array (FPGA), Complex Programmable Logice Device (CPLD), and Application-Specific Integrated Circuit (ASIC) subcores, right down to the transistor level involving *combinatorial logic* (also known confusingly as *combinational logic*).

Combinatorial logic is logic whose output depends only on its input, once a certain minimum time has passed. Hence it underlies all *sequential logic*, since it determines what happens between the clock-in of input and the clock-out of output in a single instruction execution. This can include instructions that take several cycles but merely let the intermediate clocks pass by without responding to them until ready state is reached.

The key to dedicated driver design is that at any time in its operation it has a SINGLE TIMING MAP. This can allow very limited multitasking (for example, full-duplex serial IO with five samples per input bit coexisting with generation of output bits at the same baud rate). The single timing map is expressed in pseudocode as a *single high-priority process* within a Transputer-style `PRI PAR` with only two members. That high-priority process is instantly responsive to a timer and—here is the key design feature—**its response to each timing activation takes a short time compared to the time between activations.**

For example, a full-duplex UART serial driver ticks five times per bit, and at each tick must determine whether to change the state of its output, and must record any input, and determine whether it's time to average five inputs and generate a digital bit. All of this, plus any tick response latency, is done in a few nanoseconds which is a small time compared with the several microseconds (or more) between ticks.

What about the rest of the time between activations? This is "idle time" from the point of view of the high-priority process. That means it is available for low-priority processes in the pseudocode. The low-priority processes deal with **control input and output** which must always result in a consistent state when decisions are made about the timing map and programming of the high-priority process. In the serial driver example, a control input could be a new baud rate, while a control output could be notification of an illegal voltage or waveform input.

There is a responsiveness delay in this control IO, which must be programmed precisely. Also, it is assumed, as in all computing hardware, that *metastability* is not a problem, and that a decision can always be made between two states, or about the winner of a race (such as whether the baud rate changed before a certain new bit was input).

There is often a cascade of responsiveness in very fast hardware. For example, the hardware of Low-Voltage Digital Signaling (LVDS) communicates far faster than RS232 serial—**it can reach gigabits per second**—using twisted-pair connections. Many hardware protocols from Spacewire to SATA then piggyback on this, using internal FIFOs to do more complex things with hardware protocol branching. All of this is available for Wide design, and the simpler protocols, like Spacewire and even bare LVDS, can be faster and better *and more stable,* setting the designer free from clumsy protocol libraries.

6.1.4.2 Embedded timer queue

An embedded chip will typically contain a timer interrupt that is finer than those associated with a standard OS. A default introduction to the MSP430 timer is found in [6]. The Kicksat uses a watchdog timer, which is pretty similar.

In Chapter 3, we discovered that the MSP430F5137 in use in the Kicksat has a clock speed of 8MHz. A search for the function `delay` in the tree rooted at `/Applications/Energia.app/Contents/Resources/Java/hardware` that was mentioned in Chapter 3 finds this system routine in `msp430/cores/msp430/wiring.c`, and the definition found there of `WDT_TICKS_PER_MILISECOND` (note spelling) indicates that the watchdog timer has a divider of 500 and interrupts 16000 times per second. The interrupt code from `wiring.c` is shown below.

```
__attribute__((interrupt(WDT_VECTOR)))
void watchdog_isr (void)
{
        wdtCounter++;
        /* Exit from LMP3 on reti (this includes LMP0) */
        __bic_status_register_on_exit(LPM3_bits);
}
```

The millisecond `delay` function simply sleeps until this interrupt fires and then checks `wdtCounter` against the target value `wakeTime`, which it has incremented by a multiple of 16.

This means that Energia's delay function is sixteen times coarser than it needs to be. We could use an MSP430F5137 to support a timer queue with a resolution of 62.5 microseconds, instead of the 1 to 14 milliseconds offered by Windows or Linux. A dedicated 16MHz MSP430 with the timer divider reduced to 160 would be able to manage a timer queue with a resolution of 10 microseconds. However, the code shown below (it covers several pages) is a timer queue with millisecond resolution.

The following code is `timeq.ino` and runs under Zac Manchester's special version of Energia. Notice the setup and loop functions. It uses a so-called "header" file `tqlib.h` which is really an include of several function calls (this is common with embedded code lacking a complex linking stage).

```
{{{ timeq.ino
struct tqmember {
  int tqtask;
  unsigned long tqexpire;
};
struct tqmember tq[5];
#include "tqlib.h"
char output[] = "     "; /* 5 chars long */
int notUnderway = 1;
unsigned long mstime = 0;
char msg[] = "Verne Rob Dan Larry ";
int msgleng = sizeof(msg);
int imsg = 0;
...  void setup
...  void loop
}}}
```

Above is the origami top view, below the folds, with the last fold split in two views.

```
{{{  void setup
void setup() {
  Serial.begin(9600);
}
}}}
```

```
{{{  void loop
void loop() {
  unsigned long ttime, tnext;
  int itop;
  long delta;

  if (notUnderway) {
    mstime = millis();
    buildTimer(0, mstime, 1); /* 0 = radio transmission */
    buildTimer(1, mstime + 5000, 2); /* 1 = voltage */
    buildTimer(2, mstime + 6000, 3); /* 2 = temperature */
    buildTimer(3, mstime + 2200, 4); /* 3 = mag */
    buildTimer(4, mstime + 3500, 5); /* 4 = gyro */
    notUnderway = 0;
  }
  itop = topTimer();

}}}
```

```
{{{
  switch (itop) {
    case 0:
    output[4] = msg[imsg];
    imsg++;
    if (imsg >= msgleng) imsg = 0;
    Serial.println(output);
    memset(output, (int)' ', 5);
    mstime = millis(); /* as in SpriteRadio */
    tnext = mstime + 1000 + random(-500,500); /* as in SpriteRadio */
    break;
    case 1:
    output[0] = 'V';
    tnext = mstime + 5000;
    break;
    case 2:
    output[1] = 'T';
    tnext = mstime + 6000;
    break;
    case 3:
    output[2] = 'M';
    tnext = mstime + 2200;
    break;
    case 4:
    output[3] = 'G';
    tnext = mstime + 3500;
    break;
  }

  replaceTimer(itop, tnext, 5); /* the same itop as got used */
  ttime = timetopTimer(); /* the next guy's time */
  mstime = millis();
  delta = (long)(ttime - mstime);
  if (delta > 0) {
    mstime = ttime;
    delay(delta);
  }
}
}}}
```

The following code is `tqlib.h`. It contains the machinery that runs the timer queue. The interesting parts are `buildTimer` and `replaceTimer`. It is worth noting that handling the timer queue requires effort in proportion to queue length. Nevertheless, this can be quite efficient if managing a short set of independent but interleaved timed response chains.

```
{{{  tqlib.h
/* Time queue of length n is in global
 * struct tqmember tq[LENGTH];
 * WHERE
 * struct tqmember {
 *   int tqtask;
 *   unsigned long tqexpire;
 * }
 */
...   void buildTimer(int task, unsigned long expire, int length)
...   void replaceTimer(int task, unsigned long expire, int length)
...   int topTimer(void)
...   unsigned long timetopTimer(void)
}}}
```

Above is the origami top view, below are the folds.

```
{{{  void buildTimer(int task, unsigned long expire, int length)
/* length is the length of tq AFTER {task, expire} is inserted */
void buildTimer(int task, unsigned long expire, int length) {
  int i = length - 2;
  while ((i>=0)&&(((long)(expire-tq[i].tqexpire))<0)) {
    tq[i+1] = tq[i];
    i--;
  }
  tq[i+1] = {task, expire};
}
}}}
```

```
{{{  void replaceTimer(int task, unsigned long expire, int length)
/* Assumed: tq[0] is invalid because used, length remains same */
void replaceTimer(int task, unsigned long expire, int length) {
  int i = 1;
  while ((i<length)&&(((long)(expire-tq[i].tqexpire))>=0)) {
    tq[i-1] = tq[i];
    i++;
  }
  tq[i-1] = {task, expire};
}
}}}
```

```
{{{  int topTimer(void)
int topTimer(void) {
  return tq[0].tqtask;
}
}}}
```

```
{{{  unsigned long timetopTimer(void)
unsigned long timetopTimer(void) {
  return tq[0].tqexpire;
}
}}}
```

A linked list is in theory better if the timer queue gets long, but it still requires the linear-effort search for the insertion point, and it is actually *not* more efficient for a short queue like this one. If capabilities like **memmove** exist, they can be used to advantage.

6.1.5   Smooth delayer programs

The interface between the choppy action of a digital computation and the smooth input/output relationship of a desirable physical response is the key to high-quality embedded programming. Its lack creates hiccups in music and pauses or fields of pixellated blocks in videos. At this point, it is clear why solving it is not merely a problem of speed.

The key to solving this problem in general is to work from the output backward. Several principles then appear.

6.1.5.1   (A) Continuity, smoothness, and good behavior must be imposed on some aspects of the output

The painting of a video picture may involve the zig-zag of successive scan lines followed by return to the top of a frame, or it may merely involve buffer swapping, but the appearance of successive frames and their content must certainly be stepwise smooth. Music must satisfy continuity, rhythm, and well-shaped waveforms in several time scales, one of which is continuous rather than fixed (the frequency spectrum). A robotic actuator responds according to the physics of Table 6.1, a response which always involves at least two time delay constants, and getting it right can be quite challenging. Think of moving an egg.

"Good behavior" can often present a problem that is the opposite of smoothness. Physical actuation is forced to pass through the smoothing effect

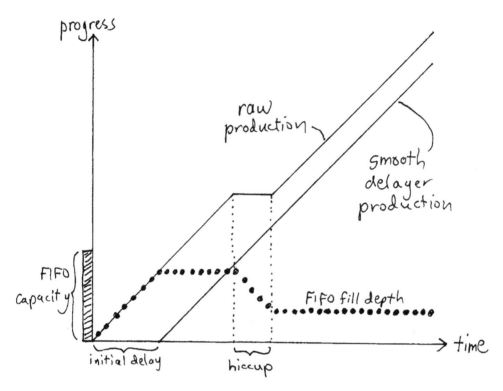

Figure 6.5: Smooth delayer FIFO and response

of the analog components, a smoothing filter, and yet is required to converge without ripple to a goal, like a distance of extension, a rotating speed, or a force. Both the smoothing and the good behavior impose exacting requirements on the digital-to-analog output, and place limits on its choppiness.

6.1.5.2 (B) Analog actuator components must be designed to cooperate with the digital output

All the physical constants of Table 6.1 are available within the constraints imposed by the physical materials and geometry. Those of form X and XT^2 are energy-conserving, while those of form XT are dissipative and heat-producing. The tradeoffs here are crucial, and whole libraries full of engineering experience exist to help. Though differential equations may be challengingly mathematical, they have one very friendly characteristic: Within the range of their good behavior (and the designer must be sure he is within that range), their solutions are a continuous function of their input data. Therefore design of the cases that give the extreme results usually implies good behavior for intermediate cases. To be sure, internal extrema (like resonance points) are a threat.

In this stage, the possible digital outputs influence the picking of the analog components. They cannot require a PWM duty cycle of less than 0% or greater than 100%, for example. But once the stable analog components are picked, their response imposes the requirements on the digital output. This includes every requirement implied by (A).

6.1.5.3 (C) Every case must produce an acceptable result

Once again, let me emphasize: **there are no exceptions!** Power loss, component failure, input "going nuts," and spilled coffee are all *normal digital inputs* to a good design. Here is where Wide foundations permit the designer to branch out. A Wide piece exists in time and has well-defined points of input and output. They can be monitored by spy pieces and, when craziness is detected, branch to an alternate path.

The key principle here is that alternate paths must be insensitive to each other's failure modes. When the Ariane V booster rocket's controller went crazy in 1996, due to an integer overflow, another system detected it and switched control to the backup, which had exactly the same programming and immediately went crazy in the same way. (Loss: $750,000,000.) Often the backup is a cruder, more "analog" control mechanism that produces a canned output that, though of lower quality, gets the job done.

6.1.5.4 (D) Input-to-output delays are inevitable and must be designed in

This is the single best component addition to avoid "hiccups." It requires careful analysis of *unavoidable* delay patterns, and may even involve feedback within the program, to catch the case, for instance, when the so-called "new and improved" OS has a coarser timer and increased latency. The actuation is then made to lag the input by a fixed (or very smoothly low-pass filtered) delay that is longer than the worst *normal* enforced delay, where "normal" is within ranges that do not cut over to one of the backup machines of (C).

This is not as simple as it sounds. It always requires a big enough FIFO (compare Figure 6.5), which is not usually a challenge these days, but also the output from the FIFO must be of constant delay. That could be done like a metered freeway entrance, but this could require too fine a timer resolution for the central CPU, at least for audio. As a rule, smart output pieces ought to receive batches of data at a time and spread the corresponding DAC responses by carefully controlled time intervals.

6.1.5.5 Summary

The result of all the above should be that the digital side of the output coding, right at the actuator, should receive data that is *natural* in value and relative timing. "Natural" means that it is equivalent to what an ideal, delay-free analog connection could create. Usually, that is not hard to determine (check the output of high-quality pre-digital technology).

This principle is rather obvious, but is rarely satisfied in the real world. Because of that fact, there is an ironic resurgence of genuine analog devices, for instance in the synthesizer world (see [8]). This quality surge would be much bigger if smooth delayers built with inexpensive digital parts and Wide technology were placed on the market.

6.2 Simple and universal operating systems

Having arranged our tasks on a time scaffolding, as described in the previous section, we can now make the flying leap to an operating system. Not just a small, half-crippled operating system that can do a few toy projects, but an operating system that can handle any problem of whatever weight and complexity.

6.2.1 Simple execution

For over thirty years, microprocessors (and earlier computing chips such as bit-slice processors) have been capable of millions of computing cycles per second. This is much faster than human-scale responses, and usually fast enough to deal with the physics of things (like music) relating to the human response, at least with the proper analog hardware support. In addition, the instruction breadth has been enough to handle dozens of independent connections, whether digital or analog. By 1980 the basics of computing as we know it were laid.

The unit of higher computing was, and is, the clocked instruction. Its incoming state includes an instruction bit pattern which, after a cycle or integer number of cycles, produces an outgoing state including "jumping" to a next instruction. Usually the jump falls down a list, but sometimes it "branches" elsewhere. Coherent tables of such jump consequences (with the rest of their state dependencies and consequences) form a microassembly or assembly program. By "coherent" is meant that the program starts, performs some understandable action or set of actions, and then terminates. "Start" can be reset or branch in, "terminate" can be fail (e.g. power off) or branch out, so these programs can be nested.

It became clear very early on that most computing devices had to multitask among independent stimuli. (This is true even in the simplest embedded systems.) From early times, "the program" and "its understandable action or set of actions" was understood restrictively, to mean those directly involved in the specific design purpose. Therefore not every instruction of "the program" was followed immediately by a next instruction of "the program." Instead, depending on state, it was possible for side programming to be executed according to need, followed by a return to that next instruction of "the program." These branches to the side were controlled by polling or by interrupts.

There is no essential difference between polling and interrupts. An interrupt is just hardware polling that happens every instruction. For yet another principle came to be understood: the "side programming" stimuli often were the "quick response" stimuli. That part of the computing that was "under the radar" of the main task was often the very part that needed immediate response, at faster than human interface speeds.

These are the only assumptions needed for a so-called single-tasking operating system, whether dependent like Arduino or self-sufficient like MS-DOS.

The reason I say "so-called" is that if interrupts are allowed, it is not really single-tasking. The externally stimulated interrupt code is not executed consequentially to the main code, so it is really a separate task. Once you think like that, interrupt coding including for multiple interrupts begins to make sense—as Wide programming.

6.2.2 Sesquitasking operating systems

I have invented the name "sesquitasking" for the OS that is being justified here. This uses the Latin prefix *sesqui* which means "one and a half." (You may have heard of a "sesquicentennial" or 150-year anniversary.) Thus I intend it to fall between single-tasking and multitasking.

As I noted in the previous subsection, these are usually called single-tasking, but in fact asynchronous interrupt response amounts to a separate task, or tasks. Truly single-tasking OSs like Ian Hirschsohn's PORT (see [3]) require a supplementary processor (Peripheral Processing Unit) to deal with asynchronous IO. Sesquitasking OSs include setup/loop systems like Arduino and Energia, and bare-bones master systems like DOS, as long as they allow interruption. They are the backbone of embedded systems.

Figure 6.6, which came from my old paper [2], shows such a system's timeline. Although the main program (W) and the interrupts and Terminate-and-Stay-Resident or "TSR" programs (T) are shown running in parallel, they

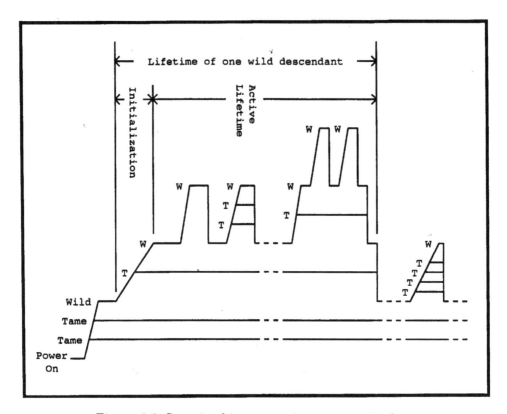

Figure 6.6: Sesquitasking operating system timeline

can actually multitask, and progress in a "dotted timeline" with only one using the CPU at a time.

Simplest is to think of a setup/loop embedded system. The setup code is called once after reset or power-up, and after that the loop code spins tightly. Such code is used in the Kicksat Sprite, and myriad other embedded projects, with a few globals (like indices in an array) surviving from one loop instance to the next. But the situation is actually a little more involved than that.

First, setup and loop are not the only code. There is also the interrupt response code. That includes code that responds to a clock tick, so it's implicit in "straightforward" calls (like sleep or delay) which wait a specific time, even if there's no user IO to the satellite.

More subtly, embedded chips almost always support low power modes. Compare [4]. The "tight" main loop itself, even if not directly dependent on an input, will normally be programmed by a command like
_BIS_SR(LPMx_bits | GIE);

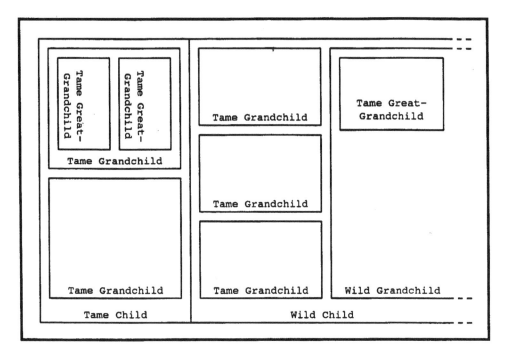

Figure 6.7: Sesquitasking OS resource allocation

to "go to sleep" when not busy, and wake up only when an interrupt, any interrupt, is detected.

Figure 6.7, also from [2], amounts to a cut orthogonal to Figure 6.6. At a certain time, it shows the subdivision of "space" among the current tasks. FROM THIS POINT OF VIEW, THERE IS NEVER A "DOTTED TIME-LINE". A task's ownership of resources remains valid, even if it is not running at the moment, as long as it is between the running of one instruction and the next, because from the task's point of view the instructions immediately follow each other with consistent state. Resources can include memory, pins, registers, interrupts, DMA slots, and similar.

Implementing Figure 6.7 in embedded code is regarded as just common sense. For example, `setup` of `timeq` calls `Serial.begin` which is clearly the initialization code (the upslope in Figure 6.6) of a `Serial` handler, which will manipulate specific pins and addresses connected with a serial Universal Asynchronous Receiver-Transmitter (UART) port. In DOS COM1 it would be register addresses 0x3F8-0x3FF, while in the MSP430F5137 UCA0 it would be 0x05C0-0x05DF (in file `periph.x`). Any such peripheral has its own "methods," normally documented in C or assembly, with several setup and driver routines

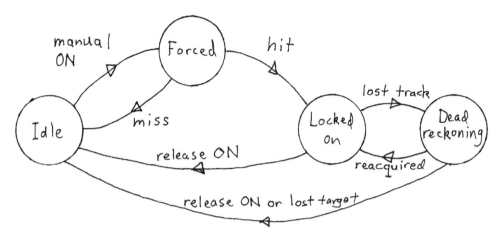

Figure 6.8: Tracker state machine

and ISRs, *but they always follow a Wide, not an object-oriented, design.* They restrict themselves to addresses proper to their "territory," respond as quickly as possible, and get out of the way as quickly as possible.

The main tasks ("loop" or main programs) usually use reassignable, generic memory and other resources, and are labeled Wild (W) in the two figures. The half-tasks (ISRs and TSRs, with their related programming such as setup) usually use fixed, limited address spaces and specific "hard" resources like pins, and are labeled Tame (T) in the figures. They can borrow resources (e.g. data records) from Wild tasks for driver work.

A fully designed sesquitasking operating system simply applies this approach consistently everywhere. **With proper hardware, a sesquitasking OS with Wide features can do any project, no matter how fast, no matter how demanding of memory, and no matter how complex.** Limits like the 1MB DOS limit and the low clock speed of some embedded chips are completely device-based and there is no limit on the general methodology. The entire problem is due to lazy programmers' use of fixed word widths and address spaces when defining their OSs. A 64-bit DOS that runs on a 2GHz core driving a 4096 by 2304 screen would be a straightforward conversion exercise for some graduate student or hobbyist—using a real-memory, Ring 0 chip setting like System Management Mode (SMM) (see [11]). Adding the features developed in [2] allows priority multitasking. With a little Wide design and a few occam-like communication primitives, you could put a sesquitasker, specialized or generic, on each one of the cores of a multicore chip.

6.2.3 Embedded example: tracker

A basic celestial tracker is a good example of an embedded project that shows the kind of design complexity to be expected here. I will deliberately avoid converging on specific hardware, only showing how the state machine's implications lead to implied needs that direct the designer's attention toward the proper hardware.

The tracker is to use feedback to track an object (star, planet, satellite, even bird) around the celestial sphere. The assumption is that the object moves smoothly (continuous position and velocity, with bounded rate of change of velocity), but not necessarily predictably, and is *usually* distinguishable by contrast with its surroundings. The tracker moves an alt-azimuth imaging device (CCD camera or telescope) to image a small part of the celestial sphere, presumably including the target.

6.2.3.1 State machine

When powered on and fully booted up, the tracker has three phases:
(A) Idle: Release is on, Manual is off, and the tracker is not aimed;
(B) Forced: Release is off, Manual is on, and the tracker is pointed according to user input from a console;
(C) Tracking: Release is off, Manual is off, and the tracker is following a selected target.

When in the Tracking phase, two states are possible (Figure 6.8):
(C1) Locked on: The target is identified and centered in the field of view;
(C2) Dead reckoning: The target is not distinguishable by the programming, but is being followed by continuity.

Dead reckoning happens, for instance, if a bird flies behind a tree, or a planet being followed is occulted by the Moon. It may drop to Idle if a decision is made that the target has been lost (has evaded the tracker). In any case, the user can release the tracker, sending it to Idle.

6.2.3.2 Wide pieces and possible implementations

The state machine and functionality description can be carried out by the Wide pieces of Figure 6.9. Although each piece has an independent existence, running in parallel with the others, it can itself break down into two or more independent pieces, depending on implementation. So Figure 6.9 is a necessary, coarse breakdown.

It may appear that the distinction between Math and Master is not necessary. A little reflection proves that it is, as long as Math operations may require a

259

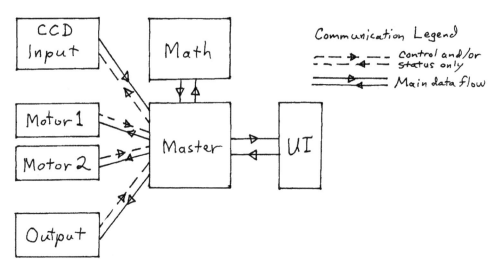

Figure 6.9: Wide piece diagram of Tracker

long period of time, too long for the hardware interrupts to wait. In essence, Math must be a "low-priority process" capable of giving way to any urgent, time-critical interactions with the physical world. The Master code which handles the interactions of all the other pieces must be highly responsive and is different in kind to the code that does Math. To merge Math and Master in the same "superloop" requires breaking up Math into short-duration blocks, while distributing Master among the other pieces requires repeating its code among several ISRs—both quite difficult. The separation shown in Figure 6.9 warns of this.

The implementations can be on one or several CPUs and can use any language or lack thereof. A conventional modern UI will normally bring with it a tablet or similar computer. The hardware implied by the upper three pieces on the left will normally be mounted on the physical device, requiring at least one embedded CPU for its high-speed operation. Where Math, Master, and Output live must then be settled.

Because Math is low-priority, one sesquitasking system, unless specifically designed for Wide use with TSRs (see [2]), is usually not satisfactory for everything to the left of the UI, as it pushes Master into ISRs as I said above. A common approach, given a *responsive* multitasking system on the tablet, is to put Math and Master (and probably Output, if that means something on the network) on the tablet.

It's important to note that **responsive multitasking** excludes some of the Object Oriented languages/systems on the market, because they are willing to talk only to communications on their "approved list," and insist (via garbage collection, interface specifications, etc) on controlling how responsive they will be to approved communications.

Prioritizing the Math is also needed. Linux and other Unices, using `nice`, make this fairly easy, if you examine the specs carefully. It can be done in Windows too, with a little more effort (see [9]). Thus it's clear that any flavor of Linux or Unix is OK, and (desktop-type) Windows can be made to work, but whether one of the Java-based systems like Android will function requires close examination, which I have not done. I'm also in doubt about iOS, although at least desktop Mac runs over a version of BSD, a Unix-like system. The problem is that iOS has multiple abstraction layers that may mask access to responsive connels.

The test, in every case, is to set up sockets, serial IO, and/or pipes and see how responsive they are when a standard UI is running over them. In the case of Windows and Linux, Connel offers the tools to handle the non-UI part of this programming. The UI (in whatever language) must support the other end of the communications (internal ones are usually sockets).

The programmer's main initial task is to make sure this machinery runs properly. Difficulties I have seen can arise from inputs separated by time intervals, which Object Oriented UI systems may decide to "batch" and send several of them through at the very end (perhaps only at the end of the entire run). Other difficulties come from Object Oriented implementations that amount to nested callbacks, which can collide with a maximum stack depth. Superloops are better in this respect.

The programmer will discover, upon close examination, that most modern event-based (GUI-centered) OSs have a hidden superloop structure. Often it is possible to reach into this and modify it to be friendly to inputs and sequences that were not thought of when it was designed. For this reason, I favor open-source OSs when possible.

When testing this responsiveness, all the off-tablet (embedded) pieces should be simulated by processes in a multitasking OS that communicate to the Master, generating (or accepting) realistic data with realistic timing. I found it convenient to have my multitasking OS running under VMWare, and to set up a *second* multitasking OS under VMWare, where the "embedded simulators" lived. That way the two could communicate via serial connections, the same as the ultimate Bluetooth hardware would.

6.2.3.3 Wide pieces, FIFOs, and embedded chips

At the same time, something has to be coded to drive the real hardware. This would be CCD, Motor1, and Motor2 (and maybe Output). All of them have unforgiving timing requirements, and therefore may need dedicated cores or subcores. Large companies like TI and Microchip Technology sell a vast array of embedded chips that are of the same basic design but offer this or that subcore to allow (for example) radio signal generation or CCD data capture. Another option is to roll your own, using logic design of the FPGA or CPLD type. This is much less expensive and difficult than it used to be.

Wherever demanding timing exists on one side (the physical side) of a link, and less responsive general-purpose programming serves it on the other side (the embedded CPU side) of the link, FIFOs are needed. These are designed into the fast-logic side. Since they are finite and small in most cases, the task of programming the CPU side is still pretty demanding. The FIFO should normally vary from 1/4 to 3/4 full, which determines the initial delay and the variation in data flow.

A standard CPU chip or board, such as a Microchip Technology PIC, a TI MSP430, an Arduino, or a Raspberry Pi, can support at least a sesquitasking OS-equivalent by using a superloop and a set of ISRs. If there is any doubt about responsiveness, use more than one CPU—they are cheap. The CPU will also have to be responsive to communication to and from the Master on the tablet, usually via Bluetooth or other version of serial. (Communication between CPU and FPGA/CPLD may use some on-board fast protocol like I2C or SPI.)

At the point where an embedded CPU communicates with the Master, there has to be a *packet protocol*. Devising a packet protocol is an additive process, building up messages that are flagged by tags, and making sure there is some way of getting back on track after a corrupted or invalid message is received. For ideas, consult any major open-source embedded project like the RepRap 3D printer.

Usually, communication is bidirectional, often with a dominating direction (solid lines in Figure 6.9). However, there may be more *kinds* of packets going in the "other" direction! A realistic protocol set should be one of the earliest things built in a project. This will imply a data flow, which may be heavily dominated by only a single message type (such as CCD in this case).

6.3 Details of embedded design

When you, the programmer, need to perform an embedded task, the huge world of available tools is best approached, as it were, backward. First, a survey of the tasks, or the kinds of tasks, that are accomplished by the embedded project. Then, the unified capabilities (OSs, protocols or cores) that address the needs of these projects. Finally, the part offered by this book: the Wide code organization that makes sense of all of these capabilities.

In the previous section I went over the first of these, for a sample project, the tracker. This section will focus on embedded capabilities, viewing them through the Wide code organization. I will pass over much, and focus on some CPUs that I am familiar with; and in some cases, I will have to allude to what is outside my experience. In my projects, others have done the closest-to-the-metal work, such as CPLD chip design and I2C, and my knowledge there is derivative. However, all of it is available in inexpensive self-teaching kits and Web-accessible tools now.

6.3.1 Embedded CPUs

I will survey a few microcontroller families (certainly not exhaustively) and then focus on the capabilities of one family, the Texas Instruments MSP430, with which I am most recently familiar. The capabilities found on the MSP430 correspond pretty closely with what other families offer, because of the design needs satisfied by embedded chips, which are Wide design needs.

A microcontroller is distinguished from a microprocessor (or standard CPU like the X86) by having many control capabilities and embedded features directly on-chip. Typically, however, they do not have a floating point unit on-chip.

6.3.1.1 Some microcontrollers

A survey of Wikipedia or other general sources will offer a large number of microcontroller families, a few of which I will mention here.

The Microchip Technology PIC has an orthogonal instruction set, as few as 35 instructions, and a Harvard architecture.

The Texas Instruments MSP430 has a CISC instruction set highly reminiscent of the DOS X86 instructions, and supports standard C compilation. It is the CPU of Energia, an Arduino lookalike, and is used in the Kicksat project Sprite satellites.

263

The ARM family of microcontrollers focuses on high-end, 32-bit applications. They bridge the gap to standard CPUs.

The Atmel family of microcontrollers includes the CPU of Arduino.

The Intel 8051 series uses Harvard architecture, code separate from data, which protects against new code and therefore against malware.

6.3.1.2 Architectures

Each family of microcontrollers has a basic architecture, often in some way characteristic, but there are certain standard features that may go one way or the other.

Memory spaces differ. Some microcontrollers have a Harvard architecture, which has code and data on different buses and even with different word lengths, though most have the conventional Princeton architecture familiar from standard CPUs like the X86. Even these may have specialized memory regions like "flash." Most treat pins and registers differently from standard memory, but a few (e.g. PICs) have *orthogonal* instruction sets that do not.

The Reduced Instruction Set Computing (RISC) versus Complex Instruction Set Computing (CISC) divide is not as well-defined as it once was, but is still notable. CISC offers many memory modes, direct and indirect, as well as register operations, while RISC is "load/store," separating memory operations from arithmetic/logical unit (ALU) ones. RISC may offer instruction-level parallelism, letting one ALU operation happen at the same time that another memory access is completing. Vector operations need RISC features.

A third architectural difference of emphasis is feature depth. Some microcontrollers have few specialized features, just pins that can be supported by external logic, while others are feature-rich. Some microcontrollers, like the PICs, have bare-bones instructions while others lean toward abstraction by supporting stacks, indirect instructions and the like.

6.3.1.3 Memory, write phasing and security

Memory organization in an embedded processor is usually more complex than in a standard, high-level CPU. For one thing, most high-level CPUs have a Princeton architecture, so that both code and data live in one memory space, while many embedded chips have a Harvard architecture. Even those which do not must deal with the fact that code cannot be reloaded every power-up. In addition, there are further subdivisions which are present, but usually not very visible, in high-level CPUs.

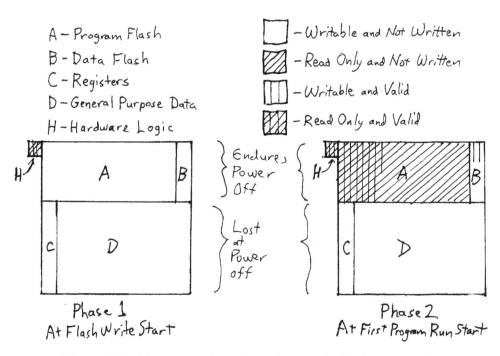

Figure 6.10: Memory write phases in a typical microcontroller

Figure 6.10 offers a minimalistic example of the consequences. Some memory contents, such as code and necessary constants, must survive power-down, but requiring all memory to survive power-down would cause technical problems. (That kind of memory, called "flash," has very slow write cycles, and can survive only a limited number of them, perhaps 50,000. I show "Program Flash" although different technologies, like PROM or EEPROM, may be used here. Another, older solution is "CMOS RAM," but that requires a battery trickle-current.) Therefore there must be (at least) two phases of writing to memory. In the first (code-writing) phase, a tiny, unchangeable program in hardware logic (H) directs "PROM burning," flash loading, or "network loading" (if done without flash, the latter is called "netbooting"). In the second phase, the chip boots to the code that was loaded in the first phase. A jumper (i.e. single readable bit) may distinguish between these, or a less secure method, like a special setting before reboot.

Further distinctions are found on Figure 6.10. In Phase 2, I show part A of the flash, including the code, becoming read-only—an elementary security precaution. (Not all the flash can be read-only, otherwise the program could store no information across power-downs. Notice that even Phase 1 must write something to the writable flash B, or else the first run of the program will have random constants.) A further distinction is between general-purpose Randomly Accessible Memory, or RAM (D), and (addressable) registers (C). The latter include all external status and IO, plus many other control registers required by state machines like serial protocols. (If they aren't addressable, then they need separate instructions, which would clutter up the instruction space.) Such registers and other startup values cannot be part of a program load in Phase 2, since there is no program load, so they must be initialized by an early part of the program run. This is concealed by languages like C, but you can find this initialization code if you expand the load image as assembly code.

Security is addressed in the same context. Network loading is inherently insecure, especially netbooting, but is often permitted for convenience since the code versions are changed often. More secure is PROM burning, which at least requires physical access, and most secure is the chip that allows that to take place only once.

Another approach to security is a Memory Management Unit (MMU), which, like memory protection in an OS-level CPU, imposes restrictions on what may or may not be written (or read) when the program is in certain states. An MMU is found in some heavyweight ARM chips, for instance, but they are more like standard CPUs than embedded ones anyway. The MMU-based chips are found at the heart of devices like smartphones whose software is continually being updated. Because of its complexity, and its conflict with ease of use, this security approach is usually "full of holes," and real danger points are better hard-coded.

THAT FACT IS A HUGE, IF UNREALIZED, POINT OF VALUE FOR WIDE CODING, WHICH PERMITS HARD-CODING OF COMPONENT PIECES WITHOUT FREEZING THE PROGRAM VERSION OR FUNCTIONALITY. With Deep approaches, each upgrade places the entire device, including its physical drivers, at risk of malware. Recent huge exploits like BlackPOS, affecting upwards of a hundred million credit card users at Target and elsewhere, have illustrated this.

6.3.1.4 Sleep states and power management

Many if not most embedded processors have to conserve power, because their power source—battery, solar, even motion—is very limited. Even the most advanced chips, like ARMs in smartphones, are built to extend battery life. To support this, sleep states are introduced.

Sleep states are a form of layered Wide programming. Whole sections of the CPU and the external pins can be shut off, leaving a few stimuli live. In particular, clocks can be shut off, so that the device is not running a polling loop to no purpose when inactive. When this is done, the device must be *awakened* by a stimulus which, at least from the point of view of the sleeping part (i.e. most of it), is asynchronous.

Clearly, there are tradeoffs here, and most embedded devices offer several sleep options. One may be so extreme as to lead to a full reset when awakened. In other cases, the code, an example of which is given above under "Sesquitasking operating systems," is run within the process that is to go to sleep, as the **last** non-branching instruction of its previous **low-priority** activity. This is a single instruction, but just happens to take a very long time to execute. It does not complete until the wakeup stimulus is received. The first full instruction executed after wakeup is thus often a branch instruction (like the one implied by the end of a C `while` loop) to the top of the "awakened" code.

6.3.1.5 GPIO pins, tristate and power needs

The General-Purpose Input/Output (GPIO) pins that bristle out around the edge of an embedded chip (or connect with the ball grid under it) are addressable by the code run on the chip. In many cases, they take or accept digital (two-valued) values, while in others analog (many-valued or continuous) values are input or output.

The digital IO pins, especially when arranged eight to a register, look a lot like single digital bits, but there is a major distinction. The *power requirements* of a bit of memory are exceedingly small, driving only a microscopic transistor. The power requirements of an external pin are relatively huge, turning electricity into heat. These are therefore called *driver pins*.

Output pins are *low-impedance*, and the internal logic of the chip should set them to a specific voltage. Input pins are *high-impedance* or *tristated*, and the internal logic of the chip is ready to read the value of their voltage. "Tristate" (© National Semiconductor) refers to the possibility of high, low, or "floating," meaning undriven. Of pins shorted together in a circuit, at most one must be low-impedance at any time, otherwise the pin or the whole chip or board may be **FRIED** due to disagreement among the drivers as to what the voltage should be.

A high-impedance pin should only be read if one of its connected pins is being driven (is low-impedance). Floating reads are bad. This is why reads of pin-valued registers are usually ANDed with a map of bits; the chip only looks at those pins ANDed with 1. Similarly, commands exist to switch a pin between READ (input or high-impedance) and WRITE (output or low-impedance), and attempts to write will only affect the WRITE pins.

In theory, a single WRITE pin could drive any number of READ pins, but in practice, this is limited to a number called the *fan-out*, usually around four.

6.3.1.6 Reset, interrupts, clocks, and crystal

Reset happens when the chip is powered up ("hard"), and under other ("soft") conditions, including the extreme sleep mentioned above. It's a slow process, since when it starts, the power distribution and the clock are not functional. There are several levels of reset in the MSP430.

Once reset has happened, and sleep has not happened, a clock begins. (A *clock* is to be distinguished from a *timer*—the latter counts up the ticks of the former, as in Figure 6.11, and performs interrupts and other jobs when a countdown is reached.) The clock is the metronome of the sequential behavior of the CPU, and is the fastest time rhythm the CPU can achieve. Often, an embedded CPU will support more than one clock, used for different power levels, for example.

The CPU contains multiple internal oscillators of differing power consumption, speed, and accuracy. In addition, an external crystal can be attached if very high accuracy is required. Techniques for switching from one clock to another are available. Each clock produces a sharp square wave signal of duty cycle about 50%, and has an associated counter.

Interrupts are a branching mechanism responding to asynchronous stimuli, though in the case of a sleep state, they take on some of the character of a reset. Thus, if the chip is asleep, the awakening event causes the sleep instruction to complete, then the interrupt code is executed (which requires a wait to avoid metastability, plus saving and restoring some state), then the branch happens in the main code. Because interrupts are, by default, disabled within Interrupt Service Routines (ISRs), interruption amounts to a two-priority system of multitasked code.

6.3.1.7 RAM, DMA and block writes

Randomly-addressable memory is the central resource of almost all CPUs, and continues to play an important role in embedded code. Compute-intensive operations typically shift some data into registers and munch away at it, but data-intensive and memory-intensive operations can profit from some parallelism. This almost always involves moving data in blocks while either using the CPU for something else, or (specialty of embedded processors) leaving the CPU asleep.

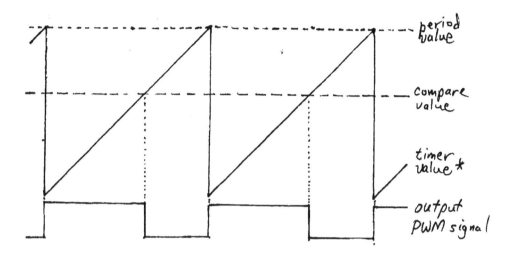

*Note: timer value is actually a step function with tiny steps

Figure 6.11: Typical PWM generation using compare output

Direct Memory Access (DMA) is the classic solution. Setting up certain registers allows counting of the data as it moves from one place to another. DMA "steals" cycles, so the MSP430 CPU operates at most at 20% efficiency while doing it. (Other chips may differ.) Nonetheless, the MSP430 documentation claims efficiency gains for I2C (external) IO, and for both the ADC and DAC, even generating a tabulated waveform voltage output.

Once a DMA transmission is triggered, something must notify the code when it finishes. Typically an interrupt is used for this purpose.

6.3.1.8   Timers, watchdog, PWM, capture and compare

In each active timer, a cycle count increments or decrements by 1 each time the system clock ticks, and triggers action (such as an interrupt or PWM edge) whenever it reaches an extreme. By setting the extreme, an accurate period can be forced on it. There are several ways this can be done. By deactivating the timer for a few cycles, typically within its own ISR, it can easily be adjusted quite frequently. The current cycle count can be read at any time.

A key specialized timer is the watchdog, which has a default behavior of resetting the whole chip if it counts down. If used this way, code should be inserted that frequently resets the watchdog, which is thus prevented from timing out unless an undesired tight loop or branch into the "weeds" indicates a code error. More typically, the watchdog is disabled and this timer can then be used as a standard timer.

Compare sets up a non-extreme value and outputs a signal (typically an edge) each time the current cycle count meets that value. See Figure 6.11 for an example of one of several ways this can be done. As long as the value is well away from the extremes, it is easy to change it during a few cycles well away from the triggering values (that is, just after a triggering value has been reached). To help with this, interrupts can be set up. This permits PWM values to track changing targets.

Capture inputs an analog timing (sharp-edged) signal and outputs the current value of the timer's cycle counter. By combining this with a value that is incremented by 1 each time the timer's cycle counter finishes counting up, highly accurate long-term cycle-counted time can be captured.

6.3.1.9 REF, ADC, DAC, and multiplexing

The voltage reference is an analog output that can take several values, which are true voltages over GND, and not just a percent of the VCC at which the chip is run. This is used in designs involving both the ADC and the DAC.

The ADC spends a short time (perhaps 10 microseconds) converging to an input voltage, and compares it to two extreme voltages, typically GND and VREF. It outputs an integer in a linear range, thus serving as a very fast voltmeter. Interrupt and DMA are at its service to get this data to where it needs to go. Analog hardware, like a temperature sensor, may be on chip to drive it, or extra analog hardware can be added by the designer. In the MSP430, an analog multiplexer (input selector) is available to feed one of several analog pin inputs to one ADC.

The DAC does the opposite task, creating an output voltage based on two extremes and an input integer. This may go to LED, sound or other actuators. Often the task of the DAC can be done equally well using PWM and a physical smoothing filter.

6.3.1.10 UART, SPI, and I2C

The UART (standard serial) has two IO pins and can support a baud rate up to 460.8kbaud, depending on the clock speed of the processor. It uses majority vote on the receiver, is asynchronous, and can be full duplex or half duplex. It's capable of autobaud and even of a special address/data protocol for multiple connections, though the latter seems nonstandard.

The Serial Peripheral Interface (SPI) is the fastest available off-CPU communication, point-to-point only and full-duplex if desired. One end is master, the other slave, and it can go as fast as the system clock, but has to be synchronous. It uses 3 or 4 pins. Multiple slaves can coexist by using a slave select line.

I2C maxes out at 400kbaud (400kbps) and uses 2 pins. It is a true arbitrated bus, and any device on it can become master and generate the clock. The master can either transmit or receive (half duplex) at any given time. Addressing is used, and low-power operation is possible. When one communicator is master, it can address and talk to any of the others as slave, and they must be prepared for this. The I2C protocol is noticeably more complex than SPI, but is economical in pin count.

These are the typical choices on most microcontrollers, but some of the details may vary.

6.3.1.11 In-circuit programming and debugging

The versions of embedded chips that are used for active code development normally have a few extra pins used for In-Circuit Emulator (ICE) or Joint Test Action Group (JTAG) debugging. (A variant on this which uses fewer pins is Spy-Bi-Wire.) These are connected to board traces that lead to board edge connectors that can be hooked up to debugging boards, which usually communicate, via USB or similar, to systems running debugging code. This kind of work is for obvious reasons associated with a loader that can re-flash the code that is to run on the embedded chip. Both the loader and the debugger are typically found in the same program on a desktop or laptop OS system.

The debugging board, like an Olimex, is a small thing that lives inside what looks like a connector or dongle. The software, like `mspdebug` running in Linux for the MSP430 family, knows how to drive this board (see the subsection on development toolsets in the Tools chapter). The debugging board is to be distinguished sharply from the board under test, with the latter usually running normal code at full speed except when a breakpoint is met or the user forces a halt. Then a lot of files that have already been prepared on the OS system swing into action, and data is pulled off the embedded chip, or even pushed onto it.

If watchpoints have been set, the embedded code will usually run slower than normal because registers or memory locations have to be checked every assembly, or C, instruction. Obviously some design thought has to go into using this, especially if physical things like motors are dependent on the timing.

6.3.1.12 USB and Ethernet

In many higher-level embedded chips, higher-level communication protocols are supported. This goes especially for chips which "naturally" live in a certain board or device, like a smartphone. If the chip is to be designed into a board that you are making, then its support of something like USB will require a lot of careful board design and probably supporting hardware.

The MSP430, for instance, can offer a "USB device" on-chip, where this term is carefully defined in distinction from the general term "device." A USB device is a slave, as opposed to a USB host (master). Independent power and clock are supported, and it has its own memory buffer, so this USB device core really is a distinct hardware piece. In fact, it can supply power to the rest of the MSP430 system.

40 pages in the manual are dedicated to this specification, and similar depth is required for other protocols, like Ethernet. However, these designs are always driven by usability, so there is always a hardware and software "recipe" that, if followed slavishly, will make it possible to "bring up" a reasonably functional communication. This process essentially amounts to fitting both hardware and software into a Wide data-flow design, with the ultimate use in mind. Difficulties typically only arise when the protocol is driven counter to its design (for example, trying to make USB peer-to-peer when it was designed to be master-slave).

6.3.1.13 Optional extras like accelerometers

Optional extras may be found in the chip, such as the radio capabilities of the MSP430F5137 (which includes CC1101 radio), or they may involve connecting up to an auxiliary chip such as an accelerometer, as in [10]. In the former case, space in the pinout, the register map, sometimes special memory buffers, and power and timing requirements are to be found in the CPU's spec. In the latter case, an "apnote" gives guidance for hooking up CPU and auxiliary chip(s).

The accelerometer case is interesting because it shows some of the lower-level capabilities at work. In this case an ADC12 with multiplexing brings in several directional data values from the accelerometer chip at timed intervals. This is because pins are usually a more plentiful resource than ADCs. Of course, the handling of such data as is received is done by code which must be designed very carefully, not only from a data-flow point of view, but also mathematically. Frequently, a special setup procedure must be used to "train" the device to function in its real environment.

6.3.1.14 Summary

In this subsection on Embedded CPUs, we have just gone through dozens of particular functions and CPU core areas. If you look at each one carefully, you will see that **each behaves as a Wide piece,** owning certain resources and receiving and transmitting certain data and control signals over time. This Wide behavior is nested, from the lowliest byte of RAM up through the DMA engine to ADC and accelerometer, for instance.

Because the subunits of an embedded CPU and its auxiliary chips can be treated as communicating Wide pieces, two consequences follow. First, designs using them can follow the Waves described in this book, and the speeds and specifications will be your friend in making sure they reach your goal. (Transputer designers in the 1980s actually used this approach, in occam, to create from scratch a floating point unit for their chips.) Second, after they have reached goal, the side-effect-free Wide character of *a complex assembly of such designs* (a big piece put together out of little pieces) means that you can be at rest once that assembly is complete. It will go on working, and other things next to it will work properly too. And its behavior can be described in detail and rigorously.

6.3.2 Beyond the embedded CPU

This is the stuff that bridges the gap between toy and real! Here Arduino and Raspberry Pi can fall short, because you can only drive what their boards allow you to drive. When you are doing a serious project involving motors or fast buffering, it frequently makes sense to design your own board and create your own physical edge logic. This is not the Boeing-scale money sink it once was. One-off or small quantity board fabrication can be found on the Web and the price be as low as a few hundred dollars.

6.3.2.1 Board design, wiring, potting and connectors

To the two normally mentioned parts of board design—*placement* and *routing*—I add a third, *shaping.* The design of the board should be a spiral process, like the Waves elsewhere in Wide design, because an embedded board essentially lives in the outside world function that it serves. Thus, the electrical and connectivity demands on board function must converge with size, shape and robustness as demanded by the physics. Think of medical devices.

The routing of the wiring is determined by the placement of the components. In doing these, you must already go beyond digital. The impedance of the traces matters, and there are several tradeoffs, especially if the signals are high-frequency (corners are bad!). Skillful hand routing can often lead to a two-layer board, including big power and ground areas; this reduces cost a lot, and increases robustness. Vias (through-holes) are a heavy cost, but usually cannot be avoided. It's worth redoing the placement and routing several times to improve these factors.

Despite over-the-air protocols like Bluetooth, connectors are almost always necessary, for data as well as for power. It's usually desirable that connectors be *keyed,* that is, so designed that incorrectly oriented mating is impossible. Power connectors, and connectors designed for hot-swapping, should be designed so that ground makes contact first, and static discharge can happen without doing damage. The process of plugging in a connector is a slow one, with bouncing voltages and currents, and this must be reflected in embedded coding, often by a delay circuit. Frequently, analog connectors have a special low-impedance design, using gold and other anti-corrosion coatings, because exact voltage matchup is more important for analog.

There is no need to be restricted to conventional board shapes, though their part accessibility is typically best for development. "Potting" (solid filling) can be used to protect the components and/or change the shape of the completed board to something physically robust. When that is not necessary, a "conformal coating" may be applied as a manufacturing step. Heat flow analysis is often of great importance, and heat can be channeled by materials of high or low heat conductivity.

6.3.2.2 Driver logic: FPGA, CPLD, and ASIC

Within the circuit, connectivity runs from the CPU on one side to whatever meets the physical world on the other. Even an embedded CPU often cannot meet all the timing demands implied by its functions, so some extra *driver logic* is frequently needed. This is the lowest level of programming normally encountered.

FPGA and CPLD, plus older arrays like PAL and GAL, are general-purpose. An FPGA is field-programmable (does not need re-burning to change the software) and often includes micro-cores. A CPLD, by contrast, has non-volatile memory and functions without aid at system startup. They are both sizable now, with thousands or tens of thousands of gates. They are programmed by Hardware Description Languages (HDLs), of which the most popular are Verilog and VHDL. If a higher-level HDL is desired, I recommend Handel-C, which is really a variant of occam and hence natural for Wide programming. SystemC is also available.

An ASIC is designed from the ground up for a specific purpose. Hundreds of *millions* of gates are possible, but ASIC design can be brutally expensive. Such Non-Recurring Engineering (NRE) can cost a million dollars in extreme cases. Still, if you are aiming for best performance in a huge market, after prototyping with FPGA and/or CPLD, it may make sense to bite the ASIC bullet.

All of this sounds intimidating, but it is only logic. The HDLs declare signals and usually operate one bit at a time. There are many tutorials at various levels, and examples of working code, so that self-teaching is perfectly practical. When carrying out such self-teaching, software emulators are your friend, and FPGAs are probably a good place to start.

Most of the HDLs are digital, but Verilog and VHDL offer variants for analog and mixed signal design.

6.3.2.3   Physics: circuit elements, sensors, and motors

Moving toward the physics, you finally exit the world of logic. Almost everything, except for a counter on the stimulus side or a stepper motor on the actuator side, is now many-valued or even smooth-valued. Differential equations and even, in some cases, quantum mechanics pose laws with which you must comply. But that is more of an opportunity than a problem, because you will discover that **physics makes sense** and tends toward negative feedback and stable behavior. It is possible to gain a "feel" for a physical response, in contrast to digital programming, which is based on tests and branches and has no bias at all toward continuity.

Electrical circuit elements are part of the physics, even though they are soldered onto your board. Linear components (resistors, capacitors, inductors) are subject to the familiar impedance equations, and operational amplifiers (op amps) are usually treated as part of linear design. Non-linear components like transistors are prominent in power and decision circuitry.

It is worth remembering that for values staying within a certain range, non-linear components can behave as if they were linear with a bias (an additive constant in the equation). The same component can have two or more inconsistent linear ranges, with non-linear behavior between. Linear circuit elements follow a fixed linear equation only at a constant frequency. As the frequency is varied, the behavior is usually rational (quotient of polynomials) in the frequency, and can therefore show such peculiarities as resonance.

Sensors can be made sensitive, or otherwise, by careful biasing so that the data moves within the analog pickup range of the ADC. It's worth taking the trouble to design circuitry that protects them from out-of-range inputs, and to characterize them very carefully for nonlinear response and for environmental dependency (e.g. temperature dependency). There is always a delay involved, and a counter (Geiger or otherwise) must be given time and mechanism to reset before the next stimulus. Metastability is a threat in the counter case: a staff, balanced on its tip, may take longer to decide which way to topple than you were willing to wait. Devices like a Schmitt trigger, plus some delay, make the likelihood of this vanishingly small.

On the actuator side, LEDs and vibrators and motors require power, and always have a nonlinear response at some point, both high-powered (usually negative or tapering off) and low-powered (often no response due to "stiction," a cause of much distress). As with the sensors, circuit protection is needed to keep outputs within the desired range. Motor delays are likely to be massive, even millions of clock cycles, due to large-scale inertia. Naive attempts to speed up response will cause oscillation, which may even resonate and lead to physical destruction. The mathematics at this end can be very challenging indeed, AND MUST BE SOLVED FOR ALL OPERATIONAL CASES. A simple example is the alt-azimuth tracker I described, for which a naive design will lead to dysfunction at the North Pole, in a manner related to gimbal lock.

There are many actuators to choose from, with tradeoffs including size, responsiveness, energy efficiency, and robustness. Things get even more interesting when the actuation is compound, as with a tracker or 3D printer. Then one actuator can cause "whiplash" with the components of the other. If you think the heyday of science and invention has passed us by, try searching any challenging problem that interests you. You are likely to find all sorts of shortcomings in current solutions, and even major directions that have not been tried.

6.3.2.4 Summary

When embedded programming makes its linkup with the outside world, a great variety of mathematics comes into its own. Of course, I enjoy this personally, being a mathematician; but I do have reason. There is beauty in analog mathematics, plus a kind of resilient toughness that springs from the continuity and limitations that are built into nature.

Flat, extensive design is the friend of natural mathematics and the friend of coherent thought and of literacy. Wide Computing acts as a bridge, reuniting Computer Science with the behavior of all the other sciences, and computer engineering with all the other kinds of engineering. Everything falls into place without all the discontinuity and exceptions that currently drive people crazy.

When the connection to the physical world is done well, the embedded design rises to the level of **art.** (That language is well known in the world of inventions, and patents always refer to "prior art.") The reason is that only here does "the stream of ones and zeroes" truly meet "everything else." And the way everything else works is much more natural and various than the structure of bit-streams. That fact is obscured because we tend to accept interfaces like screen displays and sound as being part of the world of computing, when in fact they are uses of art, dependent on brain and psychology to narrowly simulate the breadth of nature.

The embedded programmer triumphantly reaches beyond this narrowness, which is already causing a kind of revulsion, leading to things like "steam punk" and the analog revival referenced in [8]. Digital images of wood don't really have grain. If computing becomes the servant instead of the master, then a right relationship is recovered between the willfulness of our programming and the huge, calm and beautiful world around us.

6.4 References

[1] Choisser, John P., and John O. Foster: *The XT-AT Handbook.* Annabooks, San Diego, 1989–1992. Booklet (3.5" by 6"), 94 pgs.

[2] Dickson, Lawrence J: "occam (TM) Road Map for the DOS PC." *Proceedings of the 1996 International Conference on Parallel and Distributed Processing Techniques and Applications* (PDPTA'96), Hamid R. Arabnia, editor. CSREA, Sunnyvale CA, 1996.

[3] Hirschsohn, Ian: "Personal Supercomputing," 3-article series. Dr Dobbs Journal, V 17 No 6, 7, 8, June, July, August 1992.

[4] grahamf72 et al: "Low Power Mode," 43oh Blog, 25 January 2013 ff. `http://forum.43oh.com/topic/3270-low-power-mode`

[5] "Network synthesis filters," Wikipedia. `http://en.wikipedia.org/wiki/Network_synthesis_filters`

[6] Garante, Enrico: "MSP430 Launchpad Tutorial - Part 2 - Interrupts and Timers," Embedded Systems Blogs, Jun 17, 2013. `http://www.embeddedrelated.com/showarticle/182.php`

[7] Keizer, Gregg: "Windows 8's complexity tax shackles Microsoft," Computerworld, January 18, 2014. `http://www.computerworld.com/s/article/9245509/Windows_8_s_complexity_tax_shackles_Microsoft`

[8] Hamill, Jasper: "Small Firms Are Making Big Bucks In The Analog Economy," Forbes, 1/13/2014. `http://www.forbes.com/sites/jasperhamill/2014/01/13/small-firms-are-making-big-bucks-in-the-analog-economy`

[9] Stackoverflow: "Windows Equivalent of 'nice'," circa June 26 '09. `stackoverflow.com/questions/4208/windows-equivalent-of-nice`

[10] Dannenberg, Andreas: "Implementing an MSP430 Accelerometer-Based Data Acquisition System," MSP430 Advanced Technical Conference, 5/21/2008. `http://focus.ti.com/en/download/mcu/Implementing-an-MSP430-Accelerometer--Based-Data-Acquisition.pdf`

[11] Dickson, Lawrence J: "Flat is Beautiful." Proceedings of the 2004 International Conference on Parallel and Distributed Processing Techniques and Applications (PDPTA'04), Hamid R. Arabnia, editor. CSREA, Las Vegas NV, 2004.

Acronyms and Abbreviations

ACK acknowledge
AD9650 a 16-bit ADC by Analog Devices
ADC Analog to Digital Converter
ARM Acorn RISC Machine, a RISC instruction set architecture
ARM1176JZF-S ARM chip in Raspberry Pi
ASIC Application-Specific Integrated Circuit

BATCH a script file used by DOS and Windows
BSD Berkeley Software Distribution, a Unix-like OS

CC1101 a radio transceiver by Texas Instruments
CCD Charge-Coupled Device, an image pixel sensor
CDMA Code Division Multiple Access, a frequency band-sharing method
CISC Complex Instruction Set Computer
Code Composer an IDE by Texas Instruments
comms communications
connel connector link
CPLD Complex Programmable Logic Device
CPU Central Processing Unit
CS Computer Science
CSP Communicating Sequential Processes
CubeSat Cube Satellite, a standardized miniature satellite

DAC Digital to Analog Converter
DARPA Defense Advanced Research Projects Agency
DMA Direct Memory Access
DOS Disk Operating System
DS Data Segment, an X86 segment register

FIFO First-In First-Out
FPGA Field-Programmable Gate Array
FTP File Transfer Protocol

GAL Generic Array Logic
GPGPU General-Purpose Graphics Processing Unit computing
GPIO General-Purpose Input-Output
GUI Graphical User Interface

HDL Hardware Description Language
HP Hewlett-Packard Company
HTTPD Hyper-Text Transfer Protocol Daemon

I2C I-squared C, a bus standard
ICE In-Circuit Emulator
IDE Integrated Development Environment
IF Intermediate Frequency
ISR Interrupt Service Routine
ITOCA In-Time On-Chip Army, a patent-pending invention by the author

JTAG Joint Test Action Group, a debugging port standard

Kicksat a Kickstarter satellite project of Zac Manchester

LAN Local Area Network
LAZM Lost Art of Zero Maintenance, a DBA trademark of the author
LC ladder a ladder circuit using inductance and capacitance
LED Light-Emitting Diode
LIFO Last-In First-Out (also called a stack)
LVDS Low-Voltage Differential Signaling

MAC address Media Access Control address, normally world-unique
MC Master Control
MMU Memory Management Unit
MSK Minimum Shift Keying, a radio standard
MSP430 a microcontroller family by Texas Instruments
MSP430F5137 an MSP430 specialized for radio
MSP430F5418 a variety of MSP430

Nooelec DVB a radio receiver dongle by NooElec
NRE Non-Recurring Engineering
NUMA Non-Uniform Memory Access

op amp operational amplifier
OS Operating System
OSC Open Sound Control, an audio protocol

PAL Programmable Array Logic
PIC Peripheral Interface Controller, a microcontroller family by Microchip
Technology
PWM Pulse-Width Modulation

R820T a variety of RTL2832U used by Nooelec DVB
RAM Randomly Addressable Memory
RDTSC a cycle counting assembly instruction
REQ Request (handshake)
RISC Reduced Instruction Set Computer
ROI Rate of Improvement
RPi Raspberry Pi
RS232 a serial IO standard
RTL2832U a radio demodulator by Realtek
RTOS Real-Time Operating System

SATA Serial ATA, a bus standard
SCS Super-Computing Surfaces, a computing development partnership
SLCE Sidelnikov, Lempel, Cohn, Eastman CDMA algorithm
SMM System Management Mode, of Intel X86 chips
SOCKLOCAL Linux socket or Windows named pipe
SPI Serial Peripheral Interface
SS Sensor Station

TCM Tightly Coupled Memory, an ARM memory prioritization system
TCP/IP Transmission Control Protocol/Internet Protocol
TDS Transputer Development System
TI Texas Instruments
TSR Terminate and Stay Resident

UART Universal Asynchronous Receiver-Transmitter, a serial protocol
UI User Interface
UPS Uninterruptible Power Supply
USB Universal Serial Bus

VHDL VHSIC Hardware Description Language, a popular HDL

WORLDCOMP an annual computer science multiconference

XCB X-protocol C-language Binding, a free graphics layer library

Index